CIVIL WAR PRISONS

Doorways to Hell

BOOK SEVEN

THE DRIEBORG CHRONICLES

By

DR. MICHAEL J. DEEB

Civil War Prisons

Doorways to Hell

© 2017 Michael J. Deeb

All rights reserved. No part of this book may be used or reproduced by any means, graphic, electronic or mechanical, including photocopying, recording, taping or by any information storage retrieval system without the written permission of the author except in the case of brief quotations embodied in critical articles and reviews.

Certain characters in this work are historical figures, and certain events portrayed did take place. However, this is a work of fiction. All of the other characters, names and events, as well as all places, incidents, organizations, and dialogue in this novel are either the product of the author's imagination or are used fictitiously.

Printed in the United States of America

Michael J. Deeb was born and raised in Grand Rapids, Michigan. His undergraduate and graduate educations centered on American studies. His doctorate was in management.

He was an educator for nineteen years, most of which saw him teaching American history and doing historical research.

His personal life found him as a pre-teen spending time regularly at the public library, reading nonfiction works of history. This passion has continued to this day. Teaching at the college, university and high school levels only increased his interest in such reading and research.

Since 2005, he and his wife have lived in Sun City Center, Florida. In the fall of 2007, he finished the historical novel *Duty and Honor*. The sequel, *Duty Accomplished*, was completed in 2008. *Honor Restored* was the concluding novel in the original Drieborg Chronicles. These were followed by *The Lincoln Assassination*, *The Way West*, and *1860.* They are all currently available at Amazon and www.civilwarnovels.com.

INTRODUCTION

When war came to the country very suddenly in April 1861, virtually no preparations had been made by either side to prepare for war. So, it should not be surprising that no plans had been made to care for prisoners of war either. Besides, the leaders on both sides predicted that the conflict would be over after a battle or two. It was also assumed that prisoners would be exchanged or paroled right after any battle that would be fought.

In April 1861, Confederate Secretary of War Leroy P. Walker told a crowd in Montgomery, Alabama, that the Confederate flag would soon fly over the dome of the Old Capitol at Washington before the first of May 1861.

That same month, Mrs. Jefferson Davis sent out invitations to her southern friends residing at the Saint Nicholas Hotel in New York City, inviting them to a tea she intended to hold on the first of May at a Confederate White House in Washington City.

Meanwhile, following the fall of Fort Sumter, the Northern press trumpeted 'On to Richmond', promising their readers an easy victory on the battlefield and a quick end to the rebellion.

None of this was destined to happen. On the contrary, four years of war followed Fort Sumter. During that time, over 674,000 prisoners were taken. At first, most prisoners were paroled or exchanged right on the battlefield. But over 410,000 were not. Instead, they were kept in camps. These, some 223 compounds, could be found from as far north as Boston, as far South as the Dry Tortugas, and as far west as Fort Riley, Kansas and Fort Craig in New Mexico.

In these prisoner-of-war camps, over 56,000 men died during confinement, amounting to 13 percent of the total prison population

North and South. At the same time, it is interesting that only five percent of the men who remained on the battlefield died. So, it appeared a soldier's chance of survival was better fighting on a battlefield than remaining in a prison.

Aside from the belief that the war would be a short one, there were other reasons the care of prisoners was not given a higher priority early in the war by either side. The most important of these was that, as with most wars, the governments involved had not prepared for a conflict; certainly, not a protracted one.

When war did come, their energy and resources were initially devoted to organizing and equipping their fighting forces. Building fortifications and a navy, as well as planning strategy, took priority over the care of potential prisoners. Besides, leaders on both sides of the conflict believed the war would not last long, so preparing to hold large numbers of prisoners did not seem necessary.

Then, when it became apparent that the war would not be a short one, the energies of both governments were primarily devoted to maintaining their fighting forces. Concern for prisoners of war remained a much lower priority.

In the North, the US Army Quartermaster-General, Montgomery C. Meigs, urged Secretary of War Simon Cameron in July 1861 to appoint a Commissary-General of Prisons. That same October, such a post was created, and Colonel William Hoffman was appointed to fill it.

In the South, the Confederate government would not take similar action until late 1864, when General John H. Winder was appointed to oversee the South's prisoner-of-war camps.

In January 1862, the Union War Department directed Colonel Hoffman to not mistreat prisoners of war and instead directed him,

"Besides the rations allowed by regulations (full Union rations), the United States will supply such blankets, cooking utensils and clothing without regard to rank as are necessary to prevent real suffering."

At the same time, in the West, Union General Henry W. Halleck ordered his Chief of Staff, General George W. Cullum, "Give (Southern prisoners) everything necessary for their comfort. Treat them the same as our own soldiers."

Consequently, between 1861 and 1863, the literature shows that Southern prisoners in Union hands were not receiving less food than Union soldiers in the field. Nor was housing provided prisoners in the North of much different quality than that supplied Union troops in the field.

For example, Confederate prisoners of war were housed at Camp Douglas outside of Chicago. This was formerly a training camp where volunteers for service in the Union army were initially trained.

Directives similar to the one issued by General Halleck were not issued by the Confederate government regarding their treatment of Union prisoners of war.

When an agreement for prisoner exchanges was finally agreed to in July of 1862, prisons on both sides emptied out. Those prisoners not actually exchanged were paroled waiting their exchange. But this agreement later collapsed, never to be renewed.

With this said, let us enter the main gates of America's doorways to hell.

THE OUTSKIRTS OF WASHINGTON CITY

"I think that be a Reb officer over there, lads," Sgt. Riley told his squad of cavalrymen. "Let's see how much trouble it's gonna be ta' get that horse off 'en him."

On patrol, outside of the nation's capital, Washington City, Sergeant Riley and his five-man cavalry squad had been riding patrol Southeast of the city. It was right after the first battle of Bull Run. Panic was still rampant in Washington, for fear the Confederate army would follow its victory and be at the gates of the virtually defenseless city at any time. Riley's mounted patrol was to provide the city with early warning of any such attack.

On the other hand, the Confederates probed, hoping to discover weaknesses in Washington's defenses. Confederate Captain Richard Pope had been leading his cavalry unit in that very effort when his horse stepped in a hole and rolled over, falling on its rider. Shortly after, Riley's squad came along.

"Keep a sharp eye out, lads," he ordered. "This bird wasn't out here alone ya' know. I'll look him over, but you form a circle 'round me and face out. I don't want to spend this night tied up in a Reb camp, don't ya know."

While his men moved into the woods ten or so yards away, Riley approached the downed Confederate officer with his weapon drawn.

"What have we here now?" he said. "Should we leave ya' here now or take ya' with us? What'll ya' have, laddie?"

"Tell ya' what, Sergeant," the trapped Reb officer responded. "Given the choice, I vote that you get this horse off me and let me go."

"Can't let ya go, laddie," Riley chuckled. "But I'll get ya' free a' this horse in a jiffy."

It didn't take long for two of Riley's men to lift the horse enough for another Union trooper to pull Pope free. He was lucky. The fall had not seriously injured him.

Richard Pope was about five-foot-six inches tall in his polished riding boots, fair-haired, blue-eyed, and one hundred fifty pounds or so. He looked like the typical cavalryman of his day.

As he sat catching his breath, he asked, "What now, Sergeant?"

"Our troop commander will decide that," Riley told him. "You're headed for exchange or a prison camp, be my guess. So, let's get ya' mounted now."

* * *

"What did ya' bring me this fine morning, Riley?" Captain Brennan said.

"We found this Reb pinned under his horse a few miles south a' here, sir. Thought he might talk to another officer. He surely didn't tell me much."

"Thank you, Sergeant Riley," Brennan told him. "You can leave the officer with me, Sergeant."

"Yes, sir." Riley came to attention, saluted and left his commanding officer's tent.

"Well now," Brennan began. "Have a seat, Captain. I'm having a cup of coffee. Can I pour you one?"

"Thank you. I would enjoy having a cup."

While he was pouring the coffee, Brennan asked, "What name can I call you?"

"I'm Captain Richard Pope," he answered. "I assume you are Captain Brennan?"

"You got that right, Reb," Brennan snapped. "But I didn't catch the name of your unit, Captain Pope."

"That's because I didn't give it to you, Captain Brennan."

Smiling, Brennan said, "Of course, I forgot. But you gotta know, Captain, the more cooperative you are, the better your chance of being paroled instead of imprisoned."

"Just how does a Yankee parole work?" Brennan was asked.

"Last I heard, you agree not to return to the fight until a Union soldier of equal rank is available to be exchanged for you. Is that how you understand it?"

"Yes, it is."

"Are you a slaver, Captain?"

"Are you asking if I own slaves?"

"Yes."

"No, I don't own a single slave, Captain."

"So, why are you in this fight?"

"To defend my freedom."

"Freedom to own slaves?"

"If I decide to do that, yes," Pope spat back. "According to the constitution of my country, citizens have the right to buy, sell and possess property without the approval of some government official sticking his nose in my business. You might recall that even your Supreme Court affirmed that right for citizens of your country in the Dred Scott decision back in 1856."

"Oh, my, I've got an educated Reb on my hands, do I?"

"Damn right, Brennan," Pope snapped.

Captain Brennan snapped right back. "According to the letters Riley found in your saddle-bag, you're from Charleston, South Carolina. That's the place where you traitorous Rebs started this war. Right?"

"I'm from Charleston, correct," Pope affirmed. "That's where you refused to leave our territory and forced us to throw you out."

"That's one way to look at it, I suppose," Brennan responded with a laugh.

"Reverse our situations," Pope suggested. "You live in Charleston and see me flying the flag of a foreign power flying over a fort in your harbor. I won't take it down and leave. I refuse to accept a deal to pay for the fort either. Instead, I attempt to resupply the place indefinitely and even tell you when I'm going to resupply the troops stationed there.

"Just between you and I and the lamp post, wouldn't that aggravate you all to hell?" Pope asked.

"That surely would," Brennan replied.

"Consider this too," Pope continued. "I appear to have made up my mind to hold on to the fort that's located in your harbor, at least that's what I've said publicly several times. If you continue to allow me to resupply the place, occupy it and fly my flag there, what does that say to your people and the rest of the world?"

"That I'm indecisive, maybe weak," Brennan admitted.

"So, you can't allow that image to continue. At some point, don't you have to insist that I leave and recognize your existence as a legitimate state? If not, don't you have to give up the attempt at independence and come back into the Union?"

"This is all crap!" Brennan almost shouted. "You people fired upon the American flag!"

"Yes, we did," Pope admitted. "President Lincoln used your flag to taunt the South Carolina authorities, and by extension the Confederate government. He put us in a box of sorts. If we let you stay at Fort Sumter and allowed you to fly your flag there, we were admitting that we were not a sovereign state independent of the United States. If we didn't choose to be passive, but forced you out, we were Rebels firing on your sacred flag. We were damned if we did and damned if we didn't."

"So, what? You started the fighting."

"And Lincoln got his way, whichever choice we made," Pope concluded.

Brennan paused and finally responded, "I can see your point, Reb. But I can't get over the simple fact that you damned slavers fired on the flag of the United States of America."

"I can't deny that, Yank. So, here we are, right?" Pope reminded him. "We're at one another's throat for sure. Is it all over a flag? I don't think so. I believe it's between two very different societies. We decided to recognize the difference to walk away and get out a' your hair. You refused to allow that.

"You said it yourself, didn't you?" Pope reminded Brennan. "I'm a slaver, even though I don't own a single one. You're a Yank who represents a region that had become rich off cotton, sugar and tobacco, and the slave labor which produces all of it."

"Captain Pope," Brennan interrupted. "I must admit that what you say has the ring of truth and common sense to it. But it's all smoke in tha' wind, my friend. You and I are just little cogs in the great wheel of this thing.

"So, drink up, and I'll take ya' to my Regimental HQ, where they'll decide what ta' do with you."

Pope stood, finished his coffee in one gulp, straightened his cap and jacket and said, "Thanks for the coffee and the stimulating conversation, Captain. I'm ready any time you are."

CHARLESTON

"Father Pope," Mary Jacqueline Pope called. "I just received a letter from Charles you have to read."

Mary Jacqueline was Dr. Charles Pope's wife. She was a northern girl Charles had met while a medical student in Philadelphia, Pennsylvania. She was the daughter of one of his professors. Charles broke with tradition when he took as his wife a woman from the north. His mother was not pleased one bit.

Now, Charles was serving in the Confederate army. As a doctor, he was assigned to the newly established military hospital in Richmond. His pregnant wife stayed at his parents' home in Charleston, South Carolina. Her only ally there was her father-in-law, Colonel Joseph Pope.

He met his daughter-in-law in the hallway. "What is it, dear?"

"Charles has written me some news about your son, Richard," Mary Jacqueline said.

The Colonel stood in the hallway reading his eldest son's letter.

* * *

My Dearest Mary Jacqueline,

I hope this letter finds you well. Be careful, my dearest. Your pregnancy is at a critical stage right now. So, please take it easy. Get a lot of sleep, and drink a lot of water. During this hot late summer, don't forget to use the netting around your bed at night and stay away from the crowded streets and markets of the city. No telling what sickness you can pick up there.

I have some alarming news about my brother, Richard. The word I just received was that, while on patrol in Maryland, he was captured. Apparently, he was not injured, but he is in the hands of the Union forces. Right now, we don't know whether he will be exchanged for one of our captives or sent to a Yankee prison in the north someplace.

My contact in President Davis' office promised to keep me informed. It would not hurt if the Colonel contacted President Davis directly and pressed for an early exchange with the Yankees for Richard.

I will keep you informed. Please allow the Colonel and mother to read this message.

I love and miss you. I am well and look forward to holding you in my arms when I next have leave. Please take care of yourself. Please do not be stubborn about letting your house servant, Helen, wait on you. That is why she was given to you. So, please set aside your Northern attitudes about slavery and let her take care of you.

You loving husband,

Charles

* * *

Finished reading the letter, the Colonel murmured, "At least Richard was not injured. Please show this to Mrs. Pope. I'm going to go to the telegraph office and contact President Davis."

Mary Jacqueline took her husband's letter upstairs. A virtual recluse, Mrs. Pope's room was darkened and she was lying on a lounge. A house servant was standing alongside, fanning her mistress.

Mary Jacqueline entered the room. "Mother Pope?" she asked tentatively.

"Yes, dear?" Mrs. Pope responded. "I hope this is important. I'm not feeling too well today."

"I wouldn't disturb you, but Father Pope asked me to show you this letter from your son, Charles."

"Oh, I hope it isn't bad news. I hate this terrible war. You'd think our men would have been able to avoid it. But give it to me if he thinks I must see it."

Mrs. Pope took the letter.

"You can leave now, child," she directed. "I don't need you to hover while I read it. Go. Leave me. Shut the door behind you."

"Yes, ma'am," Mary Jacqueline meekly responded. And then she turned and left the room.

Her husband, Charles, had received his medical degree from the University of Pennsylvania the previous spring. By the time she and Charles had returned from their honeymoon in Bermuda, war had broken out between the new Confederate States of America and the United States.

Doctors were in great demand, so Charles had volunteered immediately. His younger brother, Richard, accepted a commission in a South Carolina cavalry regiment and headed north to join Confederate forces in Virginia. The youngest son, David, and his mother's favorite, stayed home. Unlike his older brothers, he lived the life of the spoiled son. His specialty was whisky, a bad temper and prostitutes. In his brothers' absence, he engaged in leering and making nasty, suggestive remarks toward his new sister-in-law from the north, Mary Jacqueline.

Her father-in-law, Joseph Pope, was a colonel in a South Carolina unit stationed in Charleston. He expected to leave home soon and head north with his unit to join the Army of Northern Virginia, led by General Joe Johnston and General Pierre Beauregard.

Somewhat tall for the time, Mary Jacqueline was five-foot-five and a slender 125 pounds. It was understandable why Charles had been attracted to this eighteen-year-old back in Philadelphia, where he was studying for a career as a doctor. She was quite a beauty with her stunning figure, very black hair, a sparkling smile and Irish blue eyes.

But despite her husband's assurances that she would be loved and accepted in Charleston society, her Yankee accent was so evident, she was shunned socially. Now, with the war and her husband absence, she was a virtual outcast, and a pregnant one at that.

Expecting her first child and experiencing all the attendant emotions with her husband away in Richmond, Virginia, Mary Jacqueline was lonely and afraid. Aside from her personal servant, Helen, and evening meals with her father-in-law, she was very much alone in the Pope household, as well as a Yankee foreigner in wartime Charleston.

Customarily, she wrote her husband daily. Today, her letter was especially poignant.

August, 1961

My Dearest,

I was so sorry to hear that Richard is a captive of Union forces. The Colonel left immediately upon reading your letter to wire President Davis. I hope Richard can be freed quickly. You father told me that it is still customary to either exchange prisoners of war for someone of equal rank, or parole captives until someone of equal rank is available to be exchanged. This war is all so confusing and terrible. Is there any chance

President Davis will be able to arrange a peace with President Lincoln? I hope and pray that the two leaders can find a way out of all the killing.

My morning sickness seems to be over for now. I hope it is. I have been so healthy all my life, I hate to even appear ill, even though I know it is because of my pregnancy. Actually, now I feel fine.

Helen keeps piling the food on my plate and telling me I am eating for two. The way my clothing has tightened up around my middle, I can believe her. I have been going to Mass at Saint Mary's Catholic Church every morning to pray for your safety and for an early end to this war. Helen accompanies me, so I am getting some exercise every day. If I continue to feel bloated, she and I will walk in the evening as well. I wish you were by my side instead.

I miss you so, my love. I am so alone here. You know how your mother feels about me. The less I see of your drunken brother, David, the better. Thankfully, Helen is a dear and very helpful. So is your father, the Colonel. Don't worry about me going into town. I feel that my Yankee origins are so evident to everyone that I am a lightning rod for the angry looks of everyone I pass at the market. I thank the war for that.

I also urge you to be careful. We hear of sickness running rampant in the training camps. I hope that is not true of your hospital. You can't catch a wound, I know. But is it possible for you to stay away from sick soldiers? I suppose not. Just be careful.

Now, I feel that I must ask the hard question.

Would you mind if I went north to Philadelphia and gave birth to our child there? Alone here as I am without you, I would be ever so much more comfortable waiting for our happy event with my parents, where I feel loved. I don't know if it is even possible for Southerners to cross the border into the Union anymore. Oh, my! It still seems funny calling myself a Southerner.

I don't mind, though. I am your wife, after all. But as you know, I am not accepted here in your home or the town. Instead, I am treated as an unwelcome Yankee foreigner. So, maybe, without you here to help me and shield me, I should return north until this terrible war is over.

I must end this letter now so I can get it off in time for today's post.

Take care of yourself, my darling.

Your loving wife,

Mary Jacqueline

WASHINGTON CITY

"What have you here, Captain Brennan?" Major Thomas asked his troop commander.

"One of my patrols captured this Reb Captain while on patrol this morning, sir. I visited with him some but didn't get anything useful from him. So, I brought him here."

"Right," Thomas said. "Bring him in, Captain. I'll see what I can do. What's his name?"

"Says his name is Richard Pope. From Charleston, South Carolina, he claims."

"Where they started this damn war, eh?"

"Not according to him, sir. He says we actually started it."

"Well, I'll be damned. He really said that?"

"In so many words, sir."

"I wonder if Lincoln knows that he started this war?"

Brennan laughed. "Probably not, sir. But this Pope presents an interesting argument."

"Well, send him in, Brennan. This should be fascinating. Then you can return to your unit, Captain."

"Yes, sir." Brennan came to attention, saluted, turned and left the major's office.

A few moments later, Captain Pope stepped inside the tent, came to attention in front of the major's desk, and saluted. He continued to stand at attention until the major returned the salute greeting. Then, he stood at parade rest with his feet spread and his hands behind his back.

"Good afternoon, Captain Pope," Thomas greeted. "Please have a seat."

"You were on patrol in the outskirts of Washington City, were you?"

"Yes, Major. I was when my horse stumbled and then fell on me."

"It happens," Thomas replied. "You're lucky the animal didn't break your neck or something else in the process."

"That's right, sir," Pope responded with a smile. "Unlucky, too, though."

"How so?"

"Your patrol came along at precisely the moment when my men were out of sight. Your men screened me from mine. I was stuck. So, all I could do was accept the hospitality of your Sergeant Riley and his squad."

"I see what you mean about being unlucky, too," Thomas conceded. "What am I to do with ya' now?"

"Give me a pass, a horse, and a wave goodbye, an I'll be outa' your hair, Major."

"Can't do that, son."

"Then parole me."

"That's not for me to decide."

"Then, sir, send me to someone who can decide the matter."

"That's a sensible request, I believe," Thomas agreed. "And I will. But first let me ask you a question."

"Fire away, Major," Pope urged.

"You really think we started this war after you fired on our flag?"

"Here we go with that piece-of-cloth business again," Pope sighed. "Major, your government was flying that thing in my country. And you, the United States of America, were occupying land in my country to fly it from. We gave you plenty of warning what would happen if you didn't leave and take the damn flag with you."

"But you had a choice, didn't you?" the Yankee major reminded Pope.

"Fine choice; allow you, a foreign power, to occupy land in my country and fly your flag over it, or force you to leave when you refused to do so, peaceably. Think about it, Major. We were going to be damned either way."

"And you chose force, thus starting this war. Right?"

"That's no choice at all, Major," Pope insisted. "When you refused to leave our territory in peace, we had to force you to do so. You forced that choice upon us."

"Brennan was right, Captain Pope," Thomas said with a smile. "You have a real way with words."

"Maybe so, Major," Pope said, smiling in return. "I would rather be known as someone who has a way with the facts."

An orderly entered the tent and handed Major Thomas a message.

"Well, Captain," Thomas announced, "It appears that we must send you under guard to the Provost Marshal in Washington City. You are to be detained until your case is determined. I wish you well, young man."

"One moment, sir," Pope said.

"Yes. What is it, Captain?"

"I was in the saddle at dawn," Pope related. "Captain Brennan gave me a scrape of stale bread and a swallow of coffee. Would it be possible for you to give me something to eat before you send me off?"

Major Thomas stood and shouted, "Sergeant Willis."

The regimental sergeant-major entered the tent.

"Yes, sir?"

"Before you send Captain Pope to the Provost Marshal, get him a meal. I believe we had biscuits and stew this noon. Get him some of that."

"Yes, sir."

"Thank you, Major," Pope said.

He stood, came to attention and saluted. Thomas did the same, signaling Pope to turn and leave the Major's tent.

FAIRFAX COUNTY, VIRGINIA

Fairfax County Courthouse was an important rail center and supply depot. As a result, it was heavily guarded by Union infantry. Among those foot soldiers was Ethan Schock. As soon as he was of age, in the winter of 1862, Ethan answered Lincoln's call and joined the Federal forces. From the western part of Michigan, he was sent to the marshaling center at Detroit and assigned to the 1st Infantry Division for training.

Ethan had a ready smile for everybody and was always ready to help any of his comrades. He wasn't all that tall, probably about five-foot-five or six. But he was muscular and pretty good with his fists. He proved that behind the barracks several times, showing that he was not to be trifled with. It wasn't long before Ethan was selected by his comrades as their squad leader and promoted to Corporal.

"I don't care if you are the squad leader, Schock," Williams complained. "You're a damned son-of-a-bitch for giving me guard duty two nights in a row, an' the first watch ta' boot."

"We're all in the same boat here, Williams," Ethan Schock responded calmly. "What makes you so special anyway?"

"Just seems that you're picking on me, giving me the first watch an' all."

Another member of the five-man squad, Bill Kelly said, "The first watch is the easiest, damn it." He reminded, "'Sides, when you had the third watch, we had a devil of a time tryin' to wake you up ta' take your turn. But tell you what, you can have my midnight two-hour watch in exchange for your 'n if you'd rather."

"Naw," Williams responded. "I'll stay with what I got."

"You're just a natural born complainer, Williams," Kelly added. "You're the kind a' guy that jus' always sees the dark side a' things."

"What's that mean, Kelly?" Williams snapped. "Are you insultin' me?" He jumped to his feet, fists clenched and ready for a fight.

"Settle down, both a' ya'," Schock ordered. "You start something, I'll finish it. You know I can, and I will fer sure if you keep this up."

"Aw, I didn't mean nothin' by it, Ethan. I was just funning with Williams; all his complaining an' such. It never ends, ya' know, sort a' gets on a guy's nerves."

"Well, both a' you stuff it for a while," Ethan ordered. "Your squabblin' gets on a guy's nerves, too. Get some rest, all a' ya."

Williams wasn't done complaining. "I don't know if I can, Ethan, after that awful stuff you fixed for our meal tonight."

"Oh, my Lord," Kelly exclaimed. "Is there no end to your whining, Williams? It just goes on forever."

Another squad member, a Chippewa Indian from up around Mt. Pleasant, Michigan, had ridden south to the Detroit recruiting center to join up and to collect the $100 bounty volunteers were offered. Everyone called him "Chief". He just ignored all the back and forth.

And so it went for weeks; guard and latrine duty, taking turns cooking their own food, washing their own clothing, drilling on the parade ground and living in a cramped and smelly tent. The routine and boredom of camp life was the worst. It made it more difficult to put up with the complainers like Williams.

It was times like this that Ethan retreated into himself. Nothing helped soothe him better than to read letters from home. Today, the one on the top of his stack was a letter he just received from Mike Drieborg, his buddy from home.

Hi Ethan,

I hope this letter finds you well. Why haven't you taken care of those Rebs by now? Leaving it for me to join you, I suppose.

There hasn't been much in the papers about fighting out in the East since you guys got your tails kicked at Bull Run. Most of what I read recently is about Grant's victory at Fort Donelson. I think that's where Willie is serving. That was a real big victory. They captured almost 15,000 Rebs in that one. Now, Grant is a big hero here. The papers are calling him Unconditional Surrender Grant.

Where the hell are you right now? I've tried to find you on a map without any luck. I suppose you can't tell me much.

Things are pretty much the same around here. I'm still up at dawn, rain, shine, snow or ice. I milk cows every morning and chop wood most every day, too. You know what life is like on a farm. Right now, we're also sawing blocks of ice out of the river and storing them in the ice shed. I've gone out to our old hunting grounds a few times. But it's no fun without you and Willie. At least I don't have to worry about one of you shooting me by accident. Ice fishing's no fun without you guys either.

Sarah Dittman has been giving me a hard time when I've seen her in town. She rags on me for staying at home and letting you guys join up without me. She claims that I stayed home by choice. She as much as called me a coward the last time we met. I'm sure others in town think that, too. Even my dad gets the silent treatment at the grain elevator. My mom complains about how she is treated at the general store and at church dinners on Sunday. Parents of boys who have joined up, been injured or even killed wonder why I'm home, safe and sound, I'm sure.

So, I know that it is hard on my parents, as well as me. I also know that one of the reasons they left Europe years ago was to escape all the wars that destroyed their villages and killed so many of their friends and family. So, I understand why they won't give me permission to join up. I know they hope and pray that the war will be over before I am of age to join on my own.

Well, I'll be eighteen this coming May, three months from now. Unless you guys whip the Rebs by then, I'll join you as soon as I can after that. Leave some fighting for me, will ya?

Take care of yourself, my friend. As soon as I get my next letter from Willie, I'll send it on to you. You can write, too, ya' know. Or have you forgotten how? Kenny's a sergeant already, my corporal friend. He always did like giving us orders, didn't he?

*You friend,
Mike*

* * *

In late February 1863, Ethan's entire infantry division of nearly ten thousand men marched south toward the Confederate capital, Richmond, Virginia. The march was called a reconnaissance-in-force. The rumor was that his division was actually the lead element of an attack on that city by the Army of the Potomac.

Ethan's company of almost one hundred men marched parallel on the right flank of the main body of the division as it moved through enemy territory. The company's mission was to gather information about the area through which they were marching and give early warning of any attack on the division from that flank.

Toward that end, the members of Ethan's unit were ordered to gather information about the terrain and try to capture and interrogate prisoners and local citizens whenever the opportunity presented itself.

His company commander needed advance warning of enemy attack, too. So, he sent out a five-man squad of men to his front as an advance guard, another squad was sent to his flank, and still another to the rear of his company of one hundred soldiers. These deployments would normally be rotated several times during the day to give relief to the squad members involved.

"Haven't we been out on the flank way too long?" complained Williams. "I bet it's been over an hour out here all exposed. Hell's bells, the five of us could be shot down easy before we even knew what was happening."

"That's why our squad is out here, Williams," Kelly snapped. "And come to think of it, I've got news for ya'. Everyone in the division hopes that you get taken out by a Reb sniper so, your constant bitching is never heard again. Lord, it is so tiresome to hear you go on and on all the time."

"Wait till we get back to camp, Kelly," Williams threatened. "I'll knock your block off for sure."

"Not until I have a shot at shutting up that motor mouth of yours, Williams," Kelly promised.

Tom Nowak, a volunteer from a Polish neighborhood on the west side of Detroit added, "Hey boss, can I take da' whole a' dem on when we get back ta' camp? In my neighborhood back in Detroit, ve would pound guys like dem until dey were too tired an' sore to talk, even."

"I'm tired of it, too, Tom," Ethan agreed. "But you'll have to let me give you a hand. We'll settle with Williams first, then Kelly. I think the Chief will want a piece of our action, too."

"That's fine wit me," Nowak said.

"Hey," Williams said. "What did I do wrong?"

Ethan snapped at him, "You're making so much racket with that mouth of yours, Williams, a whole company a' Rebs could be roaming around out in these woods without our hearing 'em. So, keep your mouth shut and your eyes an' ears open."

"Everybody picks on me all the time," Williams moaned.

"That oughta' tell ya' somethin'," Kelly told him, laughing.

Just then, a shot rang out. Dozens of birds flew out of the trees to their right. The Union soldier walking at the point of Ethan's squad fell to the ground.

"Hit the dirt," Ethan shouted.

Then there was nothing but silence.

"Report," Ethan shouted.

Three of his men shouted, "Here!"

"Williams?" Ethan shouted. There was no response.

"Crap," Kelly said. "I didn't mean that I wanted him ta' get shot."

"Shut up and open your ears," Ethan ordered.

Suddenly, the silence was broken by high-pitched yelling and a wave of Reb soldiers running out of the tree line toward Ethan's squad.

His men fired a volley, and one or two Rebs fell. But before his men could reload, the Rebs were on top of them. Ethan's squad was taken captive. Now, they were the ones who would be interrogated.

First thing, Ethan's men were forced to strip off their uniforms. The Reb soldiers donned the blue clothing and replaced Ethan's men on the flank of the Union infantry company.

Shit, Ethan thought. *Now the squad replacing mine will be walking right into a trap. My company and the division will have no warning of a Reb attack either.*

The change of uniforms completed, the rest of the Confederate soldiers melted back into the forest to wait for orders to attack the Union flank.

But Ethan and his three fellow squad members would not be there. Instead, they were quickly led away into captivity, wearing the Confederate grey uniforms.

"Move along now, laddie," a soldier in Confederate grey ordered in a deep Irish brogue.

Kelly noticed the guard's Irish accent and was surprised. "What er' ya' doin fighting fer these secessh?" he asked. "No true Son of Ireland should help the slavers after the treatment we Irish have taken back home from the bloody Brits."

"Things 'er not always what they seem, boyo," the Reb Irishman told Kelly with a smile. "After all, I be born in North Carolina, don't ya' know. Why wouldn't I fight for me own people, now? Tell me that."

"Hey," Kelly responded. "I thought most of us Irish lived in Boston or someplace up north, anyways," Kelly responded.

"Well now, me Irish friend," the Reb guard continued. "You're about to get a bit a' educatin' now, aren't ya'?

"Ya' see," he began. "When my pap left Ireland, he was determined to get a wee bit a' land fer himself in America. He didn't want ta get packed inta' a big city like Boston with all the other Irish leaving Ireland fer there. Nope, he was a farmer, don't ya know. He wanted the feel of soil on his hands and fresh air in his lungs.

"So, he headed where he knew he could get his hands on both. Happened ta' be in North Carolina," the Irish Reb continued. "He doesn't have much, sixty acres a' ground and a healthy stand a' trees with a good stream running through it. Pretty good weather there year 'round, too. None of your harsh northern winters in North Carolina.

"He has a good nearby market fer his corn an' hogs in Greenville. He's even got a bunch a' sheep just a'fore I left. My mum and sisters have a good size garden and look after the chickens an' the smoke house."

"You own any slaves, Irish?" Kelly asked.

"Nary a' one. No need, Yank. Me and my younger brothers work with our pap. We clear a couple a' acres every winter and have our eye on a forty-acre plot nearby fer me an' me wife."

"If'n you don't have slaves, why are you in this fight anyway?" Kelly continued.

"Fer most of us from North Carolina, it tain't about slavery, Yank," the Reb told Kelly. "But it is about defending our country against you Yanks. That's why me an' my mates are 'a fightin' anyways; fer our freedom."

"You got a family, Irish?" Kelly asked.

"Not yet," Irish told him. "But I got my eye on a good Catholic lass living nearby. She's Irish ta' her toes, with freckles, red hair, blue eyes and the prettiest smile ya' ever did see."

"So," Kelly asked. "Why ya' here and not home making babies?"

"Strange ya' should ask that, Yank," Irish chuckled. "I would be a' doing just that if'n you bastards had just stayed in yer own country and left us southerners alone. But I will, as soon as we kick ya' out. I'll be a' marrying that sweet Irish lass as quick as I can. You got family?"

"Naw," Kelly told him. "I got a maw and paw, a young brother and two irritating sisters. But none a' my own."

"So, why ya be in my country and not at home up north arguing with those irritating sisters?"

"I lost my factory job. So, I was at loose ends when Lincoln sent out his call for troops. I had nothing better ta' do. 'Sides, it sounded exciting and gave me some money ta boot."

"Well, now the excitin' part is over fer you, laddie," Kelly's Irish guard predicted. "Instead, you'll be spendin' some time in a prison camp, I'm thinkin'."

Ethan and the three remaining men of his squad were forced by guards to walk into the woods away from their unit. It couldn't have been more than an hour later when Ethan heard the roar of a cannon from that direction.

The Rebs are attacking, Ethan decided. Damn. They probably attacked the flank of my company from right where we were captured. With us gone, the boys of our company would not have had any warning either; no chance at all. I suppose the Rebs will capture a bunch more of us before this day is done. We'll all be heading to a prison, I'm thinking.

Ethan walked alongside of Joe, the Indian they called the "Chief". He whispered to Joe, "Do you think we can escape?"

"After dark," Joe answered. "Guards will be tired; no moon tonight; they can't see us. We head north. I'll tell you when."

"All of us?"

"No. Just you," Joe said. "The others make too much noise."

"We can't just leave them," Ethan insisted.

"Then I go without you. You decide, stay or go."

The column stopped at dusk by a stream. The captives were told they would stay here for the night. Some biscuits were passed out, and they scooped cold water from the stream.

"Damn," Kelly said. "These biscuits are as bad as ours. I like to crack a tooth on 'em."

"Better dan nothing," Novak corrected him. "If' ya' don't want yours, give it ta' me. I ain't fussy like you."

"My Lord," Ethan said, "looks like we got another Williams in our midst."

"I'm just funning, Ethan," Kelly said. "Nobody could be as bad as him. God rest his soul."

As the dark of the night deepened, the men fell asleep.

The Chief slid alongside of Ethan. Both men were lying on their stomachs.

"Ready?" the Chief asked.

"I can't just leave Kelly and Novak," Ethan whispered.

"They too noisy," Chief responded. "We all get caught easy."

"I can't leave 'em, Chief," Ethan insisted.

"I go, you stay."

"Good luck," Ethan said.

The Chippewa Indian crawled silently deeper into the dark of the woods.

It was soon dawn. Ethan awoke with a start.

How long did I lay here listening last night? Must 'a dozed off. I didn't hear any commotion, so maybe the Chief made it.

Kelly stood up, which alerted one of the guards.

"Hey, Reb," he almost shouted. "I got ta' take a leak. That be all right?"

Holy shit, Kelly, Ethan realized. *I suppose those guards will start countin' heads now that Kelly has called their attention to us. The Chief was right about him making too much noise. We would've all been caught for sure. I'll bet the Chief is miles away by now. I sure hope so.*

Kelly was escorted back after relieving himself.

He sat down next to Ethan. "Where's the Chief?" he asked.

"Quiet, damn it!" Ethan whispered.

"What'd' I say?" Kelly responded. He still had not caught on.

"Shut up, for God's sake," Novak whispered to the loud Irishman. "I'll tell ya' later."

There were no more biscuits passed out, but everyone was on the march south just the same. The guards had not said a word about the missing member of Ethan's squad.

Strange they haven't even taken a head count. The guards haven't sounded an alarm either. I suppose that means the Chief has made it north.

The three men of Ethan's squad trudged through the woods for what seemed like several miles.

"Will one of you tell me what happened?" Kelly insisted.

"No thanks ta' your loud mouth, Kelly," Novak said. "It appears dat da Chief has managed ta' escape."

"What did I do?" he whined.

"Well, first of all, you woke da camp up and got da guards to look us over 'cause you wanted to take a piss dis morning."

"So? I had to go."

"So, you're the reason he refused to take us with him," Ethan told his two mates.

"Why is that my fault?"

"Because he figured your loud mouth would get us all caught, that's why," Ethan added. "So, he left without us."

"Truth be known, though," Novak added, "none of us could walk as quietly as he does. Never saw a guy who could pick his way through a forest without a sound. I seem to snap every twig in the woods as I walk through, no matter how I try to avoid doing it."

"See," Kelly protested. "I'm not the only reason he left without us."

"Hey, you over there!" shouted a big, burly Confederate guard. "No talkin', or I'll put yas over here with the troublemakers."

The Reb walked menacingly over to Ethan's group.

"Yas hear me, Yank?" he shouted at Kelly. "I'm talkin' ta you."

With that, he hit Kelly in the shoulder with the butt of his rifle.

"Hey!" Ethan shouted, jumping to his feet, fists clenched. "No need for rough stuff."

The guard turned toward Ethan and swung the butt of his rifle around. Ethan jumped back in time to miss the blow but in time to hit the off-balance guard in the jaw with his right fist.

Ethan stood over the fallen guard, ready to hit him again.

Other guards rushed over to their fallen comrade. Kelly and Novak jumped up to defend Ethan, and a melee broke out. Other Union soldiers joined in the fist fight. For a while, it seemed they would overpower the guards.

But fists were no match for rifles and bayonets. After a few Yanks went down with blows and wounds, the fighting stopped. Ethan lay on the ground, doubled up from a blow to the midsection. Kelly and Novak stood over him protectively.

A pistol shot rang out. "All right, you Yanks," shouted an officer from on top of his horse. "Line up in front a' me," he ordered.

As soon as all the prisoners were lined up, he warned them, "Another crazy outburst like this, an' I'll have ya all shot.

"Sergeant," he ordered. "Control yer men, or I'll have yer stripes. Is that clear?"

"Yes, sir."

Kelly and Novak helped Ethan to his feet.

"Thanks fer standin' up fer me, Ethan," Kelly whispered.

Having gotten his breath back, Ethan cautioned, "Just remember how that loud voice of yours can be heard across a room full of soldiers. So, don't expect I'll be up to it every time, Kelly."

"I'll be watchin' you, Yank," the guard Ethan had knocked down warned him. "Jus' give me one excuse, and you're a dead man."

"Listen ta' dat," Novak suddenly said. They could all hear the thunder of artillery to their rear. Those sounds of fighting faded as the small column of prisoners were marched most of the day southeast toward Richmond.

Never thought I'd wish to be back there with the fighting, Ethan thought. *It's gotta be better 'en this, though.*

By the end of that day, he could see the spires of the Richmond churches. They camped for the night on the outskirts of the city. Only then were they given some tepid water to drink and hardtack to chew.

In the heavy fog of the early morning, they were marched through the city and across a narrow bridge onto an island in the middle of the James River.

"Here ya' are, lads," one of the guards told them. "This is Belle Isle, yas new home. Sit down now and take off yer boots."

"What the hell!" Kelly murmured.

"Don' worry about it, Irish," the guard told him. "You'll not be needing 'em. You're a prisoner, after all. An yer not going anyplace real soon, I'm thinkin."

As he unlaced his boots, Ethan thought, *I haven't gone without shoes since I was a kid. From all the barefoot Rebs I've seen, they probably want my boots for themselves. Damn, I've just broken in these, too.*

Kelly asked the Reb guard standing by him, "What is this place anyway?"

"Well, Irish," he responded. "I'm told it was sort a' playground for the local high an' mighty gents and their ladies. They would ride out here on Sundays in their fancy carriages to picnic and paddle their sweethearts around in funny little boats called 'rowboats', don't ya' know."

"Don't look like much of a playground ta' me now," Kelly remarked.

"That was all before you Yanks decided to invade our country, a' course."

"You started the fighting," Kelly fired back.

"Did we now?" the Reb guard responded. "As I hear it, you wouldn't leave that fort in Charleston Harbor; we had to force ya' out."

"Ya," Kelly responded. "But our flag was flying over that fort. Wasn't it?"

"So, you and me are fighting this war over a piece of cloth flying over a pile of rocks, are we?"

Kelly laughed. "Does seem sort a' funny, don't it?"

"Ya, it does," the Reb guard agreed. "Hey, Yank. I gotta go. Good luck to ya'."

Ethan, Kelly and Novak sat on the ground back to back. Ethan looked around at his surroundings and all the activity around him.

This island can't be more than ten acres from one end to the other, he figured. *We're jammed into less than half a' that. Full a' guys. What's next, I wonder?*

"Hey, Ethan," shouted Kelly. "See all those tents goin' up over there?"

"Just noticed that," Ethan agreed. "I hope there's one for us. Likely be pretty chilly out here on the open ground."

Before long, shelters had been erected all over the area.

"When they goin ta' let us use a tent, ya think?" Kelly asked.

"Why don't you jus' go over an' ask dem, Kelly?" Novak teased.

"Ya, an' git my head bashed in?" Kelly responded. "No, thank you very much."

"You guys just keep your mouths shut," Ethan told them. "The Rebs will let us know what they have in mind soon enough."

Kelly spoke up again, "I don't like not knowing what's happening; not one bit."

Both Ethan and Novak broke out laughing.

"What are you guys laughing at?" Kelly asked, feeling left out.

"You, loudmouth dummy," Novak said. "So, da Rebs should give a damn vat you vant?"

"I'm not loud," Kelly protested.

Ethan and Novak lay back on the ground and howled with laughter again.

"Well, I'm not."

"Whatever you say, Kelly," Ethan conceded.

Strangely, the tents remained empty for days. The prisoners huddled outside in their windy island prison without overcoats or blankets

They were served some warm soup, though.

"Did you find any meat in your bowl, Ethan?" Novak asked.

"One piece," Ethan responded. "But I think it was moving. Does that count as meat?"

Kelly added, "At least the soup wasn't cold and the bread was not too old. When do we eat again?"

"Beats me, Kelly," Ethan told him. "I asked. But the Rebs who doled out this stuff didn't know anything. At least nothing they were willing to tell me."

LOWELL

Michelle Schock was waiting in front of Brady's General Store for her husband, Carl. He had gone to the grain elevator while she did the weekly shopping. He pulled up with their wagon and loaded the supplies she had purchased.

As soon as she climbed up on the wagon bench, she said, "Father, there was a letter for us at the Brady General Store."

"From Ethan?"

"Yes. Do you want me to open it?"

"Ya! We can't know what he says until you do," he said, chuckling.

"I'll read it to you."

Hi Everyone,

I hope this letter finds you both well. You know, Papa, we worked harder and longer on the farm than we do in this army. You get up earlier, and by dinner time you have done more work than we do in almost a week.

After reveille, we clean up and eat, then we have roll call. Then, our platoon sergeant drills us by marching us around for an hour or so. After that, we practice battlefield movements in response to bugle calls and voice commands.

Then, we rest and clean up before we fix something to eat for our noon meal. Some of the city boys call it lunch. That is followed by more drills. We are done early in the afternoon. Then, some of the guys play cards, others read, some even repair their clothing. I haven't gotten the knack of that sewing business. I guess you spoiled me at home, Momma.

Let me tell you, Momma, your cooking is so much better than ours. I can't wait for my next leave when I can come home to your cooking. I will even welcome doing chores again, Papa. Aside from the poor food, the worst thing about camp life is the boredom. I had thought I joined up to fight the Rebs.

Instead, we just drill, then sit around, then drill some more.

The latest rumor is that we are going to march on Richmond. The newspapers we read here keep urging Lincoln to attack the Confederate capitol. If that city is captured, they say it will end the war. Wouldn't that be great? The latest rumor is that we are going to attack that city very soon.

Most of us believe that General McClellan would win the war if it was a marching contest, or if the winner was decided by which army looked the best. Anyway, if the rumor we hear is correct, and they seldom are, we push off first thing tomorrow morning and head south to attack Richmond.

Thank you for your last package, Momma. The socks and underwear you included came just in time. I had worn through the ones I had. The boys loved your oatmeal cookies. They were really good.

I will write you as soon as I get a minute. I don't know how mail is handled when an army is on the march. We will see. So, don't worry if my next letter is not in your hands quickly. I miss you and love you both.

Your loving son,

Ethan

"Oh, Papa," Ethan's mother exclaimed. "I miss our boy so much." She began to cry.

"Ya. I do, too, Momma. But Ethan made his decision," her husband Carl reminded her. "He is not a boy any longer, you know. He is a man now, and we must respect that. I miss him, too. We will pray for his safety, of course.

"But no more crying now, Momma. We have work to do at home. Besides, we must live our lives just as our son has to live his, God bless him."

"Yes, Papa," Michelle responded. "I understand. But it is so hard. You have the daily chores, the planting and all that to keep you busy. My house is so quiet and empty."

"Maybe we need a little one in our house again, Momma?" Carl suggested.

"What are you thinking? Maybe a baby?"

"Ya," Carl responded with a big smile. "A baby, Momma."

His wife stopped her crying and sat up straight. "Papa," Michelle reminded him. "Where did you get such a crazy idea? I am too old to have a baby."

"Maybe you are. But it would be fun to try," Carl said with a smile.

"Papa! The way you talk." Michelle then changed the subject, sort of. "You know what Emma Hecht and her husband did, don't you?"

"Ya, I do. Everybody knows they went to the old country and came back with two little girls and a nanny."

"I'd like to talk with them about how they are managing being parents again," Michelle suggested.

"Fine with me, old girl," Carl said. He put his right arm around his wife and gave her a squeeze. "Does that mean you don't want to try the old way, the way that brought us Ethan?"

"Oh, Papa."

WASHINGTON CITY

Captain Richard Pope was joined by thirty or so other prisoners and jammed into a boxcar headed for the Union capital. The side slats of the car allowed a brisk flow of air to penetrate the walls of the car. There was room for most of the men to sit, but because one of the prisoners fouled himself, most of the men chose to stand as far away from him as possible for the short ride to the Capitol.

Early in the war, Washington City was the Union's eastern distribution center for prisoners. After a stop of a few days at the Old Washington County Jail, prisoners were usually sent to the Old Capitol Prison.

Located on the corner of 1st and A Streets, this brick building was one of the earliest structures in Washington. Built in 1800, it was first a tavern and boarding house prior to the War of 1812. After the British burned the Capitol in August of 1814, the building was purchased by the government, refurbished and used by both houses of Congress and the Supreme Court for many years. Even after the new Capitol was completed in 1819, it was referred to as the "Old Capitol Building".

After the Civil War began in 1861, the rundown Old Capitol Building was taken over by Washington's Provost Marshal. It was then converted into a prison for political prisoners, local prostitutes, insubordinate Union officers and Confederate prisoners of war.

* * *

Pope and other Confederate prisoners of war were marched to the Old Capitol Building. Enlisted men were sent to the second floor, the officers to cells on the first floor, along with political prisoners.

"You don't have ta' push," Pope told the guard who shoved him into a stuffy ten-by-eight-foot cell. Before he could get adjusted to the darkness of the room, the steel door slammed shut behind him.

"Welcome to our little piece of heaven," someone sitting on the stone floor said. "You must be someone important to be housed in this shit hole."

"I'm Richard Pope, Captain of a South Carolina cavalry unit. Who are you?"

"I am the mayor of Baltimore, Maryland," came the response. "Or at least I was until Lincoln ordered me arrested and sent here." The man stood and approached Pope with his hand extended in greeting. "My name is George Brown. I've been in here since September 13th."

"Just like that? You were arrested and imprisoned?"

"Yup! Just like that. Lincoln, the Dictator in Chief, decided that I was a danger to the Republic. There are others like me in cells around Washington. They, too, criticized official federal policy."

"When does your case come before a court?" Pope asked.

"I have been held without charge for several months now," Brown told his new cellmate. "I've not been allowed legal representation or even contact with my family. The last message smuggled to me said that the Supreme Court has ruled that arrests like mine are illegal, as is the suspension of my right to a speedy hearing. But Lincoln's people have ignored the ruling."

"I've read somewhere that Mr. Lincoln is a real stickler for the rule of law," Pope related. "Now you're telling me that he ignores the law?"

"It appears so," Mayor Brown said. "At least in my case.

"Maryland is a slave state, you see; always has been. Since early Colonial times; at least two hundred years anyway," Brown continued. "The members of our legislature and the secession convention, like those in Virginia, North Carolina, Tennessee and Arkansas, held back during the secession winter, hoping that the issues would be resolved peaceably."

"So, what did your legislature do after Fort Sumter and Lincoln's call for troops to put down secession?" Pope asked.

"That was the rub, you see," Brown said. "Members of Maryland's legislature were split on the issue. It was sort of up in the air whether or not we would join our neighbors in Virginia and secede. But before a proper vote could be taken, Lincoln's goons arrested the Speaker of the House, Kilburn, and other pro-Confederate legislators. Then the pro-Union faction in the Maryland legislature was in the majority. They voted to stay in the Union."

"But you're not a legislator," Pope protested. "Why were you arrested?"

"The city of Baltimore is considered a Southern town. It is also the rail center through which Northern troops must pass to reach Washington City. The mayor of that city controls the local police force. The police force controls the decidedly pro-Confederate citizens of the city."

"How so?"

"Early in the war, a column of Northern boys in blue marched from the train station in Baltimore through that city toward Washington City. The event drew a crowd. Violence broke out. With today's high feelings, the difference between a crowd of onlookers and a mob is still the Baltimore police."

"So," Pope said. "It was decided that you could not be trusted to maintain order and protect Northern troops marching through the city."

"Correct," Brown agreed. "Thus, I was arrested and have been held without bond being set or charges made against me before a magistrate. Baltimore has been under martial law ever since, too."

Pope responded, "To my knowledge, nothing like that has happened in the South under President Davis; he hasn't arrested anybody. Not even Unionists.

"In fact, the Charleston and Richmond papers I have been reading are full of criticism of President Davis. No one has been arrested for that. But I must admit that I don't read of any Union support in those papers, either. Once the war began, Unionists and supporters of secession pretty much closed ranks against Lincoln and the North."

"So, where does that leave us, Captain Pope?" Brown asked.

"I'm supposed to be exchanged. At least that's what I'm told," Pope responded. "What about you?"

"I don't rightly know," Brown said. "Martial law hasn't been used in this country since the Revolution, when the Brits used it to try and control the colonials. So, it's a new thing in this country. Lincoln's breaking new ground in a lot of areas. Hell's bells, he's even making war without a proper declaration from his own Congress."

"I have read that he insists he doesn't need a war declaration from Congress to suppress rebellion," Pope added.

Brown continued, "Lincoln also says that he is only doing the job he has sworn to do. He says that even though the Constitution does not expressly forbid secession, he insists that the document implies the permanency of the Union. Thus, secession is illegal and must be considered rebellion.

"On that basis, he contends that he must use Federal troops to put down a rebellion too difficult for local Federal officials to manage. Bottom line, he can do what he is doing because it is the president's obligation to suppress any and all such uprisings."

"Before war broke out," Pope told his cellmate, "I attended the Citadel College in South Carolina. My Constitutional Law professor spent a good deal of time on this subject during the recent Secession Winter.

"We spent practically the entire winter reviewing Madison's writings on the Constitutional Convention," Pope went on. "It was pretty clear that the framers thought the new union of states they were proposing was a compact, always subject to the consent of the member states.

"Nowhere did we read that the future union would be permanent under any and all circumstances. In fact, voters in three states made their approval of the document and future membership in any union dependent upon whether or not that membership continued to be in the best interests of their people."

"Which states were those, Captain?" Brown asked.

"The constitutional convention delegates in New York, Virginia and Rhode Island decided to approve membership in the new arrangement, the United States of America. But they did so only if it was understood that they could withdraw from that union if participation ceased to be in the best interests of their citizens."

"That appears to be pretty plain to me," Brown stated.

"Sure, in the safety of our classroom," Pope said chuckling. "My college classmates and I thought so, too. For sure, none of us thought then that we would soon be fighting a war to decide that very issue."

"I doubt if Mr. Lincoln cares what you and your college classmates decided anyway," Brown added, joining the laughter.

"By the way, Mister Mayor," Pope said, "this heavy conversation is making me hungry. When do our jailers feed the prisoners around here?"

"What day is this, Captain Pope?" Brown asked.

"What in hell does the day of the week have to do with eating?" Pope snapped.

"Everything, young fella," Brown informed him. "On Monday, we had a little nearly raw ham, some very hard and almost moldy bread and a cold cup of coffee. We don't get any more until Thursday. So, what day of the week is it today?"

"It's Wednesday."

"That means we're due for another delightful meal tomorrow: Thursday."

"Damn! I haven't eaten anything for two days already," Pope told Brown. "By tomorrow, my stomach will think my throat's been cut."

"Be patient, my young soldier; patience," Brown urged. "Just relax. Save your energy. Neither you nor I are going anyplace real soon anyway."

* * *

As Brown had predicted, the next day the two cellmates were in a food line. Into each man's bowl a ladle of hot liquid was poured.

"Is this it?" Pope whispered. "This is all for the next two days?"

"Shush!" Brown urged. "Complaining will only get it taken away."

At the end of the serving table, each of them received what amounted to a half loaf of course, dry bread.

They found a sunny spot in the prison's exercise area, leaned against the sunlit wall and ate their food.

"You might notice that the bread is rather dry," Brown told Pope. "The stale bread seems more appetizing if you dip it into the hot soup. Sort of reminds me of dipping freshly baked bread into hot beef gravy. It isn't, of course. But it does add some substance to my food fantasies. Oh, look!" Brown exclaimed. "I think I see a bit of meat at the bottom of my bowl."

"If you have any meat, you're the only one of us who has any a 'tall," Richard Pope chuckled. "I don't suppose we're going to get any coffee?"

"What you have right now, my friend, is probably all you're going to get today. Don't expect any dessert either."

"Do you have any good news, Mayor Brown?"

"Only that you're probably going to be exchanged sooner than I will be allowed to return to my Baltimore home."

"I hope I am, Mr. Brown," Pope answered. "But why are you so pessimistic about your chances of release?"

"Because your side very probably has a captive they're willing to exchange for you. But in my case, no one is the least bit interested one way or the other. If I'm released, it will most probably be because I'm no longer considered a threat to Union control of Baltimore and that they're tired of feeding me."

"Were you ever a threat to Union control of Baltimore?"

"Most definitely," Brown chuckled. "I would have used whatever power I had as Mayor of Baltimore to have that city and the state of Maryland become part of the Confederate States of America.

"I never thought President Lincoln was stupid, only that he was a dictator acting outside the Constitution. So, I wasn't all that surprised when he had me arrested and replaced."

Pope responded, "You don't seem bitter about what has happened to you, I must say."

"I try to be a realist, Captain Pope. There's not much to be gained being angry in any case. But I will do my best to get even one day."

"I don't think I'd want you as an enemy, Mr. Brown," Pope told him.

"I'm not very dangerous to anyone at the moment, but one day."

The next morning, the two were awakened when their cell door was opened. A Union soldier stepped into the room.

"Captain Pope, the commandant wants to see you in his office, sir."

Mr. Brown commented, "I expect that exchange I predicted has been arranged, Captain."

"I hope so, sir," Pope responded, extending his hand to his cellmate. "I also hope you see the inside of your home soon, too."

"Take care, my friend."

"Goodbye, Mr. Brown."

CHARLESTON

"Mother," Colonel Pope shouted as he entered his wife's darkened room. "I've just received a telegram with wonderful news from the War Office in Richmond."

"Is it about Richard?"

The colonel moved across the room toward his wife. She was sitting upright on her bed.

"Look for yourself, dear." He handed her the telegram.

"The Yankees released him. Thank the Lord!" she whispered, holding the paper to her chest. Tears rolled down her cheeks.

"Yes," the colonel confirmed. "The Yankees exchanged him for some Union troops captured a few days ago during a recent skirmish near Harper's Ferry. President Davis arranged it personally for us."

Mrs. Pope snapped, "That's the first decent thing that awful man has done since he became president."

"You're being very harsh, dear."

"He bungled our relationship with the Union and got us into this ruinous war," she spat. "My sons, Charles and Richard, have been pulled into it. And now, even you. I won't let him drag my youngest son into this hopeless conflict."

"We must all do our part, dear," Pope insisted.

"No," his wife insisted. "David will stay home with me."

The Colonel sighed. "You baby him too much, my dear. He has become a weakling. Do him good to be among men fighting for a good cause."

"No, I tell you," she shouted at her husband. "None of your damnable holy cause, you hear? I've borne you three sons. You will leave me at least one. David is mine!"

"But dear…"

"Don't you dear me. You will use all that influence of yours you brag about to keep David home safe with me. You hear?"

The colonel's shoulders slumped. He rose from his chair and walked toward the bedroom door.

"Promise me!" she shouted to his back.

The colonel paused and looked back at his wife's tearful face.

"Yes, dear," he promised.

* * *

A week later, the Pope's Charleston home was the scene of celebration. Richard was home, freed from the Yankee prison. His brother, Charles, escorted him home from Richmond. Even Mrs. Pope was downstairs to witness the homecoming.

"All my sons are home at last," she told everyone who would listen. "Would that they never had to leave me again."

Dr. Charles Pope, in the grey Confederate dress uniform of a major, stood alongside his wife, Mary Jacqueline. They joined his father, Colonel Pope, in the home's entryway to greet the arriving guests, the cream of Charleston. Everyone wanted to congratulate Captain Richard Pope on his release from the Washington City Yankee prison.

It wasn't long before all the men had a glass of wine in their hands.

Charles raised his glass and gave the first toast. "To the safe return of my brother, Richard!" he shouted.

"Hear Hear!" everyone agreed.

Someone else shouted, "To the Confederacy and President Davis!"

"Hear Hear!" everyone agreed. Almost everyone agreed, that is.

"No!" Mrs. Pope shouted.

Surprised, a hush came over the crowd and every eye turned toward her.

Colonel Pope and his sons hurried to her side.

"Help me get her upstairs to her room, boys," he whispered.

"You can't keep me from telling the truth in my own home," she shouted. "Davis is a bumbling fool who got us into a war that will ruin us all. Mark my words: we are all doomed, I tell you."

Charles and Richard, her two sons, picked up her chair and carried their frail shouting mother up the stairs. Mary Jacqueline followed them into her mother-in-law's bedroom.

"I won't hear of a toast to that villain in my home," Mrs. Pope shouted again. "His war is destroying my family."

Her sons put her on her bed, and Colonel Pope closed the bedroom door.

Charles turned to his wife. "Mary Jacqueline, would you fetch my medical bag? It's under the bed in our room."

"Calm yourself, Mother," Richard soothed. "Please. We are celebrating my return from the North and a Yankee prison. It is time for joy, not angry talk. Please."

She grabbed hold of her son Richard's hand and said, "Don't return to Davis' war. Stay home, safe with me, son."

"Mother," he responded. "I love you dearly. But I must help defend our country. I must return to my post and do my part."

His mother pushed him away. "Go, then. You're just like your father, never thinking of me."

By now, Charles had soaked a cloth with chloroform. "Father, Richard," he asked. "Hold Mother down for me." He held the cloth over her nose while she struggled.

"Stop it, Charles," she shouted. "I'm your mother. Stop it!"

Rather quickly, she slumped back on the mattress and was quiet.

Colonel Pope called his wife's personal servant into the room.

"Prepare your mistress for bed," he ordered. "Stay by her side. Should she awaken, get Doctor Charles immediately."

"Yes, sur," the Negro slave promised.

"Would you like me to stay with her, Father Pope?" Mary Jacqueline asked.

"Thank you, my dear, but no," he told her. "You must now act as the Pope family's hostess downstairs. Come, boys, we must all rejoin our guests."

* * *

The Popes left the room and went downstairs.

After they did so, they circulated the news that Mrs. Pope's outburst was due to the great anxiety she suffered over the imprisonment of her son, Richard. Her outburst was due to her relief at his release. She is resting in her room, they said, and would not rejoin the gathering.

Later, Colonel Pope asked for everyone's attention.

"Thank you for joining us today to celebrate the safe return of our son, Captain Richard Pope," he began. "I want to take this opportunity to announce that President Davis has assigned him to the staff of our hero of the Battle of Bull Run, General P. T. Beauregard."

After the shouting and cheers died down some, Colonel Pope added, "Richard does not know it yet, but that assignment carries with it a promotion to major." More cheering erupted.

"Very soon, I fear that I will be taking orders from him." Laughter.

"We hope to fatten him up some before he leaves for his new assignment. For now, though, please join us for refreshments in the garden."

* * *

Later that evening, Charles and Mary Jacqueline were lying in bed side by side after making love.

"I wish you could hold me in your arms forever, darling," she sighed.

"I wish I could, too," Charles responded.

"Why can't I stay with you in Richmond?" she asked for the tenth time since he was assigned to hospital duty there.

"In the first place, it is too dangerous for you there," he reminded her. "In the second place, my father needs you here to help care for my mother."

"Your father must be aware that your mother hates me," Mary Jacqueline insisted. "She welcomes my help as much as she wants the pox. She considers me a Yankee opportunist who stole her first born from her. You must know that, too. So, you've got to come up with a better reason than that for my staying here."

"The danger in Richmond is very real," Charles began. "The city is virtually under siege by the Federals. If you think you are suspect here in Charleston because you're from the north, that's nothing compared to the hostility you'd encounter in Richmond. There are two large prisons in the heart of the city. The largest hospital in the South is located there, and the danger from infectious disease is very real."

"While we're discussing my not being welcomed in your home or in Charleston, what do you think of my suggestion that I go to Philadelphia and stay with my loving parents in that friendly city to await the arrival of our baby?"

"Please, dear," Charles pleaded. "We've had this discussion before. Let's enjoy the evening and not argue. Please."

"All right, if you insist."

Charles pulled his wife closer. "What do you wish for the most this night?" he asked.

"That you hold me close and make love to me until dawn. What about you?" she asked.

"That you tell me what is most important to you," he continued.

"That you survive this war and promise to love me as long as I live," his wife responded.

"I can't guarantee the first, but I make that second part of your request with all my heart," Charles assured her.

"And you? What do you wish for the most, Charles?"

"That I soon return to you safe and sound, never to leave your side again."

Mary Jacqueline moved her hand down her husband's body.

"Oh!" she said. "It appears that you have already returned to me." With that, she pushed him on his back, slid over his body, and took him in.

Charles granted her wish.

* * *

In town, Richard Pope spent the night with his favorite Charleston lady of the evening, Molly.

Covered with perspiration, they were both relaxing on their sides, facing one another. Richard was more than a client to her, so she had cleared her schedule to remain with him the entire night.

"So, ya 'all is headin' west to join this Beauregard general?" she asked, leaning against him and groping Richard with her experienced hand.

"You're making it difficult for me to think clearly, Molly."

"You want me to stop?"

"Absolutely not!" he confessed hotly.

"But to answer your question," Richard managed to say, "yes. In a few days, I'll head back to Richmond. From there, I travel west to Vicksburg. There, I'll join the general in Corinth, Mississippi. At least that's the plan."

"What I wants ta' know is, what is da plan for the rest a' tonight, Major Pope?"

Richard turned Molly onto her back and gazed down at her beautiful tan face. Watching for her reaction, he ran his hand down her body until he reached her wet core.

"Ummm!" she sighed. "You sure 'nuff know how to get Molly goin'. Don't ya?"

"I had a good teacher."

"Now who cud a' dat been, I wonder?" she chuckled.

"I was just a sixteen-year-old kid when my father brought me here the first time," Richard reminded her.

"I remember. An dat doctor brother a' yours was brought to me before dat, too," she reminded him as she stroked him gently. "How he doin' wit dat Yankee gal he brought back from up north?"

"They are madly in love, Molly," Richard told her. "She is expecting their first child. And as a matter of fact, I'm guessing they are in their room at my father's house this very minute, doing pretty much the same thing we're doing."

"Charles must be enjoyin' dat girl, too. 'Cause he ain't been ta' see me since he brought her back to Charleston.

"Your brother, Charles, I 'member he be a good learner. He be a gentle lover, too," Molly revealed. "I spect dat Yankee lady he took as his wife is enjoying da training I done give him."

"I'm sure she is enjoying it, Molly."

"Speakin' a' bein' a good lover an' all," Molly reminded Richard, "when you gonna stop talkin' an start showin' me how good a lover you be?"

Richard moved between Molly's legs and showed her.

Later, they rested side by side again.

"Whatever happened to the son you had with Charles?" Richard asked.

Molly looked at her lover. "Dat beautiful little boy be wit a good Christian white fambly up in Boston," she told Richard.

"He be getting a good education, so he be someone important one day."

"You think he will be accepted by those snobby New England Yankees?" Richard asked.

"Time will tell. But he so light-skinned, I spect' it be easy fer him to pass," Molly judged. "I bet nobody up der even knows he be da chile of a Negro woman. Him wid all dat yellow hair he got from your brother.

"I'll forever be grateful dat da colonel, your father, he took care a' everything," she continued. "I don' think your brother even knows dat I had his son, or even what happened to our little boy."

"You do, though?" Richard asked.

"I don't know his white name or anythin' like dat, only dat he be wit a good fambly in Boston," Molly responded quickly. "An I don' want ta know more. Da boy is better off not knowin' anything 'bout me either."

"For a lady who enjoys a man, you do an awful lot a' talking," Richard accused Molly.

"You caught me there, I must admit," Molly chuckled. "It's jus' been so long since I seen you. Come here ta' Molly. Show me how much you missed her."

Richard didn't leave her until after dawn.

RICHMOND, VIRGINIA

General P.T. Beauregard was getting ready to join General Albert Sidney Johnson in Corinth, Mississippi, as the second in command of the Western Theatre of operations. Colonel Thomas Jordan, Beauregard's assistant, was pulling a staff together for the general and organizing the move west.

"Who the hell is this Major Pope who's just been assigned to my staff?" Beauregard asked.

"He's a cavalryman from a South Carolina regiment," Jordan informed his boss. "He was captured, imprisoned in Washington City, and just recently exchanged. He was promoted to his current rank and assigned to your staff by President Davis himself."

"Do you think he's a spy for Davis?" Beauregard asked.

"Could be, sir," Jordan responded. "Pope's father used his influence with President Davis to obtain this assignment for his son. Remember, sir, you are still the hero of our victory at Bull Run. So, being on your staff is considered quite an honor. It could be as simple as that."

"Maybe so," Beauregard grumbled. "But I don't trust Davis to do me any favors. Remember, he's sending me out west to get rid of me. He's jealous because of my popularity with the people and the Richmond press crowd.

"Keep an eye on this Pope fella, Jordan," Beauregard continued. "I don't want him to have any access to the telegraph lines. Everything he hears, sees and does goes through you. Understand? He's your responsibility."

"Yes, sir," Jordan responded. "I'll take care of it, sir."

"See that you do. I don't want to have to look over my shoulder all the time. Davis is just looking for a reason to leave me out in the west away from Richmond and the press, or maybe ask for my resignation. I don't want this Pope to give him any ammunition."

"I understand, sir."

CHARLESTON

Colonel Pope was standing with his two sons at the railroad center in Charleston, South Carolina. His son Charles, the doctor, was returning to the military hospital in Richmond. His son Richard was on his way west to Vicksburg, and then Corinth, Mississippi, to take his place on the staff of General P.T. Beauregard.

"Richard," he urged, "be careful of Beauregard. He's known to be a highly emotional man. If he thinks you're on his staff as a spy for President Davis, you're in serious trouble. Remember, you're there to serve our cause, not take sides in a petty feud between Davis and the general. Convince Beauregard that you're loyal to him, and you'll be fine."

"Yes, Father," Richard responded. "I understand. I don't like all this infighting. We have our hands full enough with the Yankees. All our energy should be directed toward defeating them. But I understand. I think I can play the game."

"Charles," Colonel Pope said. "Look after yourself in that hospital. You've got a family now. I expect to see you survive this war for their sakes at least."

"Yes, Father. Some things, I cannot avoid. But I will be careful."

The three men hugged.

"Remember, boys, I love you and will pray for your safe return."

"Thank you, Father," his sons answered, almost in unison.

Colonel Pope then turned and walked away with a heavy heart.

* * *

The Pope boys relaxed in their railroad car as it traveled northwest toward Columbia, South Carolina. They had enjoyed a family dinner the previous evening and consumed a good deal of wine. The rest of the night, Charles was awake with his wife; Richard was with Molly again.

So, it was not surprising that the first hour or so of the journey was spent sleeping. They were awakened by the railroad conductor.

"Get your baggage, everyone," he shouted as he walked through the railroad car. "We have ta' change trains at the next station."

The two Pope men were instantly awake. They gathered their baggage and prepared to leave one train and board another.

"You'd think this important railroad link between Charleston and our state capitol, Columbia, would all be on one gauge track, for heaven's sake," Charles commented.

"You'd think," Richard agreed. "But I fear big landholders like our father opposed spending money on such things. They wanted to keep most of the income from their exports to buy more land and slaves. As it was, they used to pay nearly a third of their income to the Yankees for shipping, insurance and bank payments. They sure didn't want to also pay higher taxes to finance railroads. They like using rivers to transport their produce; it's free."

"Their argument that South Carolina has an excellent river system to transport goods to the coast couldn't be denied. So, spending their money on railroads never seemed that important to them," Charles added.

"Even so, that was certainly short-sighted, in my view," Richard said. "Remember, last summer it was Joe Johnston's troops from the west who turned the tide at Manassas in our favor. His troops were brought to the battlefield by train. So, it's obvious now that we need a better rail system if we are ever to defeat the Yankees."

"We need a lot of stuff, actually," Charles continued with a chuckle. "Before the war, nowhere in the South did we make shoes, nails, plows, railroad cars or rails, rifles or cannon. Most all our pre-war capital was devoted to agriculture. That's where men like our father made their money. We're paying the price now, believe me."

"How you doin' with medicines, Charles? You have enough?"

"Thus far, we do," Charles answered his brother. "If we have another big battle around Richmond, it will put a strain on stuff like chloroform and laudanum. And if this war drags on and the Yankee blockade becomes more effective, we will have a serious problem getting the medicines we need.

"Truth be known," Charles continued, "our mother was not far from the truth. For all the bravado about gaining our independence after one or two battles, war with the North was and still is a damned foolish enterprise."

"You're sounding pretty defeatist, brother," Richard told Charles. "Don't you see any hope for the South?"

"You're the military man, Richard. You tell me. But the way I see it, we still have no navy. The Yanks have enough ocean-going ships to blockade our coast and still protect their trade relationship with Europe.

"This past winter, they launched an ironclad naval force on the Mississippi and began to recapture control of that river, the Ohio, the Cumberland and the Tennessee Rivers, too. As a result, we've already lost Kentucky and western Tennessee, along with its capital of Nashville."

"It appears that you're pretty much on top a' things," Richard told his older brother, Charles.

"I haven't got much to do with my time in Richmond but read. I find that the Richmond press gives out a lot of information, much to the displeasure of President Davis."

"So, what is your prognosis, Doctor Pope?"

"There is no magic pill in my medical bag, I'm afraid. Remember, while you were at the Citidel College studying military tactics, I was in the University of Pennsylvania's medical school. While there, I got to know a lot of Yankees. By firing on Fort Sumter, we got them all mad, real mad. And they are a stubborn lot. So, losing a couple a' battles will not discourage them. I expect them to be in this for the long haul."

"No chance for us, then?"

"I believe that our only chance is to keep killing Yankee soldiers in such large numbers that the people of the North will tire of the war and will force Lincoln to let us go."

"So," Richard interrupted, "we have to keep fighting until at least the next presidential election up North and hope that Lincoln is defeated."

"That's the way I see it," Charles chided his brother. "'Course, now that you and your General Beauregard are headed west, you could change everything with a series of smashing victories."

"That's the plan, I'm sure," Richard said.

Their train was moving out of Columbia now. The Pope brothers watched as the city flashed by their windows.

"I don't know about you, Richard," Charles told him, "but I didn't have much more than a cup of coffee and a biscuit this morning. I'm hungry."

"I could use a snack, too. Let's see what cook packed for us."

Their baggage revealed an amazing spread of food: hard boiled eggs, fruit, slices of honey ham, cheese, baked chicken and chocolate cake.

"This is a feast," Charles told his brother. "She even included a flask of wine and another one of water."

"Don't you think the Irish linen she sent along is a good touch, too?" Richard chuckled.

"We mustn't forget our table manners, brother," Charles reminded him humorously.

"I guess."

BELLE ISLE PRISON

Belle Isle is an island in the James River. It was a favorite Sunday picnic spot for the people of Richmond, Virginia. The waters of the river swirled rapidly around the 100 acres of the island.

It wasn't long after the first battle of Manassas that the city of Richmond was crowded with prisoners of war. Union officers were assigned to the Libby tobacco warehouse in Richmond, while enlisted men were sent to Belle Isle.

The river between Richmond and the island was between a third and one half a mile wide. A long bridge connected the island to the mainland. This island was a low piece of ground that the winter's chilly winds easily swept across.

Water was not healthy to drink, and the stench of the island was terrible. Only one-third of the prisoners had shelters. The rest had to huddle together in the open.

View of the Belle Isle prison camp from the island's high ground overlooking the compound Downtown Richmond, including the Confederate Capitol, are visible in the background. (From "Frank Leslie's Illustrated Famous Leaders and Battle Scenes of the Civil War.")

Prisoners on the island had huddled together the last few nights. They had little to shelter themselves from the chilly, damp and miserable rainy conditions. Many of them walked around this morning just to get the blood circulating before standing in formation for roll call. It took two hours in the rain for the Reb sergeants to get the count right. By that time, everyone was soaked to the skin. Dozens of prisoners had fainted and lay in the mud.

The miserable prisoners could see the rows of tents that had been erected by the Rebs but still stood empty.

"When the hell are they goin' ta' let us use those tents?" Kelly moaned. "Don't make any sense ta' leave 'em empty like they is, an' us standin' in tha rain an' all."

Novak said, "It don't have ta' make sense, ya' stupid Irishman. They's in charge. So, they makes the rules."

"Maybe, but that still don't make any sense ta' me," Kelly responded. "What you think, Ethan?"

"I don't," Ethan Schock answered. "I can't do nothing to change the situation, so I jus' don't think about it."

"Now, if that don't beat all," Kelly exclaimed. "Ya gotta think about somethin'. Don't seem right that you don't."

"Right or not, I'm not going to waste my time worrying about stuff I don't control. End of story. You need to worry about something? Go right ahead, but don't expect me to wear myself out, too."

"Jus don't seem natural, that's all," Kelly concluded.

Novak laughed. "For Lord's sake, Kelly, let it go. Listen to da man. He ain't gonna moan an' groan about stuff. But you go right ahead if'n it makes you feel better. Knock yourself out. Moan an' groan all ya' want.

"Did we get any new prisoners today, Ethan?" Novak asked.

"I don't know. But John Ransom told me a bunch came in last night."

"Ransom's from the Michigan Cavalry Brigade, isn't he?" Kelly asked.

"That's the way I hear it," Ethan confirmed. "He grew up in Battle Creek; heard about the regiment forming in Grand Rapids, left home and joined up. He was captured somewhere in Virginia while on patrol. Just stumbled on a Reb unit while on point. Bad luck is all."

"Didn't he say dat he had something to do mit passing out clothing sent from da North?"

"Yes, he did, Tom. He said he'd see to it we got boots as soon as possible, too," Ethan told him.

"Dat sure sounds good to me," Tom responded.

Kelly told his two squad members, "After dinner, I think I'll walk over to that area where the new guys are gathered an' see if I know any a' them. Wanna go with me?"

"Be careful," Novak warned. "Not good to wander around dis place alone while dat bunch of thieving prisoners prey on lone soldiers and newbies to da island. Sure, I go with ya'."

"How about you, Ethan? Want to go over there with us?"

"Sure. Haven't got anything else ta' do. I'll go right after noon chow, if they give us any food today, that is."

***

There was something called food served that day. The representatives of each one-hundred-man Mess met at the cooking tents to collect the food for their men.

They all had escorts to guard the food against the thieves who preyed on the unwary.

John Ransom was there getting the ration for his Mess, along with Ethan, doing the same. Ransom had been brigade quartermaster of the Ninth Michigan Cavalry when he was taken prisoner in Tennessee. They had gotten acquainted.

"Remember how I told you that a Union officer will be here soon to pass out clothing?" he told Ethan.

"Sure, I remember," Ethan assured him. "My men and I can't wait to get boots and some decent clothing to replace these rags the Rebs gave us."

"Well, it's going to happen tomorrow morning," Ransom revealed. "Right after roll call, meet me back here at the cook tent. I'm not sure we'll have enough of everything for all three of you. But I'll do my best for you."

"Thanks, John," Ethan said. "We've been barefoot since the day we were captured. With winter almost upon us, we sure need boots and decent clothing if we're going ta' survive."

"I know, I know. By the way, six of the guys in my Mess died during the night. I told our leaders that I had three good Michigan men who wanted to join us. You and your men want to join our Michigan Mess?"

"Damn right we do, John."

"That's fine with me, Ethan. But I need to be sure your guys will fit in. Let me talk to them. Can I meet with you and them right after chow today?"

"Not a problem," Ethan assured Ransom. "We've got nowhere to go anyway. Where do you want to meet?"

"At my Mess, right over by the new tents the Rebs just put up. Ya know, the empty ones?"

"We'll be back here in one hour. All right?"

"Sounds good. One hour it is then, Ethan."

Ethan returned to his area and passed out the food to the squad leaders. Then he joined his two squad members.

The three men sat quietly chewing the stale bread and sipping the hot soup.

"This crap is hardly worth eating," Kelly complained. "The soup is hardly more than hot water poured over some old corn. My bread must be at least a week old. How about you guys? You got anything better?"

"Not dat I can tell," Nowak responded.

"You, Ethan?" Kelly probed.

Ethan almost shouted, "It don't make any difference how poor my food is. It's all I got. I'm just happy I got anything a'tall!"

"Jees, ya don't hafta' take off a guy's head fer askin'," Kelly told him.

"Yes, I do, Kelly. And you, too, Novak," Ethan snapped. "We've got a chance to join a really good bunch a' guys. It could make the difference between dying or surviving."

"What's a matter with the bunch we're with?" Kelly responded.

"Nothing, actually. But they're guys from all over the North," Ethan explained. "Ransom's bunch is all from Michigan, and they're determined to help each other survive this sinkhole. I want to be part of that kind a' group."

"What's stoppin' ya', Ethan?" Novak asked.

"You two are. That's what."

"I don't understand," Novak went on. "If we all join dis Michigan Mess, what's da problem?"

"The problem is that they might not take us all in."

"Why the hell not?" Kelly wondered aloud.

"Because of you, mainly," Ethan told Kelly.

"What the hell you gettin at? What I got to do with them not takin' us into their Mess?" Kelly wanted to know.

"Because they have rules that everyone in their Mess has ta' follow. One a' them, you break all the time."

"What's that?"

"They don't tolerate anyone complaining."

Novak started to laugh so hard, he rolled over and beat the ground with his hand.

"Holy crap," he wailed. "They'd throw da likes a' you out da first day, Kelly. You complain from dawn till dusk, and den some."

"I'm not that bad," he objected. "Sure, I complain some. But we got a lot ta complain about, don't we?"

"Whether we do or not, they do not tolerate complaining," Ethan reminded both his squad members. "They want to encourage one another. They want to ignore the bad things they can do nothing to change and concentrate on the positive things that will help them all survive the bad stuff."

"Ya mean, they lie ta' one another?" Kelly asked.

"Call it anything you like," Ethan told them. "But like Tom just said, you wouldn't last more than a day in that Mess with your attitude."

"I don't have any problem with keeping a positive attitude," Tom Novak insisted. "'Specially if'n everybody else is doin' tha same thing."

"Are you two saying you'd dump me for this Michigan bunch?" Kelly said in surprise.

Ethan spoke first, "I can't speak for Tom, but yes, that's about it. I'm joining the Michigan Mess whether you decide to join them or not. I'm determined to survive this, and I'm thinkin' I'll need help ta' do it. I'm not going ta' pass up that chance out of loyalty to you, Kelly. I did that once. I'll not do it again."

"When tha' hell did you pass up a chance to survive 'cause a' me?" Kelly asked.

"Remember when the Chief snuck off the first night after we was captured?"

Novak remembered. "Ya, he left alone. Didn't even ask any of us ta join him."

"Well, that's not exactly true, Tom," Ethan said.

"He asked me to go with him. But he refused to include you, Kelly, because he said you made too much talk, too much noise. He was sure we'd all be recaptured if you were included. I refused to go without you, Kelly; that's when I passed up a chance to escape.

"But I'm not passing up a second chance to survive. I'm joining the Michigan bunch, if they'll have me."

"What about me, Ethan?" Novak asked.

"It's an individual thing, Tom. They'll talk with each of us and make their decision. I have no reason to think they'd refuse you."

"But you think they'd turn me down, don't ya?" Kelly asked.

"That's going ta' be up ta' you, Kelly; totally up ta' you."

"Oh, ya," Ethan continued. "I have some good news, too." Ransom told me, we should meet him at the cook tent tomorrow morning right after roll call to pick up some boots and some warm clothing."

"All right!" Kelly shouted. "That's more like it. Probably don't have anything near my size, I'll bet. Whoops! I mean, I'm sure they'll have something ta' fit me."

Ethan laughed heartily. "That's the right attitude, Kelly. You just may survive this hellhole after all.

"We meet with Ransom and his bunch in a few minutes. Remember, no dark thoughts. Instead, be positive. Got it, you two?"

"Right. I hear ya," Novak said.

"Kelly?"

"Ya, ya," he responded. "I got it."

"Let's go, then."

* * *

Ransom greeted the three men.

"Welcome to the Michigan Mess," he began. "We call it the Astor House of Belle Isle."

Then he introduced the two men who accompanied him.

"These men are members of our board of governors. I know this might appear to be pretty formal, but we consider membership in our Mess a privilege. Everyone in our Mess depends upon one another for survival, so we are careful who we let in. The first step is an interview.

"This is Osburn Colburn. He's a 6th Michigan cavalry man from Big Rapids. This is Bill Johnson from Jackson, who was also a cavalryman in the Michigan Brigade.

"Ethan, you'll be interviewed by Osburn. Bill, you talk with Novak. We'll meet back here when you are done."

As Colburn and Schock walked away, Ethan opened the conversation.

"Big Rapids is just a bit north of where I come from, Osburn," he said.

"And just where is that, Ethan?"

"I was born and raised in Lowell. Just a small farm town near Grand Rapids."

"I know where Grand Rapids is, a' course," Colburn responded. "But I can't place Lowell."

Ethan chuckled. "I'm not surprised. We're ten miles or so east. Just a block-long street full of shops and a grain elevator. Nice town to raise a family."

"What'd you do back in Lowell, Ethan?" Osburn asked.

"Nothing, actually," Ethan laughed. "I was just a whiny snot-nosed kid who couldn't wait ta get inta this war. How about you? You seem a good deal older than me."

"I was a lawyer back home in Big Rapids. Wish I was back there now. I'd be married with a law practice an' letting you young whipper-snappers fight this damn conflict.

"Too late for that, though. Right now, you and I need to go over our rules. All right?"

"Sure. Fire away, Osburn."

Ten or so yards away, Ransom began, too. "Do I call you Kelly?"

"Sure. Everybody does."

"You were with the Michigan 4th Infantry Division?"

"Yes," Kelly responded. "Out a' Detroit, it was. I was born and raised there, too."

"Tell me how it was you were captured."

"Our squad was on our company's flank when we was attacked real sudden. Our point man was killed, an' the rest of us were taken captive. One member of our squad escaped on the march to Richmond."

"Is that where ya' lost yer boots?"

"Yep. The Rebs took our uniforms, too, an' gave us theirs. Ratty things, as you can see. Ethan told us you were gonna get us some new stuff tomorrow. Boots, too?"

"I surely hope so, Kelly. I should find you some boots."

"That would be a fine present."

"What do ya think a' tha food here, Kelly?"

"It is a bunch a' wormy... I mean, I know I've lost some pounds, but the food's better than nothin'."

"Ever eat rat meat, Kelly?"

"Not that I know of. Hard tellin', though, what the Rebs put in our soup, don't ya know."

"Well said, Kelly."

"Let me tell you the rules we insist on in the Michigan Mess. Then you tell me if you think you can live by them. All right?"

"Fire away."

"There are six of them, all equally important to our survival: first, everyone must exercise every day. Second, every soldier must keep clean. Third, every member of the Mess must keep clean of vermin. Fourth, no one can drink any water that has not been boiled. Fifth, each of us must avoid despondency. Sixth, each of us must talk, laugh and make light of our situation. Do you have any questions about these rules?"

"That second rule," Kelly began. "How does anyone keep clean livin' in the mud like we do?"

"Good question, Kelly," Ransom responded with a chuckle. "We expect everyone to do the best he can."

"This vermin business," Kelly continued. "I expect you're talkin' about graybacks?"

"Right."

"Everybody's got em'. Only a damn fool'd expect to be free of em."

"Right," Ransom admitted, laughing. "We work at ridding ourselves of them. We have grayback contests and pick 'em off one another to see who has the most, and we even race them on a hot piece of tin. But you're right, no way for us to keep free of them entirely."

"What does that word, despondency, mean?"

"A member of our Mess was a teacher in civilian life. He insisted that that word was the only one that described the problem. All it means is that we don't allow our members to go around moaning and complaining all over the place. The negative stuff we have to endure is obvious to everyone; we don't need reminders of it."

"An' I'm supposed to laugh about the situation, too?"

"Can you change our situation?"

"Hell no. I'm a prisoner under guard who's lookin' down the barrel of a cannon up on that hill. I'm just tryin' ta' stay alive till I'm exchanged."

"So make light of it. You'll be surprised how much it improves your health. We decided what we can't change, we'll either ignore or laugh about. You think that's stupid, Kelly?"

"If'n it works, hell no. I'm all fer talkin' and laughin'."

"Then do you think you'd be able to abide by the rules of the Michigan Mess?"

"Try ta stop me, Mister," Kelly said sternly.

"I'm happy to hear it."

"Ya really call yerself the Astor House?" Kelly asked. "Ain't that a fancy hotel somewheres?"

"It is a fancy hotel in New York City, actually," Ransom explained. "And yes, we do call our Mess by that name. It's meant to be humorous, to make light of our dismal situation here on Belle Isle."

"Then that's part a' that rule about laughin' at stuff we can't change anyways."

"Now you're catching on, Kelly."

It wasn't long before the others joined them.

* * *

Back in their Mess area, Ethan, Tom Novak and Bill Kelly talked.

"Hell, Ethan," Kelly began. "That whole thing didn't turn out so bad. You had me scared shitless. When we were done, Ransom as much as told me that I was welcome ta' join his Mess."

"Me, too," Tom Novak offered." I don't think their rules are so bad. Make a lot a' sense ta' me, actually."

"You must 'a really put on an act for Ransom, Kelly," Ethan accused. "He's a pretty sharp guy. If he welcomed you into his Mess, you pulled the wool over his eyes, fer sure."

"Maybe you've judged me too harsh, Ethan," Kelly complained, smiling.

"I must have. But you'll have to keep it up if you want ta' stay in the Michigan Mess."

"We'll see who has trouble; we'll see," Kelly challenged.

* * *

At roll call the next morning, the men of the Michigan Mess stood in a cold, wet drizzle. The Confederate head guards, Sgt. Hight and Sgt. Marks, made their prisoners endure several attempts to get the count right. By the time they did, several prisoners had collapsed in the mud and everyone else was soaked to the skin.

Right after dismissal, and true to his word, John Ransom led Novak, Kelly and Schock to the shelter of a tent where Union Colonel John P. Sanderson awaited.

Northern charitable organizations and the northern government provided shoes and clothing for Union soldiers held prisoner by the Confederates. Ransom was one of those enlisted men who assisted the Colonel with the distribution.

Sanderson was an unpleasant man. A quartermaster officer captured at Harper's Ferry during one of Stonewall Jackson's lightning attacks, he was bitter that his government had not hastened to arrange an exchange for him. He took out his irritation on the enlisted men who were prisoners on Belle Isle.

On the walk to where the clothing was stored, Ransom gave a bit of advice to the men with him.

"Keep yer mouths shut while I try ta find something to fit ya," he advised them. "This Colonel Sanderson is a nasty piece of work who looks for any excuse to close up shop and return to his warm quarters over at Libby Prison in Richmond. Let me handle him."

"Who've ya got for me today, Ransom?" Sanderson asked.

"Prisoners whose boots and uniforms were taken by the Rebs, sir. Our men just need some replacements."

"Well, get on with it, will ya?" Sanderson snapped. "I don't like being out here in this damn lousy weather. When you're done, I'm gonna close up shop and get back across the bridge before the rain really comes down."

"Yes, sir," Ransom answered. "I'll get right to it, sir.

"You heard the Colonel," Ransom bellowed. "Get to it. I'm not yer nursemaid. Pick out some pants, underwear, a couple a' blouses, an' suspenders, too. They're in those boxes over there. The boots are in that box. One a' ya' go over there and find something that fits."

The three prisoners scattered. Kelly went for the boots first. Ethan found some trousers that fit, along with underwear and a set of suspenders. Novak picked out two blouses and a wide-brimmed hat.

"Just so yas know," Ransom shouted, "they don't make shoes ta' fit left an' right feet anymore. All shoes are made to fit either foot. So, you're only concerned about length. Ya got it?

"Ya'll find socks in the box alongside the boots. Take a couple a' sets a' those. Dry socks are important, don't ya know.

"Don't try ta change yer clothing now," Ransom ordered. "Wait till ya get back ta the mess area."

It wasn't long before everyone had a hat, boots and an armful of clothing.

"You done yet, Ransom?" Col. Sanderson shouted.

"Yes, sir, we are."

"Then get back to your mess area. I'm getting outta here, too."

On the way back, Kelly spoke up.

"Is that prickly bastard always like that?"

"Yup," Ransom revealed. "That pompous ass sometimes closes up early fer no reason a' tall an' leaves clothing in the boxes with men still waiting in line for stuff intended for them."

Novak made a quiet comment, "He's the kind a' officer who would probably die early in a battle."

"A shot in the back, most likely," Kelly added.

Ethan said, "I'm told it happens."

* * *

Despite the rain and cold, once the men were back in their mess area, they stood in the open and shed their threadbare Confederate uniforms to put on the new clothing they were just given.

"Now we can get thoroughly soaked and chilled in our new uniforms," Kelly quipped.

"Don't be backsliding on me now, Kelly," Schock warned. "Doesn't sound ta me that you're very pleased with your new stuff."

"I'm pleased as punch; just statin' a fact, is all."

"I 'spose."

CORINTH, MISSISSIPPI

It was late in the afternoon of March 5th, 1862. Major Richard Pope stood at attention in front of Colonel Thomas Jordan, Chief of Staff to General Beauregard, Confederate Army of the Mississippi.

"Major Pope reporting for duty, sir," Pope announced while saluting Jordan, who was seated behind a table.

Jordan returned the salute. "At ease, Major," he announced. "Stand easy. I don't require a lot of saluting and such. Our boss, General Beauregard, surely does. But around here, I'm more interested in performance."

"Yes, sir," Pope answered, not quite knowing what to do next.

Jordan continued, "You're going to be my liaison with General Johnson's staff. That makes you an errand boy. Any problem with that, Major?"

"None at all, sir," Pope answered quickly. "I'm happy to do whatever you find helpful, sir."

Jordan continued, "I'll expect to see you in this office at 0700 hours, unless I tell you otherwise. Make sure you check in with my aide, Sergeant Major Murphy, when you arrive. I want him to know where to find you should I need you for something. Understand?"

"Yes, sir."

"For now, Major Pope, Sergeant Major Murphy will take you to your quarters in town and show you the officers' mess. Any questions?"

"No, sir."

"Sergeant Major," Jordan ordered, "show the major to his quarters."

As the two men walked the short distance into Corinth, Richard Pope asked his guide, "You've been with the Colonel for some time, I take it, Sergeant?" Pope asked.

"Yes, sir," Murphy responded. "Since before the war."

"Is the Colonel always so prickly?"

"He just wants everyone to clearly understand what is expected of them, sir," Murphy revealed. "So, he often is a bit blunt, especially with people he doesn't know well."

*   *   *

At breakfast the following morning, officers were helping themselves to eggs, bacon and freshly baked bread. Some were just enjoying a cup of coffee and smoking their pipes.

A young lieutenant walked into the room and shouted, "Attention!" Thus, he announced the arrival of an officer superior in rank to everyone in the room.

Sure enough, General Albert Sidney Johnston strode into the room.

"At ease, gentlemen," he said soothingly. "As you were."

Most of the officers returned to their food or conversation. Some still stood at attention in awe of the commander of the Army of the Mississippi.

Observing them, Johnston chuckled, "It's quite all right, gentlemen. You can stand there if you wish, or you can go about your business. I'm only going to bite a bit of breakfast, not you."

"Thank you, sir," one of the junior officers said in relief.

"You're welcome, young man," Johnston said. Then he noticed a new face. He strode over to an officer eating his breakfast alone at a side table.

"I don't think I've had the pleasure of meeting you, Major," Johnston said, extending his hand.

Richard Pope stood and shook his commanding officer's hand.

"I'm Major Richard Pope, sir. I just arrived from Richmond yesterday."

"Pray, tell me, Major," Johnston asked, sort of mischievously. "Why did Richmond send you here? Not as punishment, I hope?"

"I hope not, sir," Pope answered with a smile on his face. "I was assigned to General Beauregard's staff."

"Now I know you're being punished," Johnston said with a hearty laugh. "What did you do that was so terrible they sent you to work with Beauregard and me?

"Before you answer, allow me to get a cup of that wonderful smelling coffee, and I'll rejoin you."

"It would be my honor, sir," Pope assured him.

"We'll see about that, son."

Settled at Pope's table with his hot coffee, Johnston continued his questioning.

"Did President Davis send you here to spy on us, Major Pope?"

"Not that I know of, sir. The only instruction I received was that you needed help."

Johnston laughed heartily.

"Very good, son. I suppose we do."

"Tell me about you. What's your family background?"

After Pope had answered, General Johnston said, "I think I've met your father. He's a colonel now, isn't he? Stationed in Charleston, I understand. I think I remember him from the Mexican War. He was a junior officer back then; infantry, as I recall, a graduate of the Citadel."

"I graduated from there last June, sir," Richard told him.

"Very good. A fine training ground for military men. Welcome to the Army of the Mississippi, Major Pope. Now, tell me what Jordan has in store for you."

"I was told that I would be a liaison between Beauregard's staff and yours, sir."

"I'd like that, Major. I believe Jordan has mistakenly done me a favor. I may steal you away completely from him and make you my liaison to his bunch. How would you like that, son?"

"That would suit me just fine, General."

With that, General Johnston called over one of his aides. "Lieutenant, see that an order is cut for my signature reassigning Major Pope from General Beauregard's staff to mine."

* * *

Later that day, General Beauregard was addressing his aide, Colonel Jordan.

"I see that our Davis spy has been reassigned."

"Yes, sir. It appears that General Johnston took a shine to Major Pope and added him into his own staff. I was just going to use him as a runner anyway, sir."

"It probably gave Albert Sidney a charge stealing staff from me. Now he has a Davis spy on his staff."

"I hadn't looked at it that way, sir. But yes, now he will have to be careful what Pope learns."

"We'll see, Colonel," Beauregard concluded. "Now, I want to go over your plans for the attack on Grant's people at Pittsburg Landing."

"Of course, sir," Jordan said, standing. "If you will come over to the map table, sir."

"I don't have the energy to stand very long, Colonel. This infection has sapped my strength. You know that, for God's sake."

"Of course, sir. I'll pin the map on the wall, sir. You can sit while we go over the plans we've come up with thus far."

"You mean they're not finished? Our target date is March 29th, damn it. If we delay much longer, Buell might have reinforced Grant before we can attack. You know we have to attack before that link-up occurs. What's holding things up?"

Colonel Jordan was used to his commanding officer's fiery temper. Patience without condescension was essential.

"Sir," he began. "As you know, General Johnston wants to wait until General Earl Van Dorn's 10,000 men arrive from the west. He also is anxious for our men to get more training. Remember, sir, the bulk of our force has never been in a battle."

"Colonel," Beauregard snapped. "I don't give a rat's ass what General Johnston wants, who he's waiting for or how green our men are at this point. We have to get the attack mounted before Don Carlos Buell moves his slow ass and his 35,000 troops from Nashville to Pittsburg Landing. We have to hit Grant first. How soon can you have these plans ready for presentation?"

After a pause, Major Jordan responded, "In twenty-four hours, sir."

"So you're telling me that tomorrow afternoon you will present not only the Order of March, but all the logistics supporting that plan of attack, our complete battle plan?"

"Yes, sir."

"That's more like it, Colonel," Beauregard said, more calmly. "I knew I could count on you."

"Yes, sir, you can."

"Well? Don't just stand there with your mouth hanging open, man. Get to it!"

* * *

General Albert Sidney Johnston sat on his horse watching the long line of Confederate troops, wagons and artillery struggle through the deep mud. Because of the heavy rain and the muddy roads, it had taken two days to move from Corinth to the point of attack. So, instead of attacking as planned on April 3rd, it would be April 6th instead. Three more days for Union General Buell to reinforce Grant's forces at Pittsburg Landing.

Next to Johnston, Major Pope sat astride his horse.

"Major," the general ordered. "Move down to Bragg's Corps and report back to me as soon as his attack begins. I'll hear his cannon, but I want to know exactly when his men hit the Yankees."

"Yes, sir."

Pope had barely left when Confederate cannon thundered the opening of the attack. But it was an hour before Pope arrived back at Johnston's side with news that the infantry had left their positions and hit Sherman's Corps at 6:30 in the morning.

"I need to get closer," Johnston told the men who accompanied him. "Major Pope, lead me to the forward elements of Bragg's Corps."

As they moved down the slope toward the battle, Pope cautioned his commander. "Sir, I gotta tell you," he began. "It was pretty hot down there when I left. Our attack surprised the Yanks, and most a' them were running for the river. But a bunch a' them were putting up a good fight."

"Major Pope, if it's my day to meet the Lord, so be it. So lead the way, if you please, sir."

He's so calm, it's unreal. My heart's beating a mile a minute, and he doesn't appear to be excited at all. I guess that's why he's the general and I'm not.

By the time, Johnston and his staff reached the bottom of the hill, they were galloping on the heels of the advancing troops of Buell's Corps. Pope could hear the shrill sound of the Rebel Yell between the screech of artillery shells passing overhead.

My Lord, he thought. There's no Union trenches or redoubts for our men to breach, only thousands of tents with scattered breakfast fires in-between. The bluecoats have run off. Looks ta' me like they left everything behind, even their breakfasts.

The hungry Confederate soldiers paused when they reached the Union tents. They began to rummage through the Yank tents and to enjoy the abandoned food. The attack slowed.

"Major Pope," Johnston shouted. "You'll take this order to General Bragg. You will find him to the rear of our position. He is to advance immediately through Hardee's Corps and drive the retreating Federals toward the river. Assure him that I will inform Hardee of his action. Now move, Major!"

Pope took the hastily written order from General Johnston. "Yes, sir," he shouted, spurred his mount and was gone over a rise to the rear.

I hope Bragg is where he's supposed to be. This hilly area is so covered with shrubbery and trees, it's hard to see more than ten yards in any direction. During the pre-attack briefings, I didn't hear anyone warn of such difficult terrain. If I can't find him quickly, the Federals may have time to reorganize and we may lose the momentum of our surprise attack.

It was only a few minutes until Pope came across the lead elements of Bragg's force.

"Where is General Bragg?" he asked of the captains in charge of the point Company.

"I don't rightly know, Major," was the response. "Somewheres back that a' way, I think." The man pointed in a general southern direction.

My Lord in heaven. He's no help a'tal.

Another ten minutes or so brought him to a rise where he saw the Corps flags a hundred yards or so to his right. The terrain between his position and where he saw Bragg's Headquarter flags was clogged with brush. It was further than he had thought, too. All told, it had taken him almost forty minutes to find the General, who was only a mile away from the fighting.

Damnable terrain. Can't see a thing past a few yards for all these gullies full a' dense brush and trees.

"What can I do for you, Major Pope?" Bragg's adjutant greeted.

"You can give him this order from General Johnston, Colonel."

"Is there anything else?" Pope was asked.

"Yes. Hardee's men have stopped their advance in order to rummage through the Yankee encampment. So our attack has slowed and the Federals have been given some time to regroup.

"General Johnston wanted me to convey his wish that General Bragg would move on through Hardee's men with all possible speed and hit the Federals hard."

"Wait here, Major," Pope was told. "General Bragg might want to speak with you."

"Yes, sir."

It was another ten minutes when Pope was ushered into Bragg's command tent.

"Major Pope," Bragg asked, testily. "Look at this map, please. I'm right about here." He pointed to a spot on the roughly drawn map. "Show me on this damnable map just where you left General Johnston."

Pope got out his compass, placed it on the map table and retraced his route.

"I left the General right here, sir."

"Describe the conditions at the front, Major," he was asked.

He did so.

"So, Sidney wants me to run my men through Hardee's to get this attack moving again, does he?" Bragg mused aloud.

"Thank you, Major," General Bragg said. "I'd appreciate it if you would rejoin my point company and lead us to the front. Assure General Johnston that we will be there as soon as possible."

"Yes, sir. I will."

As soon as Pope left, Bragg turned to his brigade commanders. "What the hell are you standing around for? Get your men on the move! Now!"

They all ran to their horses and sped off.

Even with Pope leading the way, it took another half an hour for the lead elements of Bragg's Corps to arrive and renew the attack.

But renew it they did. Pope watched as they ran through Hardee's men and hit the Federals hard, causing the bluecoats to retreat again.

Johnston's quick response just may have saved our attack from failure, Pope mused. *Hardee lost control of his men. Johnston recognized it and took the necessary action. No wonder he is regarded as the best battlefield general the Confederacy has.*

"Major Pope," Johnston shouted. "Come with me. I sense that our right flank needs some encouragement." Leading the way, Johnston and his staff rode off to the sound of the guns on their right.

As the day wore on, General Polk's Corps followed Bragg into the fray. Breckenridge's Corps had been committed before the sun was high in the sky, too. All the while, General Johnston seemed to be everywhere; moving men forward, always forward.

In the process, a bullet had clipped off a piece of his wide-brimmed hat, and another ball made a hole in his right sleeve.

"General," Tennessee Governor Isham Harris, who had been with him the entire day, urged. "Don't you think it wise to stay back some? We can't afford to lose you, sir."

"Won't make a bit of difference, Governor, what happens to me if we lose this battle. Besides, our men need to see their leader up close and taking risks, just like I ask them to take. So I'll go where it is necessary for me to go. Thank you for your concern, though.

"Major Pope," Johnston shouted over the sounds of battle. "Take an order to General Beauregard. Back at the Shiloh Church, he's operating in the dark and I want him to know what's happening up here. Make sure he understands that with one more push, Grant's people will have their boots in the river. If we are to end this thing successfully, he must send all available troops and ammunition forward to this position immediately. Dusk is coming on, and I'd rather not fight in the dark. Got all that, Major?"

"Yes, sir, I do."

"If you would, Governor," Johnston continued. "I'd appreciate it if you would accompany the Major. Beauregard and his man Taylor might need convincing."

"Be my privilege, General," Governor Harris responded. "If they won't listen to Pope, I'll make sure they hear me loudly and clearly."

"That's what I had in mind, Governor. Make it quick, though. Our boys are mighty short of ammunition. Many are down to bayonets and rocks."

* * *

On the way back to the Shiloh Church, Pope and Governor Harris passed through an area devastated by fighting.

"You ever seen the like?" the Governor said to Richard Pope.

"No, sir. I thought the battle at Manassas last summer was hard on the land. This is unbelievable. Trees are just shattered stumps. There are so many bodies and dead horses all over the ground, it's hard for us to ride through the area."

The two shortly arrived at General Beauregard's headquarters. Colonel Taylor was there to greet them.

"You have word from General Johnston, Pope?" he said testily.

"Yes, sir," he responded. "A written order and a verbal message."

"I'll see if the General is well enough to see you."

Governor Harris dismounted and whispered to Pope, "I've heard that Beauregard was sick. But I didn't realize he was this badly off."

Colonel Taylor returned. "I've given the dispatch to the General," he said. "You can wait here if he has a response."

At this point, Pope spoke up.

"Colonel Taylor," he began. "This is Tennessee Governor Harris. "He has a personal message from General Johnston for General Beauregard."

"Possibly you two didn't hear me," Taylor snapped. "The General is ill. Whatever message you have, you can give it to me. I'll see that it is passed on."

Governor Harris spoke up, "It is obvious to me, Colonel, that from your safe position back here you are not aware of conditions at the front. They are critical. We are in dire need of ammunition. General Johnston believes that one more push will have Grant at the river's edge before dark.

"But many of our troops are down to using bayonets and throwing rocks. We need to take that ammunition back with us now, Colonel."

Taylor did not seem to be impressed. "We're low back here, too, Governor. I don't know if we should deplete our reserve stocks of ammunition right now."

Governor Harris exploded. "My Lord, man! You've got no use for those supplies back here. We need them where there is fighting, at the front. And we need them now."

"I'll ask the General," Taylor answered. "I can't authorize the release of those supplies without his agreement."

"Allow me to remind you and the General," Governor Harris continued. "You have been given a written order by the commander of this army. If you do not obey it, I will see you are brought before a court martial, Colonel."

"As I said, Governor," Taylor responded coldly. "I will speak to General Beauregard."

* * *

On the Federal side of the fighting, there was even greater confusion.

General Sherman had not believed reports from his own patrols when they warned him of enemy activity from the direction of Corinth. Nor had his men been told to establish defensive positions as a precaution in case of attack. It was Sunday morning, after all.

So, he allowed his men to stack their weapons and fix breakfast instead. Enjoy the morning. After days of rain, the warm sun was a welcome relief.

But when the shells began to fall, general panic set in. And as the first sounds of the Rebel Yell were heard, most of Sherman's men fled in panic.

Sergeant Willie Petzold's squad of five men were camped nearer to the river. They were fixing breakfast when the shells of the attack began to explode overhead.

"Grab your rifles, fellas," Willie directed his men. Quickly, their platoon sergeant ordered them to establish a defensive line facing the sounds of battle. They did, and waited.

Suddenly through the trees and brush to their front, thousands of Union soldiers ran toward them. Some wore blue uniforms, some only parts. Others were barefoot. Few had weapons. All were in a panic to escape the attacking Rebels.

Petzold's sergeant shouted at them to hold their fire, to hold their positions. Nevertheless, some members of his platoon panicked and joined the retreating men running toward their rear.

Petzold shouted to his squad, "Anyone makes a move, I'll tell everyone back home you were a coward and ran." No one wanted that to happen. They stayed put as the flow of retreating soldiers running past them to the rear increased.

Then, the first of the Reb infantry appeared in front of their defensive line.

"Fire!" the platoon sergeant shouted. That rifle volley ripped into the Confederates and stopped the first line of attackers. But before Willie and the other Federals could reload, another mass of gray-clad soldiers emerged from the tree line. Their Rebel Yell broke the sudden silence.

This time, Willie's platoon was overrun and he and two men of his squad were taken captive.

The battle moved away from them in the direction of the Tennessee River to their rear. As prisoners now, they were forced to join a growing group of Union soldiers being marched to the rear.

"Look for a chance to escape into the brush," Willie whispered to his friends. "The Rebs can't watch us all." Sure enough, it wasn't long before the line of Union prisoners marched around a bend. Willie slipped behind some thick shrubbery and hunkered down, hidden by the thick underbrush.

Just be quiet and wait, Willie thought. *With all this noise and confusion, I'll bet they'll not miss me. Then I can get back to our lines.*

Willie was right. In the confusion, he wasn't missed. After a while, he moved. As he slowly worked his way through the confusion toward his own lines, he picked up a discarded rifle. He continued to look for a way through the Reb line.

Suddenly, artillery shells began to burst overhead.

Shit! he thought. *That came from the direction of the river. Our guys are firing back. I had better get out a' here.*

He moved more quickly toward the Tennessee River.

Another overhead burst, and everything went black for Union Sergeant Willie Petzold.

When he awoke, it was dusk and he was lying on the ground between two other men. He could hear someone talking.

"What about that Yank over there, Doctor?"

"As soon as he's conscious, give him some water and turn him over to the Provost Marshal. He does look fit to be moved, I think."

"But Doc," the aide reminded him. "Blood is still running from his ears."

"I know it. But there's nothing I can do about it," he told his medical aide. "Probably the result of a nearby shell burst. He was also nicked by a piece of shrapnel. I cleaned that up. Otherwise, if he can stand, he's fit to travel. So turn him over to the Provost Marshal."

"Yes, sir."

And so, Willie Petzold was a prisoner of war again.

* * *

It was getting late in the day, dusk. But the battle still raged. The Confederates were still attempting to turn the left flank of the Union line and cut them off from the Tennessee River and escape.

But the deep ravine separating the two forces had filled with water during all the rain of the last few days. So, the Confederates could not cross to the high ground on the other side and complete the job of encirclement. In addition, the river was up as well. This allowed two of the Union's timber-clads to rake the Confederate-held bank with canister fire.

Just the same, General Johnston urged his men on. He seemed to be everywhere, pushing his men to attack one more time.

"I don't care if you're low on ammunition, Colonel," he told one subordinate. "Use bayonets, if you must. But we've got to bust through their lines before dark. If you can't do it, say so, and I'll replace you. What is it going to be?"

"I'll get it done, sir."

"Then get to it, man. The sun is going down."

"Yes, sir." The officer rode away.

Johnston turned his horse, started to say something, but suddenly felt faint and fell forward.

He would have fallen off his horse completely, but Pope saw the General begin to fall.

"General," he shouted and reached over to steady him. Pope slipped off his horse and stood on the ground as General Johnston fell into his arms, unconscious.

"Where the hell is the surgeon?" he shouted over the din of the battle. "The General's been wounded."

Governor Hayes said, "Johnston ordered him to attend to some Yankee wounded a while back. I don't know where the hell he is right now."

They lay their unconscious leader on a blanket and waited while men scurried around looking for medical help. It was a few minutes before a doctor arrived on the scene.

After examining the general, the doctor found a wound on the back of his right leg and noticed that blood was dripping into his boot. A tourniquet was applied, but it was too late. General Johnston had lost too much blood; he was dead.

A messenger was immediately sent to inform General Beauregard.

It wasn't long before Colonel Taylor appeared on the scene. He was there to deliver orders to the corps commanders from General Beauregard.

"Pope," he asked. "Do you know where General Bragg is right now?"

"I know where he was a few minutes ago, sir. I delivered a message from General Johnston to him."

"Take me to him immediately."

When the pair found Bragg, he was directing the battle from atop his horse.

"General," Taylor began. "I regret to inform you that General Johnston has been killed."

"Son of a bitch!" Bragg exploded. "I warned him about riding around too close to the battle. Shit almighty!" He sat quietly on his horse for a moment.

"That right, Pope?" Bragg asked. "Johnston really dead?"

"Yes, sir. Happened just moments ago, sir."

My God! He thinks I would make up such a thing? Bragg really is the hard case others claim he is, Taylor thought angrily.

"All right, Taylor. So, General Johnston is dead. You didn't ride all the way up here to tell me that. What does Beauregard want?"

"General Beauregard wants you to pull back off this ridge. He believes his army is scattered and disjointed. He wants you to take the night to reorganize and resupply for a push tomorrow."

"By damn, Taylor," Bragg shouted in the messenger's face. "One more push, another hour is all we need, and we'll have kicked Grant's ass right into the Tennessee River. Doesn't Beauregard realize that?"

"The general has examined all the options, General Bragg. It is almost dark. Everyone is running out of ammunition, and with this terrain, our forces are broken up. We need to reorganize and solidify our gains. We'll finish Grant off tomorrow."

"But we've got him on his heels right now, damn it!" Bragg countered heatedly. "Besides, what if Buell reinforces Grant during the night with his army? What then, Colonel?"

"That's not likely to happen. Our information is that he's two days out. You have your orders, General. The attack is called off until dawn tomorrow."

"Sitting back at your safe headquarters, Taylor, you and Beauregard don't know what it cost us to take this ridge. We're so close to the river, the Federal timber-clads have been hitting us with canister. Another hour, and we'll control the landing area at the river's edge," the general shouted. "The Yankees won't even have a place to land their reinforcements."

"You have your orders, General," Taylor reminded him.

"What if I don't pull back?" Bragg challenged. "What are you gonna do about that?"

"General, our forces on your flanks are already pulling back. You would be exposed."

"So, we're gonna half ta give this ridge back to the Federals? We're gonna give them all night to fortify it and then have ta take it back in the morning? Is that it, Colonel?"

"You have your orders, General."

"Are those orders in writing, Colonel?"

"No, sir."

Bragg turned to an aide. "Is that pistol of yours loaded?"

"Yes, sir. It is."

"Give it to me."

Bragg took the pistol, cocked it and put it under Taylor's chin. "I'd as soon put a bullet into your slimy head right now, Colonel. So, you had better write that order out and sign it for your General Beauregard."

Colonel Taylor wrote out an order for the General.

The attack would be renewed in the morning.

Then Colonel Taylor wrote out another order and directed Major Pope to deliver it to General Breckenridge. Pope had to find him first, though. No small task given the terrain, the confusion of the battle and the fact that it was getting dark. It was a dangerous assignment, as well.

Breckenridge was off to our left an hour ago, when I took him a message from General Johnston. I'll try that area first. It's getting dark, too. Hope I don't lose my way getting through this mess.

He urged his mount down a narrow path through an area thick with high shrubs and trees.

Damn. The sun just went below the trees, he realized. *I might have taken the wrong turn back a bit. I best turn around.*

Backtracking along the trail, he rounded a bend. As he came along some high brush, he found himself right in the middle of a group of Yankee Soldiers.

"Lookee what we have here, boys," a Yankee sergeant said to his men. "Looks like we got ourselves a real live Reb officer come to visit."

He stepped forward to Pope's horse and pointed his rifle at the Confederate officer.

"If I be you, I'd get down real slow like, Major," he said. "Tommy, grab the reins a' this here horse."

Major Richard Pope was a prisoner of war, again.

BELLE ISLE PRISON

"My Lord," Ransom exclaimed. "Another bunch of railroad cars loaded with Yanks."

"Must be hundreds of 'em. Looks like we lost another battle, don't it?" Novak commented.

"Hard ta' tell," Ethan Schock said. "Can't never tell anymore who won or lost. If we were the winners a' this one, hate to see the casualty 'an captured lists for the other side."

The three men walked to the area where the new prisoners were assembled. The camp commandant, Lt. Virginius Bossieux, and his aides were organizing the newcomers.

Sgt. Marks, assisted by Sgt. Hight, were giving instructions.

"Sit on the ground, back straight, arms around your knees. Do it now!"

After a bit of shuffling, the several hundred men did as they were told.

Hight then shouted, "Any sick or wounded among you, raise yer hand."

Several hands were raised.

"You men," he continued. "The ones with yer hands up, come forward."

"This man needs help, Sergeant," someone shouted.

"Who spoke right now?" Hight asked.

A hand went up. "I did, Sergeant. The man next to me can't walk very good. He needs help getting to the front, like you ordered, that's all."

"Bring him up here, Soldier," Hight ordered.

The wounded man was helped to the front of the assembly. He was a broad-shouldered soldier about five-foot-ten. He moved rather well; didn't look wounded. But he did have a bandana around his head.

"Looks all right ta' me," Sgt. Hight said. "If'n you're trying ta' pull something, Soldier, you're in a heap a' trouble."

"No, Sergeant," the soldier insisted. "He was my squad leader. He took a hit in the head back at Shiloh. Ain't been right since. Don't even talk much anymore. Hardly answers to his own name."

"All right," Hight said. "Leave him here with the others. I'll have the doc look him over. What's his name?"

"Willie Petzold, Sergeant. Sergeant Willie Petzold is his name."

"All right, Soldier," Hight ordered. "Return to your position. I'll take charge of your squad leader."

"Yes, sir. Thank you, sir."

* * *

"Hey! Did you hear that, John?" Ethan said to Ransom.

"Can't say that I did. What didn't I hear?"

"That man's name is Willie Petzold."

"So?"

"You know that soldier, Ethan?" Novak asked.

"I sure do. We grew up together back in Lowell, Michigan. Went to school together 'an joined up together, too. John, we gotta get him into our Mess."

"I don't know if we can manage that, Ethan. They're sending him to the infirmary. That makes him someone special; outside of our reach, probably."

"Ya gotta try though, John. Willie is hurting right now. I just gotta help him. Will you help me, John?"

"Sure, Ethan. I'll try."

LOWELL

It was a Saturday, and Ethan Shock's mother was in town to get her food order at Brady's General Store. She was standing at the pick-up area of the store with her purchases, waiting for her husband to bring the wagon around. One of the store's bag boys had piled her purchases there for her. Her son, Ethan, had done that on Saturdays before he joined the army.

Her husband, Carl, would load up the wagon as soon as he was finished at the grain elevator.

While she waited, she opened a letter from Ethan.

"Oh, my," she exclaimed at one point. She held the letter to her chest and closed her eyes as tears began to drop from her eyes. She didn't see her husband walking toward her.

"Michelle," he asked. "Whatever is wrong, woman? Nothing happened to Ethan, did it?"

His wife held out the letter to him. After he read a bit, he looked at her and said, "Oh, my Lord. The Petzold boy is alive!"

"He's a prisoner and hurt somehow, but Ethan is looking after him."

"Are any of the Petzolds in town?" Carl asked. "I didn't see Gustov at the grain elevator this morning. Did you see Mary or any of her girls in Brady's store?"

"No, but I heard someone say Mary Petzold was down at White's Boot and Shoe Shop this morning. Let's load up and stop down there on the way out of town. She may not have heard the news about her son being alive."

CAMP DOUGLAS, ILLINOIS

On the outskirts of Chicago, Illinois, a 45-acre poorly drained plot of land had been used by the state as a training ground for volunteers during the first year of the war. Thereafter, it was abandoned for this purpose because it was considered too unhealthy a site for the Union men trained there.

However, in February of 1862, a Union force captured Fort Donelson. This was a facility that controlled the Cumberland River at one point, and with it, access to western Tennessee. With that victory, an entire Confederate army of 12,392 men was taken captive.

General Grant refused to exchange prisoners after the battle was concluded. Instead, he sent almost 6,258 of his Confederate captives north to this Chicago camp, now named, Camp Douglas, as prisoners of war. They were housed in the same barracks used by the departed Union troops who had trained there.

So, in early February 1862, prisoners, both enlisted men and officers, were sent north by steamer. Some were taken to St. Louis, Missouri, others went to Cairo, Illinois. From both sites, they traveled by the trains of the Illinois Central Railroad directly to downtown Chicago.

The Illinois governor complained to General Halleck that the citizens of Chicago were in danger bringing the captives into the city. The general told him that there were not sufficient troops to satisfy his concern. But a spur was built just 400 yards from the camp to satisfy the security worry. Shortly, Colonel James Mulligan and his 23rd Illinois Irish Infantry regiment were assigned to the camp.

After the April 1862 battle of Shiloh, it was also to this site that 2,450 of the Confederate troops captured there were sent. CSA Major Richard Pope was one of those captives.

* * *

"So, you were part of General Johnston's staff?" Colonel Randal McGavock asked.

"Yes, sir," Richard Pope responded. "I had that privilege."

The two officers were sitting in the corner of a small compartment on the third deck aboard the USS Boston. The boat had been stripped of all furniture, so they sat on the floor leaning their backs against the wall. Even though it was almost mid-April, western Tennessee was still chilly this time of year. And the wind on the river was strong enough to rock the boat as it traveled north through the swollen Mississippi waters toward Cairo, Illinois.

"I thought the plan of attacking one corps behind the other was madness," McGavock said heatedly. "Soon after we hit the Yankees, everything got confused. Our reserves were stuck behind another attacking unit instead of being free to swing one way or another. How did the general ever come up with that plan?"

Major Pope sat silently for a moment, gathering his thoughts.

"General Johnston assigned General Beauregard, his second in command, the job of designing the attack. I was told that Colonel Taylor, Beauregard's aide, came up with the attack plan. It was presented so late in March that, had General Johnston refused the plan, it would have taken another week or more to correct things."

"With the advantage 'a hindsight," McGavock interrupted." Seems ta' me it would have been a good idea to do just that; delay, get it right in the first place."

"The problem with that, Colonel," Pope responded. "Was that Grant had troops in sort of equal in number to ours. He was camped at Pittsburg Landing, awaiting General Buell's 25,000 or so troops. That would least double Grant's strength once Buell arrived. Johnston wanted to hit him before that happened, defeat him and then turn on Buell's force.

"So you see, he didn't have the time to scrap Beauregard's plan and put together another one. As it turned out, Buell's people arrived during the night of the first day on Sunday evening and turned the tide against us Monday morning."

"Why we stopped Sunday night is a mystery to me, too," McGavock went on. "I keep running it around in my head. I was with Bragg, ya see. We had gained some high ground bordering Pittsburg Landing."

"I was there with Bragg that evening," Pope revealed.

"Then you could see it," McGavock said excitedly. "We were in position to roll Grant right into the river. All we needed was another hour of daylight and some ammunition. Hell's bells, some a' my men were throwing rocks.

"If you were with Bragg, you'd know why we stopped, wouldn't you? Why didn't we get the ammunition we needed? Why was the attack called off, dammit ta hell? Why?"

"After General Johnston was killed, Colonel Taylor had a message for us from General Beauregard. The order directed that the attack be stopped."

"Why in hell?"

"Taylor said with daylight almost gone, it would be difficult to continue. Besides, he said our troops were all disorganized. We needed some time to get our units straightened out and resupply them. He said Beauregard believed we would finish Grant off the next morning.

"Then Taylor ordered me to take him to Bragg, which I did.

"Once we found him, Bragg objected strongly. He said pretty much what you said. In fact, he put a loaded pistol to Taylor's head and ordered him to put the order in writing.

"Taylor said that he believed Buell's Union force was two or three days away and would therefore be no threat."

"We sure found out that was a bunch of hooey next morning, didn't we?" McGavock said heatedly. "Buell's Federal troops arrived Sunday night and kicked our butts the next morning."

"That's what I'm told, Colonel," Pope agreed. "I was captured Sunday night trying to find General Breckenridge in all that confusion. So, I wasn't there when Buell's fresh troops attacked us Monday morning and pushed us back to Corinth."

"Not our worry right now, Major," McGavock said. "I suppose we'll be exchanged soon. But for now, our job is to stay alive. I'll want your help in keeping everyone's spirits up, Pope. My hope is that we'll return to this fight and kick some Yankee rumps."

"Absolutely! I'm all for that, Colonel."

"Any idea just where we are, Major Pope?" McGavock asked.

"All I know is that we turned north when we hit the Mississippi River. That means, I think, that we are not going to St. Louis. What's north is Illinois, and eventually Minnesota. Must be a prison up that way, seems to me."

"Now I know why they made you a major."

CHARLESTON

The very pregnant Mary Jacqueline Pope was shopping in the city market with Helen, her personal slave.

"Oh, my God!" she exclaimed, staggered and gripped Helen with one hand and her distended belly with the other.

"Hold on ta' me, girl," Helen ordered. "Let's sit you down."

"Just let me catch my breath a minute," Mary Jacqueline urged.

"I tol you we should stay home. You so close to givin' birth. But you a stubborn Yankee girl and won't listen to Helen. Gotta go out to da market like always. Well dis ain't like always. You havin' a baby. You listen to me now?"

"Yes," Mary Jacqueline gasped. "I'll listen now."

"Good. Den let's get you home."

The cramps continued, so the two ladies had to stop several times on the way. But they made it to the Pope home before Mary Jacqueline's water broke.

Helen shouted for Amos, one of the other house slaves.

"Get your black ass out'a here and find Doctor Childress," she ordered. "Tell him to come quick. Tell him dat da misses is havin' her baby right now!"

Helen had her mistress undressed and in bed well before the doctor arrived. Then it was not long before a healthy baby boy was placed in Mary Jacqueline's arms.

Mrs. Pope sat on a chair by her daughter-in-law's bed. Colonel Pope stood by her side. "The doctor said you have a healthy child, my dear,"

Mrs. Pope informed Mary Jacqueline. "What are you going to call your son?"

"We'll call him Charles; after his father, of course."

"Does my son know of the birth yet?"

Colonel Pope answered, "I sent Alexander off to the telegraph office with a message for Charles as soon as I heard the child cry."

"I hope they'll give him leave to come home before the child is grown," Mrs. Pope said.

Then she sarcastically asked her husband, "Possibly you can use some of your famous influence to see to it."

"I will do my best, dear."

"I'll contact the father at St. Mary's to arrange for the baptism here," she said to no one in particular.

Mary Jacqueline asked, "Won't we have it at the church, Mother Pope?"

"That's out of the question," she snapped. "I'm not well enough for all of that. We will have it here. I think my son David would make a splendid godfather, too."

"No," Mary Jacqueline responded firmly. "I will not have that awful man anywhere near my child, much less as his godfather. Richard would be fine. But never David. He is an evil man and would be a terrible choice."

"Well, I never," Mrs. Pope huffed, standing up. "Handle it yourself, then." She walked toward the bedroom door.

"I intend to. Thank you."

Colonel Pope listened to the exchange and watched his wife leave the room. He couldn't help but smile.

Good for you, young lady, he thought. *Stand your ground.*

"Just you rest now, my dear," he cautioned. "I will do what I can to get Charles back here quickly."

"Thank you, Grandfather," she said. "Would you mind so very much sending a wire to my parents in Philadelphia?"

"That may be difficult with the war and all. But I'll try."

SALISBURY, NORTH CAROLINA

In March of 1861, the people of North Carolina were sharply divided on the issue of secession. Unionists there were not convinced that secession was the answer to the election of Abraham Lincoln.

John Bruner, owner and publisher of the Carolina Watchman, the oldest newspaper in North Carolina, was a Unionist. In late March, he wrote that secessionists were looking for an event that would "...rouse the passions of the people" and unite both Unionists and Secessionists.

That event would be the firing on Fort Sumter and the subsequent call by Lincoln for troops to put down the rebellion. Bruner wrote that,

"...had Lincoln spent a whole year discussing a method to unite the southern people, he could not have brought out anything more successful."

Zebulon Vance said that it was Lincoln's proclamation calling for troops that united public opinion in North Carolina against the Union. Governor Ellis replied to that call for troops,

"I can be no party to his wicked violation of the laws of the country and to his war on the liberties of a free people. You can get no troops from North Carolina."

On May 20, 1861, Bruner told the story of North Carolina secession in his news article.

The (secession) convention then declared North Carolina to be a "sovereign and independent state."

Now, even Unionists like Bruner supported secession for North Carolina and were resigned to fighting a war against Lincoln's Union government.

That summer, the governor of North Carolina was the only Confederate chief executive to respond positively to Richmond's call to establish a prison camp for Union Soldiers. The city council of Salisbury had notified his office of their willingness to have a prison in their area. A failed manufacturing venture had abandoned a factory building at the outskirts of Salisbury.

Negotiations for its purchase by the Confederate government were completed in November 1861. Renovation began at once.

Bruner reported on that date,

"The government has bought the old Salisbury Factory and is now preparing to fit it up for a prison to accommodate some thousands or more Yankees who are encumbering the tobacco factories of Richmond."

As Bruner hastened to explain, not everyone in Salisbury was thrilled with the plan.

"Our citizens don't much like the idea of such an accession to their population; nevertheless, they have assented to their part of the hardships and disagreeable aspects of war. So, bring them along. We will do the best we can with them."

Even though the prison was ready by late fall, for the lack of proper guards, it was left empty. Few able-bodied men wanted to serve as guards and joined to fight Yankees instead. Once this problem was solved, the project moved forward.

The first Union prisoners of war arrived on December 9, 1861. The 120 Yankee captives were immediate curiosities for the good citizens of Salisbury. They didn't know what to expect, actually. Prior to the war, there had been little, if any, travel for most residents outside of the immediate area, much less their state. Bruner wrote that these prisoners:

"had neither hooves nor horns but looked very much like other men."

The prison was serviced by a railroad spur and surrounded by a high palisade. So, the local community was well separated from the inmates. Strangely though, early on, the prisoners were allowed to wander into town. That strange freedom didn't last too long, but the visitors from the North were still treated with kindness by the locals, being brought food from the nearby gardens and sweets from southern kitchens.

And while the prison population grew, there was increased interest, at least on the home front, for a prisoner exchange system agreement.

In the meantime, Union prisoners on Belle Isle, Virginia, were moved. Some were sent north to Salisbury, North Carolina. Corporal Schock and his squad were among those moved there. Even Willie Petzold was included. Ethan and his men were standing at a Richmond, Virginia, railroad siding.

"Must be a thousand of us going north," Tom guessed. "Wouldn't you say?

"Probably right," Ethan replied. "Crowd in here, guys," he urged. "I don't want the guards to spot Willie. I didn't hear his name called with ours, but they probably won't miss him in this crowd. Come on, Willie. Keep your head down and stay close."

"I got that bad headache again, Ethan," Willie moaned.

"Hang on, buddy, we're getting you out of this cesspool; hang on," Ethan urged.

Willie had been with Ethan and his group since his arrival on Belle Isle. He had been captured out west during the battle of Shiloh. Near as Ethan could figure, something had caused his friend to become addled. He was strong as a bull but didn't hardly speak even. Instead, Willie just followed Ethan around like a lost soul. The men of the squad took care of him. Just like now. They were not going to leave him behind.

They didn't stand around very long before Ethan and his men, along with Willie, were jammed into a boxcar. There was so many prisoners crowded into the car that all of them had to stand.

The stench and the heat from their bodies were suffocating. But once the train began to move, they got some relief from the air that whistled through the openings in the sides of the car.

"I hope this damn ride ain't too long, us jammed inta here like we is," Bill Kelly complained.

"Bitchin' 'bout it won't make da ride any shorter or easier, Kelly," Tom observed. "But I don't suppose a bit 'a truth like that will shut ya up, though."

"Got that right, you dumb Polak," Kelly snapped back. "You're the kind 'a guy would search through a pile 'a horse shit thinking sure you'd find a pony under it all."

Schock had heard enough. "Keep yer trap shut, Kelly. We got enough trouble without you causing more. Got it?"

"Ya, I got it. Sorry, Tom. I just got all worked up with being jammed inta this coffin-like thing like we is."

"That's all right," Tom responded with a smile. "I was too busy searching for that pony you mentioned ta' pay much attention to what ya was sayin'."

Even Willie laughed at that comment.

Their boxcar rattled and jerked from side to side as the train continued its slow northern trip to Salisbury, North Carolina.

LOWELL

The Shocks were home from town. The supplies were put away, the livestock fed and the two cows milked for the day. Michelle Schock had the evening meal cooking in her Dutch oven. Carl had washed up after completing his chores and was relaxing in his rocker smoking a fresh pipe and reading the recent newspaper he had picked up in town, *The Grand Rapids Eagle*.

He lowered the paper and said, "So, Mary Petzold already knew that their son Willie was alive and a prisoner at Salisbury, North Carolina, eh?"

"Yes, she did. She told me that our government was informed of his capture and location. She and Gustov were told just this week. Pastor Emerson is going to announce it at church this Sunday. She was excited that our Ethan was looking after him. She had not known that Ethan was in the same prison. She still doesn't know anything about Willie's injury."

"If Willie is as injured as Ethan wrote us, you'd think the Confederates would send him home just to get him off their hands," Carl Shock observed.

"You'd think," Michelle agreed.

"There is an article in this week's Eagle I think you would find interesting," he added.

"What's it about, Father?"

Carl handed her the newspaper. "You read it for yourself."

Michelle took the newspaper. "All right. If you insist."

"I do," Carl said. Then he sat back in his chair, relit his pipe and just watched his wife.

Shortly, she put the paper down on her lap.

"Are you serious, Papa?" she gasped.

"I think we should look into it, Momma. Don't you?" he responded.

"The Orphan Train. I never heard of it, Papa. It sounds sort of cruel putting little children on a train headed west and just giving them away to anyone who wants to take them."

"It seems ta me that's better than the life they had in New York or Boston living on the streets an all."

"I suppose," Michelle sighed. "Those poor little ones. They must feel so alone and be so frightened."

"But dear," Carl interjected. "Don't you think they must be excited, too? To have the chance for a new life out of the dirty and dangerous big city must be exciting, too."

"Maybe for the older children, Carl," she responded. "But I fear for the little ones. They must be so terrified."

"Look at this, Momma. The article in the paper was written by someone working for *The New York Times*, a newspaper out there," Carl told his wife. "He reported that the trains have stopped running because the government has taken them over for use in the war."

"So, we cannot expect there will be an Orphan Train until the war ends?"

"Probably not, Momma," Carl answered. "But the article talks of another place in New York that takes and cares for infants; a foundling home."

Michelle picked up the newspaper. "Yes, here it is. The Sisters of Charity run a home for newborns there. Some of the mothers stay and nurse their babies, but many children are just left on the doorstep in a basket that the Sisters leave outside for that purpose.

"Why did you mention this place, Papa?"

"Seems to me, Momma," Carl responded. "We would want a little child, not an almost grown boy or girl. What do you think?"

"But the baby would probably be a Catholic. We're Lutherans."

"The reporter says that the Sisters are only concerned that the children they place are in good Christian homes. They didn't say anything about only Catholic families."

Michelle paused to take it all in. She looked over the article again and then said, "Papa, I think we should write these Sisters of Charity in New York. We can tell them about our good Lutheran farm home full of love, just waiting for children. If you are right, they would welcome the chance to place one or two of their babies here."

"Two babies!" Carl exclaimed, taking the pipe out of his mouth. "I thought we were talking about one child."

"I want a little girl this time, Papa," Michelle said softly. "And I think you want a boy to help you, like Ethan did?"

"Certainly," Carl said firmly. "That's what I thought we were talking about, a boy."

"Can't you see my point about a little girl, though?"

"I suppose," Carl said, sitting back in his chair. "Two babies, eh?"

"So, Papa, it is settled," Michelle said. "Let us write these Sisters of Charity and see what happens. Eh?"

It was Carl's turn to sit quietly and think.

"But you write the letter, eh Momma?"

"Oh, thank you, Papa! I will write the lady mentioned in the newspaper article, Sister Irene Fitzgibbon, at the New York Foundling Hospital."

Carl smiled and added, "That doesn't mean we can't still try to have a child the old-fashioned way, does it, Momma?"

"Oh, Papa."

THE RICHMOND RAID

After dark on Sunday, February 28, 1864, thirty-five hundred cavalrymen and an artillery battery left their winter encampment. By midnight, the advanced guard of this force had crossed the Rapidan River at Ely's Ford.

Another force of six hundred troopers, commanded by Colonel Dahlgren, crossed the same river upstream to the northeast. This advanced force, of which Captain Drieborg's troop was a part, took the Confederate pickets by surprise without firing a shot. Since all the Rebel guards had been captured, no alarm was given. The raid had begun well.

But events did not continue to favor the raid. At the very hour scheduled for General Kilpatrick's forces to begin their attack, he ordered retreat to be sounded instead. Colonel Dahlgren's force, in position outside of Richmond, had no choice but to retreat.

During their withdrawal, Captain Drieborg's troop led the way. His point squad of six riders was some fifty yards ahead of the main body and led the way to secure the critically important Goochand Bridge.

Fifty yards behind the point followed two platoons of twenty-five troopers each, spread over another one hundred yards or so. These platoons had riders out on both flanks, as well. A rear guard followed another fifty yards behind.

Because of the winding nature of the turnpike, the three parts of this troop would sometimes lose sight of one another when sharp turns were encountered. Their greatest danger was attack from the flanks, especially when passing through a wooded area.

As Drieborg's point squad moved around a sharp curve, they were momentarily out of sight of the main body. Suddenly, rifle fire from the flanks was directed at the two platoons in the middle of the formation. This was followed by fire upon the point and rear guards.

Then, rebel soldiers charged out of the woods and attacked the two platoons which formed the middle of his formation. By the time the point squad and the rear guard had turned and attacked, the Confederate force had withdrawn and taken their prisoners with them; Captain Drieborg with them.

In Drieborg's absence, First Sergeant Riley took command. He broke off the fight, took care of his wounded and moved west. His troop had been charged with the responsibility of capturing and securing the Goochland Bridge. Some five-hundred mounted men were following him and depended upon it.

So, he reformed his men and headed west. His wounded would wait for the medics following with Colonel Dalgren and the main body.

* * *

"All a' you, get a move on," a gray-clad soldier shouted. "Prod them prisoners."

Michael Drieborg slowly recovered from the blow he had received to the head. Finally, he asked a reb soldier, "Do you know where we're being taken?"

"Richmond, probably," was the response. "There's a prison they keep there for officers. It's called Libby Prison. No one has ever escaped from that place. It seems ta me that your fighting days are over, Captain. Till this war is over, at least."

As Mike became clear-headed, he looked around to access his situation.

My God. The men guarding us are mostly old men and boys with squirrel guns. There are only a few who look to be regulars. I've got to look for an opportunity to escape.

But there were just too many of them. They swarmed around Michael and the other prisoners. It was clear they were angry about these Union troopers they believed were attacking their homes and womenfolk.

After an hour of walking cross-country, they reached a solid road.

* * *

It was just after mid-day when Mike and the other prisoners reached the outskirts of Richmond. They were marched in a long column of twos through the city, while local citizens gathered all along the street to watch. The crowd was made up of mostly women, children and old men. They were all angry, many shouting, "Leave us alone, you Yankees."

"Your momma would be ashamed of you," shouted another.

Some threw mudballs or stones.

The entire column was marched to the James River. The enlisted men were then marched over a narrow bridge to Belle Island, a prison-camp in the middle of the river. The officers were headed to nearby Libby Prison, one exclusively for Union officers.

LIBBY PRISON, RICHMOND, VIRGINIA

Michael and the other officers in the column were marched to a nearby four-story building. An officer emerged and approached the column.

"This is going to be your home, men. It is called Libby Prison. This street you're standing on is called Carey Street. Over to your left is the James River. With your arrival, this building will house over one thousand Union officers.

"Libby has the reputation of being escape-proof, and we intend to keep it that way. Our guards and other Confederate military personnel are located on the first floor. All prisoners are housed on the upper three floors.

"If you're hoping to be exchanged, a few of you might be important enough for that. But most of you are not, since we haven't had an officer exchange since your people ended the practice.

"So, once you enter these doors, the chance of your coming out before this war is over is slim to none. I suggest you get used to it. My advice is to cooperate, and you will survive.

"The first order of business today is to find out just who you are so's we can notify your people. Our clerical personnel will take your information at the desk to your right. We will appreciate your cooperation.

LIBBY PRISON

The prisoners captured in Kilpatrick's Richmond raid stood in single file. A clerk seated at a table addressed them.

"Give me your full name, rank, unit and home address," he ordered.

When Mike's turn came, he said, "Michael J. Drieborg, Captain, I Troop, Sixth Cavalry, Michigan Brigade, Lowell, Michigan."

The clerk finished recording that information. Then he looked up at Michael.

"Before I was assigned to this desk job, Captain, I was with Fitz Lee's cavalry regiment. We an' the rest of General Stuart's cavalry met you boys a bit west of Gettysburg. Do you remember that, sir?"

"I was there, Corporal," Michael answered cautiously.

"Those repeating carbines a' yours sure caused us some problems. You took us by surprise with those weapons, for sure. After that, we called you the Michigan Devils. Put me in this chair, too," the clerk told Mike.

"It gives me great pleasure to get you out of this war, Captain." The corporal grinned. "Jus' you move along to that stairway over there an wait, sir."

Soon thereafter, Michael and the other officer prisoners were moved to the third floor of the building. There, they were addressed by two Union officers.

"I'm Colonel Rose, and this is Major Hamilton. I was infantry, and the major was cavalry. We share responsibility for the internal organization and discipline of the Libby prison.

"Tomorrow, each of you will be interviewed by personnel of the prison commandant's office. They will assign you to one of our six rooms. We suggest that you respond to their questions with courtesy and dignity. We further suggest that you not reveal information about your unit's strength, disposition or movements. Using the basic information, you have already given they will notify our War Department of your internment and general health. Our government will notify you family of your situation and how they may send you mail and packages."

Major Hamilton cut in at this point.

"Remember, they control our food and medical services. They can also withhold our mail. They can deny us our packages, clothing, blankets or anything sent us from the North."

A newly captured prisoner, a young-looking lieutenant, spoke up.

"Major, you make it sound like we're supposed to just give up and act helpless."

"That's not what we're saying, Lieutenant," Colonel Rose answered. "But a bad attitude just challenges them to punish everyone. If you have a problem with the rebs or another prisoner, you Room Committee is the first place you take it. That committee will handle most problems. If the problem can't be solved at that level, the major and I will take it to the prison commandant's office."

At this point, Major Hamilton re-entered the briefing.

"Disrespect for fellow prisoners will not be tolerated. We must help one another if we are to survive prison. We must also exercise and keep as clean as possible, given the circumstances.

He continued. "The membership on all Room Committees Colonel Rose referred to is changed every month. The men on those committees are responsible for passing out food, mail and clothing that might be sent here by our government. The committees assign latrine duty and determine clean-up assignments, supervise daily exercise and handle group problems. We rotate committee membership monthly. So, each of you can expect to serve.

"Also, you will soon realize that the rooms are very crowded with prisoners. That makes it even more important for each of us to treat our fellow prisoners with respect."

Colonel Rose asked, "Do any of you have a question?"

The same young lieutenant raised his hand.

"Yeah. I got one, with respect, of course." After the laughter died down, he asked his question. "When do we get fed around here?"

"Well, Lieutenant, you just missed our main, and usually only meal of the day. It was moldy hard-tack soaked in warm corn soup. How many kernels of corn did you find in your portion of sour, Major?"

"I saw at least four kernels, Colonel. I was lucky today. Yesterday, there were none."

"I have some good news, though," Colonel Rose mentioned. "Each of you will receive a new blanket today, compliments of our Union War Department."

"On the subject of your personal possessions, like this blanket, I want to warn you," Major Hamilton said. "As much as we preach about caring for one another, and as severely as we punish prisoners for stealing, stuff like this is routinely stolen. This blanket, your greatcoat, and your boots and other possessions are important to your survival here. Guard them well. Do not leave anything unattended. If you do, I guarantee that it will be gone faster than you can snap your fingers."

"And," Colonel Rose added, "it will never be found."

"That will be all for today, gentlemen. Water will be brought to you shortly. In the meantime, I suggest you get some rest."

* * *

There would be only one successful escape from Libby Prison. And, on the one occasion when an attempt was made, more than half of those who did tunnel their way out were recaptured.

Colonel Rose, who led that escape effort, was one of those recaptured. He was eventually exchanged. Captain Drieborg was also a part of that escape group. He was recaptured too. But, he was not exchanged.

ANDERSONVILLE PRISON, GEORGIA

John Ransom was pushed into a boxcar, too. There were so many others pressed against him, he could only stand. By the time the door was pulled shut, the air was already stifling. Instead of heading north as Ethan Schock's train had, Ransom's train was headed in a different direction; south.

For the next few days, the train lumbered along heading south. None of the prisoners was given any water or food. Even though the train traveled south, the weather cooled some. That was a blessing. Still, it was hot with body heat, and the putrid smell caused many to throw up, even on empty stomachs. The train didn't stop for latrine breaks either, so the smell got even worse with all the human waste in the cars.

The train stopped occasionally on a siding, but only for fuel or to allow another train traveling north to pass by on the main track. At these stops, the prisoners were left in the locked boxcars. No food or water was provided. No opportunity was given to stretch their legs or to properly relieve themselves either.

Virtually numb from standing packed into his car, John was surprised when suddenly after the train came once again to a stop, the door to his car was rolled back.

"Get outta' there, Yanks!" shouted a Confederate soldier.

Most of the men could barely stand without support. Many just fell to the ground through the open door of the boxcar. As each car was emptied of its human cargo, the men who could stand were quickly herded from the train to just inside the wide gate of the nearby prison. Once inside, the guards withdrew and closed the doors of the prison behind them.

The men were given no instructions, just left standing there.

Now what do I do? John wondered.

"Hey, Ransom!" he heard.

Getting used to the bright sunlight, John squinted, shading the sun with his hand. He looked around and tried to find the familiar voice. He did notice someone pushing his way through the crowd toward him.

Suddenly, he saw the man who was shouting at him. "Hendryx, is that you?" John shouted.

The men hugged one another.

"I thought you were dead, George."

"Damned near was, John," Hendryx responded. "When the Rebs took me to that so-called prison hospital a' theirs in Richmond, I thought I was a goner. But I got stubborn, I guess, and came out a' the fever. Next thing I knew, I was on a train to this paradise."

The two men were standing near the main entrance to Andersonville. John noticed that the entrance was on higher ground than the general camp. From where he stood, he could look across the entire prison all the way to the far stockade wall. What he saw stunned him.

"This place looks ta me to be worse than Belle Isle."

"You got that right, John. Can't drink tha water, fuel for fires is scarce as the dickens and you're always in danger from attack from other prisoners. A real delightful place, all right. But it's home for now."

"How many men are here, George?"

"Don't rightly know, exactly. The Rebs just keep bringing in trains like yours most every day, full a' men with just the clothes on their backs, an' most times not much a' that."

"Doesn't anyone ever get out of here?" John asked. "You know, exchanged?"

"Far as I can tell, no one has been exchanged since the prison opened a few months ago. As you can see, the place is overcrowded. If that weren't bad enough, we're also in danger all the time from a pretty large gang of prisoners who prey on the weak. We call 'em Raiders. Other than that, this place is worry-free; a paradise on Earth."

Like John, George Hendryx was from Michigan, and a cavalryman, too. John thought his old friend from Belle Isle prison looked to be a lot thinner than when they had last met. What was left of Bill's uniform was filthy and worn; dirty, too. But he still had that ready smile, and John was happy to see his friendly face.

"Come on over to my area, John," George suggested. "Ya hang around these new arrivals and lookin' lost, ya might just get beaten up an' robbed by the Raiders. We're mostly cavalry guys in my mess. Ya probably will recognize Phil Lewis of the Michigan 5th. But ya will have to abide by our rules if ya join us."

"What kind of rules, George?"

"Not much different than what you had on Belle Isle," George explained. "We exercise together every day. We take turns preparing and sharing what food we get. We even pray together twice a day. And even though we never win the war with the graybacks, we pick 'em off one another all the time, anyway. We want one another to stay clean, ya know. We also take turns on guard duty all through the day and night. You got any problem with these rules?"

"No complaint from me," John responded. "They all make sense to me. But standing guard? We're all Union soldiers here who are confined in a Confederate prison. The Rebs allow these Raiders to terrorize everyone?"

"Afraid so, John. These guys roam throughout the camp, day and night. They take what they want. Most men in this prison are not organized like us. In fact, most prisoners are too sickly and weak to put up much of a fight. So, the Raiders rule the roost here. We figure the Reb guards get bought off to look the other way.

"Here we are, John," George announced. "Hey guys, guess who just arrived on the latest train? You remember John Ransom from the Michigan 6th?"

John looked at the men huddled under a tattered tarp. All of them were dressed in tattered clothing. None of them were very tall, maybe five-feet-five, but all of them looked emaciated.

Then he saw two very small members of the group huddled in the shadows.

My Lord, those two soldiers look like children. he thought.

"This is Phil Lewis from the Michigan 5th. That's Jimmy Devers of the Michigan 9th. Sam Hutton over there and Joe Sergeant right next to him are from the 9th, too. Warren Goss is the odd guy out. He's a lawyer from Massachusetts. But we don't hold that against him. We even have a couple a' young'uns from Illinois with us.

"That's Cory McElvain over there, and next to him is his brother Ephraim, the eldest of the two.

"Unless any a' you object, I asked John here to join our mess. Is that all right, or do you guys want him to move on?" Each of the men nodded toward Bill in approval.

"No one seems ta mind. So, welcome to our mess, John. This little spot a' heaven is now your home away from home."

"Thanks, guys. I appreciate it. Anything I can do to help each of us to get out of here alive, just tell me," John assured them.

* * *

Before long, John had caught on to the routine and the demands of living in an open-air sewer. The men of the mess boiled all water used for drinking or cooking. John took his turn getting his group's share of the food, when there was any to get. He stood guard watching for the predator Raiders. He kept his clothing and his body as clean as he could, and he prayed with his mess mates and joined the others in their never-ending battle with lice.

"Hear anything about food today, Phil?" John asked.

"Word is, we're getting bean soup and cornbread again. We're supposed ta get it sometime this afternoon. If it's anything like the last so-called soup we were given, we'll be drinking barely warm water with a few worm-infested beans hidden at the bottom of a bucket of dirty water."

"Doesn't sound too appetizing to me," John judged.

"Complain ta the cook," Phil Lewis said, chuckling.

"Let's see if I can't do something about that, Phil. Give me George's straight razor, will you? See if I can get us some meat for that soup."

"Oh, my Lord! Are you talking about rat meat? And you were the guy who said you would retch at the mere thought of eating rat meat."

"That's right, Phil," John admitted. "But I've decided to survive this prison. If eating rat meat will help me keep up my strength, I'm going to eat the damn stuff. So, get me that damn razor. I'll trade a shave or two for a juicy rat."

Later that afternoon, the men of John's mess were eating their portion of the bean soup and cornbread given them earlier that day.

"Not bad soup today, Phil," observed Sam Hutton. "The Rebs threw in some bits of meat this time. Amazing!" one of the men commented.

"I had a bit of pepper stashed away that I threw in, too," Phil volunteered.

"It's sure welcome, Phil," Ephrain said.

Joe Sergeant swallowed the last bit of his cornbread. "Our mess eats better right now than any other around. We are healthier, cleaner, and better dressed, too. Any a' you guys have a problem with this mess and our rules, I suggest you look for another group where you can do better."

"Calm down, Joe," Phil urged. "No one here has a complaint I know about. In fact, I think we're the only ones with any meat atoll. Right, John?"

"Hey, Phil," Joe asked. "Are you sayin' the Rebs weren't the ones put the meat in our soup?"

"Want me to tell 'em, John?" Phil asked.

"No!" exclaimed Joe. "Not you, John."

"It's like you said, George," John admitted. "We can't survive very long on the weak stuff the Rebs give us. We gotta have meat sometimes, too. I gave three shaves for the two rats we used in our soup. Just don't any of you guys ever tell my wife or mother that I did that, OK?"

"Joe won the pot on that bet," George said.

"Right. He did, John. Everyone else thought you would hold out longer. But Joe said you would eat rat meat, on purpose, in ten days ta two weeks after your arrival. So, he won an extra share of grub next time we get any."

Joe assured him, "I just made a lucky guess."

"If that don't beat all," John said, shaking his head, chuckling. "You guys would bet on most anything. I know you bet on who can pick the most graybacks, who can do the most sit-ups, even who relieves himself first after reveille. Is there any end to the things you guys bet on?"

No one said anything. They just smiled and looked at John.

"You guys didn't," John exclaimed. "Not when my baby will be born?"

"You're close, John," George said. "But that's not what we're betting on this time. It's much more basic than that. Sex has something ta do with it, though."

"Whether it's a boy or a girl?"

"You got it, my friend."

John laughed, "Is nothing sacred around here?"

"Nope," George snapped. "No harm done, John. Besides, what else is there to do around here?"

"Stay alive," John asserted. "Stay alive. Doing whatever it takes to survive. That's what."

* * *

"Hey, Cory," John asked. "Why does everyone call you, 'Doc'?"

"I think it's because I vaccinated everyone in our mess against smallpox."

"Well, I'll be. You're too young to be a school trained doctor. So, how'd ya learn that stuff?"

"Back home, there's an old lady lives nearby who knows all kinds a' weird stuff. She lives in the woods by our house. She appears ta me ta be a bit crazy living alone with her animals an such. She showed me how ta do it."

Cory's brother Ephraim added, "People in our town have her treat all sorts of problems."

"Really works, eh?" John asked.

"Cory vaccinated all of us. Since none of us have come down with the pox, I'd say it does," Phil added.

"How about you work your magic on me, too, Cory?" John asked.

"I will be able to do it as soon as I can find someone who's had the smallpox recently."

* * *

A few days later, George Hendryx stumbled into their area and collapsed.

"George." John rushed up to his messmate. "What happened to you?"

"Raiders roughed me up, that's what!" he answered. "I was on watch in our enclosure and saw a guy getting beaten up. I ran to help him. But they outnumbered me."

"Damn it! Ya should 'a waited for help, George."

"I know it," George admitted. "But I didn't. So, just leave me alone."

That night, the men of John's mess gathered.

"Feeling any better, George?" Sam asked.

"Ya, but I'm still pissed that I got suckered in like I did. "

John Ransom broke into the conversation.

"Damn it! We've got to stop these guys."

"Easy ta say, smart guy. And how are you going ta do that?" Sam snapped.

"Take the fight to them, that's what."

"Look, Sam," John hastened to explain. "I'm not criticizing. I know I'm the new guy here. I sure hope you guys realize how grateful I am to you for taking me into your group. You probably saved my life.

"But I'm not blind. Every day, I can tell that I'm losing weight and strength. As a result, it won't be long before I could be that guy who got beaten up this afternoon. It could be any of us, actually; even you, Sam.

"I for one don't intend to just sit here and let that happen," he concluded.

The men sat silently.

Finally, George spoke up.

"Do you have a plan, John?"

"Yes, I do," John answered. "Want to hear it?"

Sam laughed and said, "I've not got anything pressing to do tonight. In fact, my social calendar is open. Go ahead, entertain me with your pipe dream."

"All right, I will," John began. "We have already admitted that we are all growing weaker. We also admit that the Raiders are not and that we can't depend upon the Reb guards to protect us from them. The Raiders have all the food they want and probably get all the packages sent to the prisoners but never delivered. They have good water and occupy the highest ground in the camp. They have good tents and decent clothing. What the Reb guards don't give them, they steal from us.

"The result is, they grow stronger while we grow weaker. We also know that none of this will change unless we do something."

Sarcastically, Sam snapped, "Tell us something we don't know."

"Let him finish, for God's sake, Sam," retorted George. "I'm the guy got beat up today, not you. 'Sides, I want to hear this. So, sit there and shut up until he finishes."

"Sure. This might be funny. Go ahead, John," responded Sam.

"We must destroy them, and we must do it very soon if we are to survive. There is no other option I can see."

"Big talk, buddy," Sam interrupted. "Just like that, we destroy them, eh?"

"Yes, Sam. We kill them!" John responded. "Organize like we did in the Army and kill them."

"Whew!" George said. "That's bold talk, John. How we gonna do that?"

"We five can't. But if we organize, grow our numbers, say to platoon size, we can. We gather about 30 strong and determined men to form an attack group. Then we could do what is necessary."

"John," George responded. "I've been in this hellhole long enough to have witnessed a couple of attempts to do what you are suggesting. Not only did they fail, but the guys involved didn't live long afterward. How is your plan going to succeed when these other attempts failed?"

John didn't hesitate to answer.

"Good question, George. I've asked around and listened to some other prisoners who were around then, like you. It seems to me that the other failed attacks were just reactions to something the Raiders did. Those other attacks were not well-organized either. They were just knee-jerk reactions. The Raiders even boasted of knowing about them in advance. So, the Raiders turned them into killing traps. And they did the killing.

"When the Raiders plan an attack, they have scouted their target thoroughly. They pick their place and time. Their attacks have superior numbers and surprise on their side, too. In the past, by the time any group of prisoners has gotten organized to respond, the Raiders were ready to trap and kill them."

"How will your deal be different?" Warren Goss asked.

"This time, we'll pick the time and the place. Nor will our attack be just a reaction to something they did. Instead, our attack will be a surprise of our own. Our intention will not be to loot, but to kill as many of them as we can and then retreat. Afterwards, we will set up a trap of our own. If they attempt a counterattack, we'll kill more of them."

"Let me get this straight, Ransom," Sam asked. "You propose to attack a group of fellow Union prisoners who are physically stronger than we are and are better armed and organized, too?"

"Yup. That's it exactly."

"How will you manage that?" George asked.

"Not me, George. Us."

"Whoa!" Sam almost shouted. "Wait just a minute. When did I for one agree to your cockamamie plan?"

"You didn't, Sam. Neither did anyone else," Ransom said with a bit of a laugh. "But even I have to admit that I can't do this alone. And if you guys won't join me, I'm gonna die in this rat hole, just like you will. That's a fact."

After what seemed like a long time, George broke the silence.

"You're probably right about that, John. So, tell us how you figure the five of us can carry this off."

"First and foremost," Ransom began. "Strict security is essential while we recruit men to join us and prior to the actual attack.

"So, I will recruit six men to find and lead five other men to make up a squad of six each. None of them will know our complete plan. I will help each of them organize their squads, one man at a time. For additional security, the members of these squads will know the squad leader and me, but not the others in his squad. And, only I will know the date and time of the attack."

"Seems like you've given this a lot of thought, John," Phil Lewis observed. "How do you know all of us are willing to join you in this madness?"

John looked at each of the men listening to him. He finally said, "If anyone is not up to it, just say so now.

Phil spoke first. "You've answered my initial questions, John. I'm in."

"I am, too," George said.

"How about you, Warren?" John asked.

"I'd rather die with a fighting chance 'stead 'a wasting away like we are now. I'm in."

The McElvain brothers nodded. Ephraim said, "We're in, too, John."

George looked at Sam Hutton.

"I guess it's down to you, Sam. What about you? Are you in?"

"Shit, yes!" Sam said with a big smile. "You know me, the doubting Thomas; always questioning everything. I was just pressin' John ta' see if he has this hair-brained idea thought out. Hell yes, I'm in. Rather die with a club in my hands than keel over from starvation or a beating from the Raiders."

Over the next ten days, John recruited five squad leaders: Ned Corrigan, of five men each were recruited. Five men plus a squad leader gave John a force of thirty men.

As they were recruited, he spoke to each of the men about the killing purpose of the raid and the type of weapon each of them had to find. He suggested each man get wooden stake three or four feet in length. He told them that a shovel with a sharpened blade would be great. Of course, a knife would be better.

At the same time, he assured them that darkness and surprise would be their primary weapons. Of course, he emphasized the need for secrecy. They were not even to tell their best friend about their role and the impending attack.

Once the squads were organized, John met with the squad leaders, one at a time.

Ned Corrigan was first.

"How is your squad doing?" he asked.

"Great, John," Ned told him. "I can't believe how eager the guys I recruited are for this. I think I could have recruited another squad easily. I hope you set a date soon for the attack."

"I will, Ned."

Tom Larkin, Ned Johnson, and A.R. Hill were next. Each man had found five men without much difficulty.

Then George spoke up. "John, I hate to bring this up. But I have had a bad case of the runs these past few days. If the attack is going to be soon, I don't think I'll have the strength to lead my men."

"Holy crap, George!" Phil whispered. "What'll we do now?"

George said, "I got a guy in my squad who I think can take over without a hitch." John then explained to the others that this fellow was a Sioux Indian named Battist.

"He's a recent arrival, so he's still healthy. He's quiet but has a bellyful a' hate for the Raiders. He was a sergeant in his unit, so he's used to ordering guys around. What do you think?"

"Will he do it?"

"Ya. I spoke to him this morning. I'll get him over here, if you want."

"Do that, George," John Ransom decided.

Later, Battist sat quietly in the circle of men. Many questions were asked of him. His answers were short and to the point.

Finally, John asked him, "How do you feel about helping to lead this attack, Battist?"

"I feel as you men do," he answered. "We must kill those outlaw prisoners or lose our own lives. Your plan is my chance to survive and return to my people. I was a warrior of the Sioux nation. I was a leader of men in my infantry unit, too. I will go with you on this attack as a squad member or a squad leader. Either way, I am very good at moving quietly and killing and leading. It is up to you to decide."

John spoke next. "If there is no objection, I will welcome Battist as a squad leader, replacing George."

There was no objection.

"We will not have time to speak with each man in your squad, George," John informed him. "So, I'll want you to stay with your squad to the point of attack. We'll leave you there, and Battist will take charge. After that, you will be in charge of that escape route. Can you handle that, George?"

"I think I should be able to do that. But what if I'm feeling better by the time you decide to attack?"

"Don't think so, George. We're attacking tonight."

"Holy shit!" Sam muttered. "It's really gonna happen."

John nodded. "That's right. I'm satisfied that everyone is ready. And you all know that the longer we wait, the greater the chance of discovery. So, with no moon tonight, it's got to be now.

"You squad leaders get back here with your squads in one hour. George, then you can explain your situation to your men and introduce Battist to them.

"All of you remember," John went on. "As you speak to the men of your squad, have each one of them bring his weapon to your rendezvous point. When they arrive, give each of them one of these strips of white cloth to tie around their head. We don't want to be hitting our own guys in the dark.

"Make sure that once they are together, no one can leave until we move out. Anyone who tries to leave your assembly area, kill him."

"Damn, John," George exclaimed. "That's pretty rough, isn't it?"

"It might seem harsh, but we will all die if the Raiders are waiting for us. Our lives depend upon surprise."

The squad leaders settled down to rest for an hour or so before gathering their men.

Cory McElvain approached John.

"Now that everything's a go, John," he said, "how about me? You told me you would have an assignment for me. What is it?"

"Cory, I've noticed that you're pretty good with all this medical mumbo-jumbo. Since I've been here, you've treated guys for fevers, cuts an' bruises; all sorts a' things. I think you picked up a lot of stuff from that crazy lady back home."

"Ya, that's right. So, what's that got to do with the raid tonight?"

"I need you at the rendezvous point to help with our guys who are injured."

"So, you're not keeping me out 'a this cause I'm small or young?"

"Not at all. Hells-bells, Cory," John assured him. "You were part of a fighting unit before you were captured. Your size has nothing to do with this assignment. You have medical skills. The men have grown to trust you. That's why I'm asking you to stay out of the fighting and help with the wounded."

"Just checking, John," Cory said. "Of course, I'll do it. I'll get some bandages an stuff together for tonight. My brother will help me."

"Thank you, Cory."

CAMP DOUGLAS, ILLINOIS

The Illinois Central Railroad train pulled onto a siding in downtown Chicago. Union guards opened the doors of the boxcars.

"You Rebs get down out a' there now an' form up," A Union sergeant ordered.

Men cooped up for days virtually fell out of the cars on unsteady legs.

A light spring mist fell on the bedraggled-looking bunch of men. The fresh air was welcomed, but most of the men were weak from lack of water and food.

So, there was a lot of pushing, shoving and leaning on one another.

"Form up, damn it!" the sergeant repeated. "I don't want ta have ta tell yas again."

Eventually, ranks were formed facing the sergeant.

"Right face," he ordered. Then he shouted, "Forward, march!"

The column of men obeyed and shuffled down the wide, muddy road that led through the center of the city.

"Look at all those people on the boardwalk," Richard Pope said to the man marching alongside.

Sure enough, the elevated boardwalk on each side of the road was crowded with people.

"They're just standing there staring at us."

"Probably never seen a Southerner afore," one of the prisoners said.

Richard Pope observed, "We've got to be a big disappointment, then. We don't look a hell of a' lot different than them."

"'Cept we're dirty and hungry lookin'," someone added.

"Well, there's that."

Just then, a mud ball hit one of the prisoners.

"Traitors!" someone in the crowd shouted.

The sky was suddenly full of mud balls.

" Murderers!" another shouted.

The cry was picked up by the crowd. "Traitors!! Murderers! Traitors!" The onlookers shouted. Some shook their fists at the prisoners, too.

"Nice to know how your host feels about you," Pope said. He held his arms up over his head to ward off the mud balls.

"Move along, you Rebs," the sergeant urged. "We've only a bit more ta go down this road."

"I never thought I'd welcome the sight of a prison," Colonel McGavock told Pope.

The front gate of Camp Douglas. *Chicago History Museum.*

The column moved through the city to the gate of the prison.

"Column, halt!" the sergeant ordered.

"Column, right," he continued. The several hundred men of the column of men turned and moved through the gate into the prison yard.

"Move along, no lollygagging now," the Union sergeant shouted.

The campground was filled with prisoners standing silently, watching.

"At least they're not throwing anything at us," Pope observed.

Then he heard the order. "Column, halt!"

"Officers, on my command, move to my position. Enlisted men, stay where you are till we assign you one of the barracks.

"Now, move."

The dozen or so Confederate officers in the column broke ranks and gathered around the Union sergeant.

"The Corporal here will lead ya to the temporary officers' barracks. Keep to yourselves. We don't want yas ta be mixin among the enlisted men. If we hear of any a yas inciting them ta causin' trouble, trying ta organize a' escape or complainin' an' such, ya will end up in solitary for a week or so."

Colonel McGavock raised his hand.

"What is it, Colonel?" the Sergeant asked.

"What was that business you said, 'temporary barracks'?"

"What that means, Colonel dear, is that you officers will be movin' on to a prison all ta yerselves one day very soon. So, gentlemen, don't get too comfortable. Afore the first snow flies, you'll be movin on, I'm guessing."

"What's snow?" one of the young officers muttered.

"I'm thinking yer not going to like it, whatever it tis," another man answered. "I'm thinking it has something ta do with cold. Anyways, I can't believe anything in this infernal North country could be pleasing."

"We'll soon see," Pope added.

LOWELL

Michelle Schock handed her husband Carl a piece of paper.

"Carl, please look at this letter."

"But I've already read it.," he objected.

"I know. We both have. But it has been several days since we received it from the orphanage in New York City. We must decide one way or another. Are we going to give a home and our love to these two little ones, or not?"

After a few moments of silence, he looked up.

"The Catholic nun who is in charge of the orphanage in New York says she has a brother and his sister available for us," Carl related.

"Yes," Michelle responded. "The nun's name is Sister Fitzgibbon. She is in charge at the orphanage. She also says that she was very impressed by the letters of recommendation she received from our Catholic neighbors."

Carl added an observation. "What really surprised me was the fine letter we got from our friend's Catholic priest. I thought he'd turn us down flat when we told him we intended to raise the children as Lutherans, not as Catholics."

"I believe our friends who are members of his parish convinced him we would be good Christian parents. After all, isn't that the most important thing for these little orphans; a good home and a Christian upbringing?"

"I suppose so," Carl said. "I agree with you, but I was still surprised the Catholic priest did, too."

"That's all behind us," Michelle concluded. "Now, the next step is up to us."

"Are we really going to do this, dear?" Carl asked earnestly. "The little boy and his infant sister are available for us to bring here right now. The nun says the little girl was actually born at the orphanage. So, they have been in her care for almost a year.

"I keep asking myself, 'Do we want to bring them both into our home? Are we really ready to adopt them as our own children?

"For God's sake, Michelle." Carl exclaimed. "These children are from the streets of New York. We know nothing about them."

"Carl, dear," Michelle responded calmly. She moved to her husband's side and knelt by his chair. She took his hands in her own and looked at him intently. Tears filled her eyes.

Finally, she said, "Sweetheart, we know these little children need a good home. We know we want to have the voices of little ones in our home again. Think about it, Carl, maybe we need them as much as they need us."

"I hadn't thought of it that way," he admitted.

"Besides," Michelle went on, "we must trust in God. He will help us raise these little ones to be godly and hardworking, just like He helped us raise our Ethan to be a hardworking and Christian man. All we have to do is give these little ones a loving home just like we did for our son, Ethan."

"I suppose."

"You were a good father to Ethan," Michelle continued. "You will be a good one for these little ones, too. I just know it."

"You really think so?" he asked, tearing up himself. "I must admit," he confessed, "I'm afraid some. You know?"

"Don't worry, Carl," she assured him. "You'll be just fine. The good Lord will help us. We'll help one another, too. All right?"

Carl reached out his arms for his wife. She sat on his lap, and they hugged for a time.

Michelle finally spoke. "I'll write Sister Fitzgibbon and tell her we will arrange to come to New York and get the children. All right?"

"Sure," Carl responded. "And I'll make the travel arrangements."

"So, it is settled," Michelle said. "We will bring the children to our home as our own." Tears were streaming down her cheeks now.

"But first, sweetheart," Michelle said, standing.

She pulled Carl up beside her and put her arms around his neck. He responded by pulling her close. They kissed. After a bit, he allowed her to step back.

She looked up at him, smiled, took his hand, and led him toward their bedroom.

SALISBURY PRISON

The first trainload of Union prisoners arrived at the newly constructed prison outside of Salisbury, North Carolina, on December 9, 1861. Most of these men had been taken prisoner at the First Battle of Bull Run in the summer of 1861.

In August of 1862, prisoners many were shipped North from the overcrowded enlisted man's Belle Isle Prison. This was located on an island in the James River outside of Richmond, Virginia. Carl Shock and his friend Willie Petzold were both prisoners there and were on one of those trains heading to Salisbury Prison.

An old four-story factory had been purchased by the Confederate government and renovated as a prison. Inside a stockade were six acres providing adequate space for baseball games. Not everyone was happy with locating such a prison just outside of their town. But generally, the locals treated the prisoners with respect.

Prisoners wrote home of their kindness and that they were allowed to visit outside the prison grounds. They could also buy fresh vegetables and fruit in the town. The prison was reported by the soldiers held there as a comfortable place. Over time, however poor sanitation and poor drainage created a stench. The smell was so strong that the locals complained loudly. The other problem encountered was the lack of adequate firewood for cooking, boiling drinking water and to heat the sleeping areas.

* * *

"Hey, Willie!" Ethan shouted. "Come on out, we've got a ball game against those loudmouthed third floor guys from Pennsylvania."

Willie came lumbering out of the barracks.

"Think they can beat us, do they?" he asked his friend Ethan.

"I guess so," Ethan responded. "We took 'em down a week ago. But some people never learn. Are you up for a game?"

"You bet. What else is there to do anyways?" Willie said.

Willie was talking more now. Whatever had affected his ability to speak seemed to be disappearing some. He still sort a' clung to his friend Ethan.

Ethan looked at his childhood friend. *Surely is great that Willie is talking more. Still sort of follows me around, though. Just not very sure of himself - but he's getting better. A good sign.*

The two friends began to throw the makeshift ball back and forth, warming up. Ethan usually pitched, and Willie was his catcher. Not many batters hit Ethan's pitches very well. Willie was probably the best batter in the entire prison population. Hard to beat that combination, pitching and batting.

"I'm going to bat first today, Willie," Ethan decided. "You can follow me. All right?"

"Sure, Ethan," Willie agreed

Sure enough, Ethan faced the third-floor pitcher first. He bunted the first ball thrown to him down the third base line and made it to the first base before the opponent's third baseman could throw the ball to the first baseman.

Now it was Willie's turn at bat. His bat met the second pitch thrown toward him squarely. Strong as a bull, Willie sent the ball to the end of the parade ground. He wasn't the fastest runner, so he only made it to third base before the ball was thrown to the other team's catcher.

But Ethan had scored.

By the end of the sixth and final inning, Ethan's second floor team was tied with the third floor team three runs to three. Willie was on second base with two out. His teammate at the plate was Tom Novak, one of Ethan's squad members.

Tom was walked on four straight pitches. Then it was Kelly at the plate with Tom on first base and Willie on second base, still with two outs and the score tied.

Tom hit the first pitch down to third base. It was fielded cleanly deep behind the base. The third baseman ran to his base, turned and faced Willie, who was running toward him; an easy out.

"Knock him down, Willie," a teammate shouted.

Willie put down his shoulder and hit the third baseman with a blow that dislodged the ball, sending it in one direction and the third baseman in another.

Willie could have stopped and been safe at third base, but he continued running toward home plate. As slow a runner as he was, he still made it there before the ball was retrieved. As it turned out, he scored the winning run.

Many of the Northern boys at Salisbury Prison didn't play baseball. The majority enjoyed more sedentary games like chess, checkers and card games of all sorts. Interestingly, some prisoners put on theatrical plays. Even locals came to the makeshift stage to see the productions. Many of them brought baked goods to the event as their contribution.

In the first year or so, Dr. Braxton Craven, who had recently been the president of Trinity College, was commandant of the prison. Under his supervision, the camp was as pleasant for the prisoners as one might expect a prison to be.

The pleasant atmosphere changed when in late 1862, Captain McCoy was given the responsibility. By this time, food shortages impacted both the community and the prison. And the attitude of the locals changed to downright surly as the war went on and the local families lost loved ones.

As with most every prisoner of war camp, North and South, sanitation was a problem.

Human waste filled sinkholes as fast as they could be dug. Ground water became polluted, and firewood was in such short supply, it could not always be boiled before use. Both Rebel and Union Inspectors repeatedly reported the problem and identified it as the cause of dysentery and diarrhea the major killers.

"Ya got some firewood today, I see," Kelly said to his messmate, Tom Novak.

"'Bout time, too," Tom responded. "We ain't been able to boil our water for a week. I'm surprised we all haven't come down with the shits."

"Townspeople don't want us let out to forage for wood," Kelly reminded him. "They're afraid we might steal from them or maybe run away, I suppose. More this war goes on, the more a' the Salisbury people lose members a' their families. They kept the Sutler from selling us stuff recently, too; forced him to leave, they did."

"We ain't got any packages from home lately either," Tom added. "Think the guards are takin' them?"

"Probably," Kelly observed. "Remember we used ta get a couple a' packages a month from Ethan's people? We ain't seen one a' those in a while either."

"I loved those oatmeal cookies his mom used ta send."

"Our rations here have sort a' tapered off, too" Ethan said. "I' think I've lost a few pounds in the last month or so."

"Don't worry about it," Tom urged. "We're going ta get exchanged any day now."

"That's wishful thinking, for sure," Kelly interrupted. "The prisoners who were here a'fore we arrived all got exchanged. You'd think it'd be our turn soon.

"But no, those guys all left here last August. This be November. Ain't nobody exchanged since we got here a couple a' months ago."

Tom piped up, "I expect our high and mighty leaders in Washington City got a burr up their butts about not exchanging any Confederates prisoners 'cause they don't want any a' them reb soldiers returning to the fighting.

"'Course that means we sit here and rot," Tom concluded.

"Seems ta me there's nothing we can do about it," Ethan said matter of flatly.

"There you go again, Ethan," Kelly complained. "A guy can't even talk about somethin' without you pouring cold water on it. Seems we can't talk about nothing with you around."

"You can talk about anything you like, Kelly," Ethan said, laughing. "Just don't expect me not to say what I think, too. You're too touchy, Kelly. Talk on all ya' like."

"Thank you very much, Corporal Shock. I'll do just that," Kelly snapped.

"By the way, guys," Ethan changed the subject, "we got a preacher from a city church coming into the camp tomorrow to give a service. Who's going with me to hear him?"

"What kind, Ethan?" Tom Novak asked.

Kelly spoke first. "What difference do it make? If'n he's a preacher, he a Protestant. I'm a Catholic. So, I guess I'll pass on hearing him talk."

"I'm a Catholic, too, Kelly," Novak reminded everyone. "But I haven't seen any Catholic priest around here lately. 'Sides, I don't think God cares very much who preaches his word. It's the same God after all. Count me in, Ethan, I'll go with ya."

"I spose he's a Confederate, too," Kelly surmised. "Probably tell us that God's on their side an' all. How we Union guys are all wrong. I don't need ta hear that kind a' preaching."

"He might say those things," Ethan admitted. "But he might just preach the word of God and maybe read from the Bible. So, I intend to give this preacher a chance. Who knows, Kelly. Even you might get something out a' his preaching. 'Sides, you don't have nothing ta do tomorrow morning, do you?"

"Ya," Novak kidded. "Check your social calendar, Kelly. As fer me, I'm going ta cancel all my appointments tomorrow just ta hear this guy."

"All right, you guys," Kelly responded. "I'll go with you if Willie goes."

Ethan turned to his quiet friend. "How about it, big guy? Want to go with me to church tomorrow?"

"Sure, Ethan," Willie responded with a big smile. "I used to go to church with my sisters all the time at home."

"Want to go tomorrow?" Ethan repeated.

"Sue, if you take me, Ethan."

"You got it, buddy."

"By the way," Ethan asked, "how is Joe Cox feeling today?"

Cox was another Detroiter picked up by the rebs about the same time as Kelly, Tom and Ethan.

"That lucky Kraut got a visit from Mrs. Johnson again. She brought him some soup and fresh bread. If he's not careful, she's about to hook him into marryin' her."

"Wouldn't be the worst thing," Tom added. "She's a good looker. And to hear Johnson talk, a damn good cook. Not a bad combination, if ya ask me."

"Before Cox, she nursed another prisoner here, Hugh Berry, till he died," Kelly reminded everyone. "What's with that lady? She got a yen fer Yanks or what?"

"Hells bells," Ethan commented. "She can nurse me any day. I think you're just jealous you're not getting some of her loving-tender care, Kelly."

"I probably am, truth be told."

ANDERSONVILLE PRISON

"Tonight!" George said. "Holy shit. I feel just like I used to the night before a battle."

"Nervous and afraid?"

"Ya, I guess you'd say that," George admitted. "I'll be all right, but it's been a while, ya know."

"Me, too, George," Ransom revealed. "Ever in a fight at night?"

"Nope," Hone responded. "This will be the first time for me. So, better stay out a' my way, ol' buddy. I'll be hitting anyone who comes across my path. I don't know if I'll even see that damn white cloth tied around the head of each of our guys."

"I understand, George," Ransom said. "Time ta go."

Shortly before dark, the squad leaders rounded up the members of their squad. All the men were accounted for as they gathered. Two squads were to lead and secure the entryway to the Raiders' area. Three squads were to follow on their heels into the heart of that area. The sixth squad, led by John Ransom, would head directly to the heart of the Raider camp to locate and kill the leaders.

All the other attacking men would work their way around the perimeter of the Raiders' enclosure, killing as many men they could. One squad would move to the right of the entrance, one squad to the left. They intended to kill all they encountered.

There was no moon, so when the sun disappeared below the horizon, it quickly became very dark.

Perfect night, Ransom thought.

But he also began to think of all the things he might have said to the men in the six squads, but hadn't.

Too late now. The squads are on their way. It's do or die for all of us.

Ransom moved past the entryway to the Raider stronghold. He noticed several Raider bodies on the ground. Once, these dead men had guarded this entrance to their stronghold. Killing the guards, the men of another squad had secured the entrance.

Now these men stood guard at the entrance. Not a word was spoken as Ransom led his other squads of killers into the Raider compound.

The first squad did their job here, Ransom thought approvingly. *Now I've got to do my part.*

Breathing heavily, heart pounding, he led the other squads into the heart of the Raider area. He had told his men to move in pairs. Side by side, they used their weapons to attack the sleeping forms.

"No mercy," he had ordered. *"Remember all the poor, helpless men they have killed and stolen from.* "Strike in anger, strike with fury and move on. Take nothing, no loot; take their lives, and we live."

John had scouted the Raider area very carefully. He knew exactly where the leaders usually slept. His information had even included the number of paces from the entrance. They did not stop along the way to attack any other targets. Instead, he led his men directly to their destination.

Once they had taken the prescribed number of steps, they stopped and began to attack any sleeping men they found. John shut out all sound and only seemed to hear the thud of his sharpened shovel as it cut into the sleeping forms. He was lost in the fury of his attack as he struck again and again.

Suddenly, the shrill sound of a whistle interrupted his killing frenzy. That was the signal to break off the attack and retreat to the entrance that was still being held by one of his squads.

At the entrance, he accounted for his squad members and led them to the rendezvous point. There, he met with his five squad leaders.

"Are all of your men accounted for?" Once he received their report, he ordered, "Great. Now return to your squads. Get them ready for a counterattack from the Raiders."

John's shirt was soaked with sweat. He wiped perspiration from his face as he crouched alongside the path he expected some of the Raiders to use. He tightly clutched the shovel he had just used to kill several sleeping Union soldiers.

After about an hour, it was obvious the Raiders did not intend to mount a counterattack. John moved to each squad leader.

"Collect the headband from each of your men. Then send the men back to their mess areas. Tell them to stay put tomorrow. Our 'doc' will visit any who are hurt then. You will contact them with any news. But in the meantime, tell them to keep their mouths shut about what we did this night."

"Will do, John," Tom Larkin said. The other squad leaders nodded in agreement.

Battist, the Sioux squad leader, whispered to John, "Any my men talk, they will never talk again." He made a slashing motion across his own throat before he moved away silently into the darkness.

Thank God, that Indian is on my side. John thought.

LOWELL

It was a November Saturday. The first bits of snow were falling, as was the temperature. The Petzold's wagon just pulled into their farm yard.

Mary Petzold jumped off the wagon and ran into her house.

"Momma, come quick!" she shouted. She didn't even take off her winter coat or overshoes.

Her mother was at the wood stove, stirring a pot of sliced apples. She intended to can some applesauce. "What is it, child?" her mother asked. "Just tell me, I can't leave my pot of apples."

"It's from Ethan Shock," Mary continued to almost shout, jumping up and down with the letter in her hand.

"So, read me what he has to say." Mary's mother was getting impatient with her daughter.

"Willie is coming home, Momma," she shouted. "Willie is coming home."

"Give me the letter, child," she ordered. "Come stir the pot for me."

She read the letter. "Oh, my Lord," she exclaimed. "How can Ethan know such a thing?"

Her husband walked in the house.

"Papa, how can Ethan Shock know such a thing?"

"I don't know, Momma. But tomorrow we go to Congressman Kellogg's office in Grand Rapids. We will talk with Mr. Kellogg's aide. He can wire Washington to find out if it is true. Ya?"

The household was in an uproar the rest of the evening. While still at the dinner table, Mrs. Petzold quieted everyone down and said, "Now we pray that it is true about our Willie coming home, ya?"

"Dear Lord, we pray that the news about our Willie is true.

In the meantime, keep him safe and bring him home to his family soon. Amen."

WASHINGTON CITY

The United States Quartermaster General M.C. Meigs was meeting with Secretary of War Cameron. The newly appointed Commissioner of Prisoners, Lt. Colonel William Hoffman, was with him.

"Gentlemen," Secretary Cameron began. "I'm told that you requested this meeting to make some sort of presentation. I don't have a great deal of time, so please get on with it."

General Meigs began. "As you might be aware, Mr. Secretary, since the battles of Fort Donelson and Shiloh, we have accumulated a great number of prisoners. While we have made do with various facilities, we have another problem we believe must be solved."

"What is it?"

"Because of limited facilities, we have had to house officers with enlisted men."

"Why the hell is that a problem?" Cameron snapped.

Colonel Hoffman entered the conversation. "Because it creates a serious security problem, sir. We can't have officers organizing resistance right in our prisons or for that matter, mass escape attempts. Enlisted men are much more easily controlled in the absence of their officers."

"So, gentlemen, what do you propose to do about it?"

"We want to build a prison strictly to hold Confederate officers, sir," Meigs responded.

"You two know most of our funds are now going to train and equip the army so we can crush this rebellion."

"Yes, sir, we know that," Hoffman said. "But we also know you want us to do a proper job of providing secure prison facilities. At present, we can't do that if we continue to mix officers in with enlisted men."

"All right," Cameron interrupted. "What's this going to cost me?"

"We estimate is should cost about $30,000, sir," Meigs informed him. "We have a site identified on Johnson's Island in Lake Erie that we can cheaply lease. We figure to house about 1,500 or so officers there. Firewood is abundant, and supplies can be obtained from the locals in the nearby town of Sandusky, Ohio."

Cameron interrupted. "I thought some island closer to the Canadian border was suggested?"

"It was, sir," Hoffman answered. "But upon inspection, I discovered that it was very close to the Canadian border; too close for security purposes, and too close to Canadian sympathizers. And as a practical matter, we would have to buy our supplies and construction materials from Canadian sources."

"I don't know about your security concerns, but I damn well want us buying supplies and such from Americans, not the damn Canadians. By the way, where'd you come up with that fifteen-hundred capacity figure you gave me?"

"We have half that number of officers at Fort Chase, Ohio, and Camp Douglas, Illinois, right now. If this rebellion isn't crushed soon, we will probably double that number before the end of this year."

"What will happen if the cartel for the exchange of prisoners becomes a reality?" Cameron asked.

"Most probably the prison would be emptied and closed, I would imagine," Hoffman responded. "But I suggest, sir, that we plan as though there will be no such agreement and the need for a prison used for Confederate officers will continue to be needed."

"Let me get this straight, gentlemen," Cameron concluded. "You want me to approve the construction of a prison on this Lake Erie island, even though it will probably be shut down if an exchange agreement makes it unnecessary?"

"Yes, sir," General Meigs confirmed.

"You can do whatever is necessary for under $30,000?"

"We believe so, sir."

"Within a month of the approval for the project?"

"Yes, sir."

Cameron thought for a moment.

"All right, I'll cut the necessary paperwork and include a list of suppliers I expect you to use as well. Now get out of here and leave me alone."

"Thank you, sir," General Meigs said.

Both officers rose and hurriedly left Cameron's office.

On the way out of the building, Hoffman asked General Meigs, "Is he always so abrupt? Or was it just me who irritated him?"

"It's been my experience that Cameron seems to be that way with everyone."

"What's this list of suppliers he referred to?" Hoffman asked.

"It is rumored that Cameron gets kickbacks from suppliers of military equipment and such.

Hoffman bristled at that. "Hell's fire. I suggest we get the best price and his list be damned."

"Listen to me, sonny," Meigs countered. "Unless you want to risk having this project somehow run out of funds before the Johnson Island prison is finished, you had best use his list of suppliers for most everything you need to construct and supply the prison."

"Simple as that, eh?"

"Right, simple as that," Meigs responded. "You get the message, son?"

"I get it," Hoffman agreed.

"Just keep good records," Meigs counseled. "If someone accuses you of having your hand in the till, you need to be able to defend yourself. You get that, too?"

"Yes, sir," Hoffman assured him. "I get that, too."

"Good. Cameron will think nothing of throwing us to the wolves if any investigation is made."

"What a hell of a way to fight a war," Hoffman exclaimed.

"Still want this job?"

"What choice have I got, sir?" Hoffman complained. "If I back off and don't build an officer's prison, I'd probably be accused of dereliction of duty. And you're warning me that if I do, I'll likely be accused of lining my pockets with kickback from suppliers.

"Seems like I'm damned if I do and damned if I don't."

"Welcome to the army, son."

CAMP DOUGLAS

The front gate of Camp Douglas. *Chicago History Museum.*

Located right on the shore of Lake Michigan, heavy lake effect snow was common. This November was no exception. It was only Thanksgiving week, and the wet snow was accumulating to the depth of a foot.

"Actually, it's sort of strange," Richard Pope said. "One day we get our exercise area full a' this stuff, an' the next day the temperature goes up a bit, then it melts."

Another member of Pope's mess said, "I don't mind that so much. It's the mud that's left over after the melting that bothers me. Wet n' sloppy snow one day, and mud the next. No wonder these Yanks are half-crazy."

"Ya," Pope added. "If you don't like the weather, wait an hour and it will probably change."

Pope and several hundred other Confederate prisoners taken at Shiloh, Tennessee, last spring had been marched here the four miles from the downtown Chicago train depot. Now there was a railroad siding dropping off prisoners of war right at the entrance of Camp Douglas.

"I guess I don't mind the snow as much as the damn wind," another prisoner from the officers' barracks commented. "Damn wind off in that lake seems ta' blow right through me. I'm chilled all the time."

"Gotta agree with you, Stan," another said. "I'm shivering all the time, too."

"Don't worry about it, boys," Pope assured them. "Sergeant Wiley told us the other day that we'd be moving to an officer's only prison right after Thanksgiving."

"What will the Yankee tourists look at when we're gone?"

That fall, the Commandant had an observation platform constructed along one of the prison walls for locals to observe the prisoners. Weekends were the busiest time. The small fee he charged each observer did not seem to deter a good crowd.

"Wonder what happens to all that money he collects each weekend?"

"Doesn't go for extra blankets or food for the prisoners, I'm promisin' ya that."

"Word is, he's going to discipline an enlisted man in the yard for the tourists to see."

"You mean one a' our guys is going ta' be whipped or hung by the wrists just fer the tourists ta see?"

"That's the word."

"Well, I'll be. Doesn't sound right."

"Once we're gone, he's gotta do something to attract the paying customers, I suppose."

"Just don't seem right, jus' tha same."

Another officer in the group changed the subject.

"Pope?" he asked. "Your buddy, the Yankee sergeant, tell you where we're going?"

"First off, asshole, he's not my buddy. Secondly, if he didn't tell me stuff, I'd have no interesting information to feed the rumor mill, now would I?"

"All right, all right, what's the deal? Do you know?"

"Wiley told me we're going to a new camp in the state of Ohio outside a town called Sandusky. The prison is located on an island in another of these lakes called Lake Erie."

"Holy shit!" one of the men exclaimed.

"On an island, out in a body of water like Lake Michigan?" another said. "The wind will sweep across that place like a gale. I don't look forward to a winter there."

"Actually," Pope interjected, "I can't speak for a Northern winter, but ya sort a' get used to the wind. My folks have a plantation on Edisto Island off the coast of South Carolina. We don't have cold like in the North, and a' course there's no snow there, like here. But we do get some pretty strong winds sort a' regular. When we do, ya' practically have ta' tie yourself to a tree or get blown out ta' sea."

"Whatever, it's gonna be an adventure for this poor Southern boy, that's fer sure," another officer mused.

"That's fer sure."

PRISONER EXCHANGE

Historically, the exchange of prisoners of war was managed right on the battlefield by the military commanders of the opposing forces present at the scene.

But during the American Revolution, there had been no formal agreement for after battle exchanges. So, during that conflict, large numbers of prisoners had been sent to a prison of some sort. It wasn't until the war with Great Britain in 1812 that an exchange system was negotiated.

During the Civil War, the Lincoln administration was reluctant to negotiate with representatives of the Confederate government to arrange for a system of prisoner exchange. After all, the war was considered an insurrection. So, prisoners taken by the Union were considered rebels at best, and traitors at worst.

It was also feared that meeting with commissioners from the Confederate States might be considered by other sovereign nations as tacit recognition of the Confederate government as an independent nation.

But due to public pressure in the North, Union commissioners were appointed to meet with counterparts from the CSA to work out a system. The result was called the Dix-Hill Cartel. It went into effect July of 1862. The agreement put in place a system of parole and exchange.

A 'paroled' prisoner was one released to the care of his government. But he was not to return to active duty. On the contrary, he was to remain inactive, that is, given no military duties, until exchanged for a soldier of equal rank from the other warring nation.

In some cases, several prisoners of lower rank could be exchanged for one of higher rank. Thus, a paroled prisoner with the rank of captain might be exchanged for thirty privates.

Until properly exchanged, not paroled prisoner was to be returned to active duty.

Sick or severely wounded prisoners were sometimes sent quickly back to their lines without reference to rank or the rules for exchange.

Under the rules of the Dix-Hill Cartel, prisons in both the North and the South were thus emptied during the fall of 1862. After that, problems arose which caused Union officials to question the wisdom of the system.

CAMP SALISBURY

BIRDS EYE VIEW OF CONFEDERATE PRISON PEN
AT SALISBURY, N.C. — TAKEN IN 1864

"Hey, Ethan," Tom Nowak said. "Did ya hear the latest rumor?"

"We're getting a turkey dinner with giblet gravy, cranberries and pumpkin pie?"

"Sure, I heard that one."

"No, smart-ass," Tom responded, laughing. "I'm talkin' about the one saying we're going ta be exchanged or paroled. Sent home. That rumor."

"Sure," Ethan replied. "Everyone's heard that one. I'll believe it when I'm walking out the gate of this place and getting on a train headed north."

"You've turned into a real sour puss, ya know."

"Maybe so," Ethan admitted. "But right now, if you want to eat, I've gotta go and get the food for our mess. All right?"

"Well, please take your sour puss with ya, too."

Ethan turned to Willie and said, "Come on, Willie. You can help me carry the food."

"Sure, Ethan." Willie stood and followed Ethan out of their mess area.

"Look at that," Kelly commented. "Just like a little puppy following his master. He tags along with Ethan everywhere he goes."

"Maybe so. But I'd not tangle with either a' them. They're a tough pair; especially Willie, if he's riled up."

"Ya got that right."

* * *

Ethan was standing in line, waiting his turn to get food for his group. Willie was standing alongside of him.

A burly guy pushed in front of them.

"Get the hell out'a the way, squirt," the man said to Ethan as he cut in line.

"I don't think so, soldier," Ethan said as he gripped the guy's shirt and pushed him aside.

The man turned and took a swing at Ethan. His fist did not get very far before one of Willie's large hands grabbed it in mid- air.

"Hey!" the man shouted in dismay. "Who the hell are you?"

Willie didn't say a word. He just began to twist the man's arm backward until the man had no choice but to kneel on the ground in front him. At that point, Willie's foot lashed out and kicked the man in the midsection.

"Willie, that's enough," shouted Ethan. "He's through."

"Are you all right, Ethan?" Willie asked.

"Yes, I am," Ethan told his friend. "You can let him go now."

The other men in line had pulled away, forming a circle around the two fighting men. Willie released the man's hand. But the man who had attempted to attack Ethan lay on the ground in a fetal position, clutching his crotch. He wasn't moving much.

"All right, Ethan," Willie said. Then he and Willie got back into line.

As though nothing had happened, the others waiting for food resumed their positions, too, and ignored the man on the ground.

Later, back at their mess, Kelly asked, "What the hell took you guys so damned long?"

"Nothing special. Just the normal hassle," Ethan responded. "Ya want to eat or complain, Kelly?"

Novak interrupted. "Stop da crap, Kelly. I vant to eat, vatever it is dey give us."

* * *

The next morning at roll call, the camp commandant stood on a raised platform in front of the prisoners. Usually, only several Confederate non-coms took roll call. But this morning, the camp's commandant was standing on a platform in front of the assembled group of prisoners.

"Gentlemen," he began. "I am here this morning to make a special announcement. There is to be a general parole of all prisoners."

Cheers erupted from the assembled prisoners, who threw their hats into the air as they jumped up and down in glee.

When a semblance of order had been restored, the Commandant continued.

"I do not know all the details yet," he admitted. "As soon as I do, you will be informed. I do know that a parole means you will be sent back to your lines; back to your country. You will not be allowed to return to the fighting until someone of equal rank in my country's army has been exchanged for you. How your government treats you during that waiting period is up to them.

"As for the Confederate States of America," he continued. "I have been informed that I am to expect a trainload of Confederate prisoners from one of your prisons to be housed here until exchanged.

"In any case, gentlemen," he concluded, "I will meet with your mess leaders immediately after this roll call to answer questions. Sergeant, dismiss the assembly."

"Assembly! Attention!"

The prisoners snapped to attention.

"Assembly, dismissed!"

With that, the men broke ranks. Some jumped around with joy, others hugged fellow prisoners, everyone was happy to hear the news.

"What'd I tell you, Ethan?" Novak gloated. "Didn't I tell ya?"

"Gotta admit it, Tom," Ethan said. "Ya got this one rumor right. But you can stop slapping me on the back an' hugging me. I think ya nearly broke a rib or something."

"Why is everyone cheering and jumping 'round, Ethan?" Willie asked.

"We all just heard that we're going home, my friend. Right now, I have to go to a meeting with the commandant. You wait here with Kelly and Novak, all right?"

"All right, Ethan."

Within days, the men were told that trains would take them into Ohio, where they would be transferred to Union trains for transportation to Camp Chase, located in that state. They would be housed there, awaiting exchange.

And that's what happened.

Once in Ohio, the prisoners from Salisbury, North Carolina, were loaded on Union trains. One thing wasn't different from their last ride. 'They were jammed in so tightly, no one could sit down in any of the train's cars.

"This damn cattle car ain't much different than the ones I rode in back in reb country," Kelly complained.

"You expected padded seats and stewards to bring you hot coffee?" Novak teased.

"Ya know," snapped Kelly, "it would have been nice ta be given somethin' to eat and at least a swallow a' clean water before we got packed inta these cars, ya know. It's going on two days since our last ration, an' come to think about it, that weren't much ta brag about neither."

"You're right about that, Kelly; on both counts," Ethan admitted. "It would have been nice, but we're back in our own country. I'm happy about that more than I'm irritated about these conditions or the growling in my stomach."

"I 'spose," Kelly conceded.

It was getting on to sundown when their train screeched to a halt. Because of all the times the train had to pull off onto a siding to let other trains have the main track, it had taken their train over 12 hours to get to their destination. Now it was dusk and getting chilly.

CAMP CHASE, OHIO

Camp Chase was located four miles from downtown Columbus, Ohio. Originally a Union army training site, it was also used to house political prisoners from Western Virginia, Kentucky and Ohio. But in late 1862, it became a holding place for Union prisoners paroled by the Confederates who were waiting to be exchanged and then sent home.

Once the prisoners were out of the cattle cars, they were marched to a field alongside the tracks.

A Union sergeant shouted, "I'm Sergeant Murphy. Yer back home now, boys. We're goin' ta take care of ya from now on, till ya get exchanged. After we figure out just who we got here, we're going to feed ya and then have our doctors examine anyone who's feeling poorly.

"So, ta get this all started, I need all a' ya who been serving as Mess Leaders ta raise yer hands."

He surveyed the several hundred men and looked for the raised hands.

"The rest a' yas, rally 'round yer Mess Leader," he continued. "Now ya'll just sit down while we try to see just who's here and who's not. While we're doing that, you Mess Leaders will be called one at a time ta take yer men to those tents over yonder for some chow. If ya need a latrine, they be over that a'way. Meanwhile, buckets of nice, clean water will be brought over ta yas.

"Cause it's so late in the day, all a' yas will be sleeping right out here. You'll get your barrack assignment after morning chow. So, just relax. You Mess Leaders come forward ta get your instructions."

Once the several Mess Leaders gathered, Sergeant Murphy continued.

"Any a' yas got sick men who need attention right now?"

Several of the Mess Leaders raised their hand.

"This medical orderly will talk with ya soon as I'm done here. These are yer numbers. You will take yer men to the tent with your number on it fer chow." Murphy passed out a card to each Mess Leader.

"This card has a number on it. Remember it, cause' after you return to your men, you will take them to the food tent with this number posted on it.

"After chow, I'll announce where ya will go ta get blankets an such. We'll do that by using these numbers, too. So keep 'em handy. Off with yas, now."

At the mess tents, the men's plates were filled with slices of beef and mounds of mashed potatoes.

"Man o' man," Kelly observed. "This is the most food I've seen since we were captured."

"No question about that," Tom agreed.

"I wonder what that green stuff on my plate is," Ethan wondered.

One of the cooks heard him.

"Them's called desiccated vegetables, soldier," he informed them. "We serve 'em with every meal."

"They look deadly," Kelly told the cook.

"They tell us it's good fer you. All vegetable help, keep the scurvy away. So, we serve 'em with everything."

"Has anyone got sick after eating them healthy vegetables?"

"Not that I know about," the cook reported. "But I see a lot a' guys throwing 'em in the trash."

Ethan told his men, "I'm going ta try 'em."

"Oh, my Lord," he said after he tasted a spoonful. "Mine tastes awful. Try yours, Tom?"

"Why would I do dat, Ethan?"

"Right. Ya already told us the stuff tastes terrible, Ethan," Kelly added. "I'm not going ta try the stuff, either."

The cook chimed in, "We've tried everything to improve the taste; salt, pepper, even maple syrup. Nothing works."

"Thanks for the warning."

END OF THE EXCHANGE CARTEL

Aside from the paperwork chaos caused by the system, each side accused the other of manipulating the system for their own benefit. Northern leaders claimed that Southern officials returned their paroled soldiers to the war before they were properly exchanged.

In addition, northern leaders claimed that Union prisoners paroled by the South were in such terrible physical shape that they were not fit for military duty. Union leaders further contended that Southern prisoners, paroled by the North, were in good health and therefore battle ready.

Also, General Grant argued that the system was inhumane. He told his Washington superiors that because virtually all Southern prisoners, once paroled and exchanged, returned to the battlefield, they all had to be killed before the war could come to an end.

For its part, the Southern government announced their intention to treat the Union's Negro soldiers in a manner that was unacceptable to the Union government. The CSA refused to treat captured Negro soldiers in the same manner as they treated the Union's white soldiers.

 On the contrary, Negro Union soldiers, once captured, would be returned to their owners or sold as slaves. And they announced their intention to execute all of the captured white officers who were leading such Negro units.

WASHINGTON CITY

"Secretary Stanton will see you now, gentlemen," a uniformed officer announced.

General Meigs, Colonel Hoffman and General Halleck were shown into the office of the new Secretary of War.

"Good morning, gentlemen," announced Edwin Stanton. "I may have to cut this meeting short if I get a message about the Army of Northern Virginia. Now that winter is over and the roads are drying out, we're anxious about Bobby Lee spring intentions. We're worried he might head north."

"We understand. Thank you for making time for us, Mr. Secretary," General Meigs assured him.

"So, what's this about the Cartel?"

General Halleck opened the discussion.

"Because the rebels have recently announced their intention to kill all captured white officers commanding our new colored units and treat captive Negro soldiers as runaways, we feel that it is necessary to recommend the suspension of the cartel agreement."

"Colonel Hoffman," Stanton interrupted. "What impact will a suspension have on our prison system?"

" Currently, Mr. Secretary," Hoffman began. "Such a directive from you would have no negative impact on our prison system. Because of the releases demanded by the terms of the Cartel, our prisons are now virtually empty. With the resumption of hostilities this spring, I expect several thousand Rebel prisoners to be taken and quickly exchanged as well."

"If you are prepared, why are you here, gentlemen?" Stanton wanted to know.

"Our concern is the impact the suspension of the Cartel will have on Union prisoners of war in Confederate camps. As we have noted in the past, they do not treat prisoners in their care very well.

"While we have no information that their poor treatment is intentional, the fact of the matter is that their prisoners of war, our soldiers, are released to us in very poor physical shape."

"And?" Stanton prompted.

"If we suspend the Cartel, our soldiers held in Confederate prisons will suffer and many more will die from malnutrition, exposure, disease or poor medical care.

"In short, Mr. Secretary, we would probably have on our conscience the deaths of thousands of our troops held prisoner by the Rebs," Hoffman concluded.

General Halleck joined the conversation. "In addition, Mr. Secretary, leaving our captured troops in Reb prisons would not be looked upon positively by the Northern public. People in the North would probably oppose such a suspension."

Stanton interrupted. "I'm surprised at you Halleck," he snapped. "We're fighting a war for the survival of the Union, for God's sake. If depriving the rebels of men to continue this rebellion is essential, we must do it. We must do it, even if it means abandoning Union troops held by the rebels. Damn the public reaction in the North."

"Of course, Mr. Secretary," Halleck responded. " I understand your point. But the next presidential election is only sixteen months away. How will President Lincoln feel about angering tens of thousands of Northern voters?"

"He will do whatever is necessary to suppress the rebellion; I guarantee it," Stanton insisted.

General Halleck handed the Secretary of War a communication.

"I received this memo from General Grant just yesterday. It touches on this matter."

Stanton was silent while he read the letter.

TO: General Halleck

FROM: General U.S. Grant

Date: April, 15, 1863

SUBJECT: The Dix-Hill Cartel agreement.

"The cartel agreement has been in place since last July of 1862. Thousands of our Confederate prisoners of war have been released from our prisons, in keeping with that agreement. My intelligence people have told me repeatedly that they know most of those released have returned to their units and the battlefield.

"So, it seems we must face these same soldiers on the battlefield again and again.

"In addition, it has been my observation that our returning soldiers, former prisoners of the Confederates, are in terrible physical shape; hardly ready for return to duty. The prisoners we release, however, are in good health and, in my opinion, ready to return to the battlefield.

"So, it is my recommendation that we scrap the Dix-Hill Cartel agreement and stop releasing battle ready soldiers to our enemy. If not, we will have to exterminate an entire generation of Southern men in order to end this rebellion."

Stanton passed his copy of the letter to General Meigs, who shared it with Colonel Hoffman.

After a few moments, Stanton asked, "So, gentlemen. What do you think of the General's observation and recommendation?

"General Meigs," Stanton asked directly. "Your response, sir."

"Mr. Secretary," Meigs began. "I have seen the reports to which Grant refers. And I have noted the condition of both rebel soldiers and our released boys. He is also correct to note the need to virtually annihilate the Confederate armies as long as the Dix-Hill Cartel is observed. So, I concur in his recommendation."

"And you, Colonel Hoffman?" Stanton continued. "Do you agree with Grant and Meigs?"

"Yes, sir. I do."

"Halleck," Stanton asked. "Have you told Meigs and Hoffman about the new Confederate policy regarding captured Negro troops?"

"Yes, sir," Halleck answered." They are fully aware of it."

"Another factor we must consider in this discussion is that the Confederate government has announced that they will treat all captured Negro troops as runaways and thus return them to slavery. In addition, they intend to execute any captured white officer who commands Negro troops."

"I doubt that a suspension of the Cartel agreement would change the rebel response to our use of Negro units, sir!" Meigs stated with some heat.

"I agree," Stanton said. "And I believe General Halleck agrees. Correct, General?"

"Yes, sir," Halleck answered.

"Be sure, gentlemen," Stanton warned. "I don't want to hear of any of you making negative comments to the press about the suspension.

"So, gentlemen," Stanton continued. "With your endorsement, I intend to recommend to the president that we pull out of the Cartel."

No one spoke.

"Gentlemen," Stanton concluded. "Since I hear no compelling argument to the contrary, I intend to proceed with my recommendation to the president."

There was still no comment.

On the way out of the building, Colonel Hoffman said, "Well, General. I believe we had better be prepared for a large number of permanent residents in our prisons."

"That's your job, my boy," Meigs responded. "Best get to it."

CLEVELAND, OHIO

On their way to New York City, Carl and Michelle Schock stopped to spend the night in Cleveland, Ohio. They did not realize that their son Ethan was about to arrive at Camp Chase not many miles away to the south, near Columbus, Ohio.

"Such an elegant hotel, Carl," Michelle told her husband. "Are you sure we can afford it?"

"Nothing but the best for you, my dear."

Michelle smiled at her husband as they walked around after their supper.

"Thank you, dear," she said. "But how did you find out about this place?"

"I asked Congressman Kellogg's office people in Grand Rapids to recommend a place for us to stay in Cleveland. They not only told me about this place, but sent a telegraph message to reserve a room for us."

"That was nice of them. Does the Congressman know you are a Democrat who voted for his opponent?"

"No," Carl told his wife. "But I am thinking of voting for him the next time."

"That would be good."

Hand in hand, they walked along the shore of Lake Erie.

"Look at that beautiful full April moon, Carl."

"It is that," he responded. "Do you remember an evening almost twenty years ago when we went for a walk on a Lake Michigan beach? It was an April night with a full moon just like this one."

"Oh, Carl. You remember after all these years?"

"Well, sure," he said, looking offended. "That's when I asked you to marry me, after all. Certainly I remember."

Michelle was in her husband's arms by now. She looked up at him, and they kissed.

"We did this way back then, too, Carl. Do you remember that?"

"As I remember it, dear, that kiss lasted much longer than this one."

Michelle laughed and gave her husband a squeeze.

"I'll give you more than a squeeze when we're back in our room," she promised.

"I'll hold you to that, young lady."

They headed back to the hotel and their room.

NEW YORK CITY

It was late in the day when the Schocks' train arrived in New York city.

"I am really tired of riding trains," Carl Schock told his wife. "Our seats were so hard; my butt is still sore."

"I agree. I'm just happy to be on solid ground and away from all the monotonous clickity-clack of the tracks," his wife Michelle said.

They walked out of the train station with their carpet bags.

"Can you believe all the carriages and people in this city, Carl?"

"There is a whole line of carriages here parked along the street. I expect we can hire one of them to take us to our hotel," Carl responded.

"Did Kellogg's office people arrange for a hotel here, too?"

"Yes, dear," Carl told her. "We have reservations at the National Hotel. With the war going on, we got a real low rate for our room, too. It seems that hundreds of people from the South used to stay there before the war."

"So, the hotel catered to them?" Michelle asked.

"It seems so. Southern men would be in New York with their families, because this city was a major cotton trading center and a center for the slave trade, too."

"But I thought the slave trade was outlawed in the United States over fifty years ago."

"It was, dear. But government officials stationed here looked the other way to allow the slave trade. A lot of money could be made on even one boatload of slaves. Lincoln changed that after he took office by making his Federal attorneys and our Coast Guard enforce the law."

"So, Lincoln shut down the illegal slave trade?"

"Sure did. And the war shut down the cotton trade. So, Southerners had little reason to come to New York."

"It would seem, then, that the National Hotel lost a lot of customers and income."

"You got it, dear."

"Oh, Carl," Michelle said, sitting close to her husband in the carriage. "I'm so excited about being in New York. When my parents brought me to the United States, our boat landed in Boston. That's a very large city, too.

"After supper, let's go for a walk and window shop."

"If you wish, dear."

When they checked in at the front desk, Michelle told her husband, "You go ahead to the room, Carl. I want to browse around these hotel shops before I go to the room."

"All right," Carl responded. "I think I'll wash up and take a nap."

Michelle went to a woman's clothing shop right off the lobby of the hotel. There was a sign in its lobby window, 'Spring Sale. Come in and Look.'

So, she did.

A very friendly lady offered to show her around the shop and to help her try on a few dresses, too.

* * *

Awake and fully dressed for supper, Carl knocked on the bathroom door.

"Aren't you ready yet, Michelle?" he asked his wife.

The National Hotel had hot and cold running water in all of their rooms. So, after she returned from shopping, Michelle took advantage of the hotel's bathroom. She took a long soak in what was called a bath-tub. Carl continued to nap.

"Relax, Carl," she said from behind the closed door of the bathroom. "I'll be right out."

"Remember, we have a supper reservation for six, and it's already thirty minutes after five."

Carl was standing in the center of their sitting room when the bathroom door opened.

His wife stood in the doorway for a moment. She was sort of posing in her new outfit and fresh hairdo. "Ta da!" she intoned with a smile.

"My goodness, Michelle," he said in surprise. "You look more beautiful than ever. What did you do in that shop?"

"While you were napping, I had my hair done in what is called a Hair Salon. Then I bought a new dress for the occasion tonight. Like it?"

"I liked the old Michelle, too," Carl responded, still sort of stunned by his wife's appearance. "But yes, I do like it. Did you take out a loan at the local bank to pay for all of this?"

"You needn't worry, dear. I brought some of my secret cookie jar money for this trip."

"I didn't know you had a secret stash of money."

"You don't know everything, Carl. And after we pick up the children, I intend to take them shopping before we leave New York."

"My Lord, what have I let myself in for?"

Michelle laughed and hugged her husband.

"You'll see, dear. You'll see. The best is yet to come. We'll talk about it later. But now we must leave, or we'll be late for our reservation."

* * *

Once seated in the restaurant, their waiter approached the table.

"Can I get you a glass of wine, sir?"

"I don't know," he responded, somewhat taken aback by the question. "What do you think, dear?"

"What would you recommend?" Michelle asked the waiter.

"We have a very nice dry red to go with a meat dish, and a nice white if you order fish."

"I intend to try your crab," she responded. "So, let me sample your white."

"Will you be ordering a meat dish, sir?" the waiter asked Carl.

"Yes, I think so."

"Then I'll bring you a sample of our red."

When he left their table, Carl said, "My lord, Michelle. Are we going to mortgage the farm on this trip?"

"I told you not to worry about it, dear. I talked to the Head Waiter when I was shopping during your nap. The meal is already paid for. It's my treat."

"Well, I'll be. You are really something."

"That's right, dear; I am," she told him with a smile. "Nice of you to recognize it."

Michelle held up her glass of wine. "Let's have a toast, dear," she said

"To our health and our new family," her husband responded as they clicked glasses.

When they had finished their meal, Michelle said, "I want to walk around outside the hotel before we go to our room. Will you go with me, Carl?"

"Of course, I will."

The April evening was mild, so they left the hotel and walked arm in arm down the street. It was dark and the streetlights were on, but the sidewalks were crowded and the street was filled with carriages.

"It seems strange that so many people are out after dark," Carl commented.

"Before we left home," Michelle told her husband, "I read that over 1,000,000 people live and work in New York City. Can you imagine that? Our little town of Lowell has fewer than a hundred people."

"And we think it's crowded back home on a Saturday morning in town."

"This is a different world, for sure," Michelle decided.

* * *

The next morning, the Schocks had coffee and rolls in the hotel dining room before the doorman hailed a carriage to take them to the New York Foundling Asylum.

"Sister Fitzgibbon expects us at 9 o'clock, Carl. We don't want to be late."

"Really, dear," Carl responded. "When have you allowed us to be late for anything?"

"I understand, but this is a strange city and anything might go wrong. Better we are early than have to explain that we got lost or something," Michelle continued.

"It is only 8 A.M., dear. But whatever you say."

They arrived at the Foundling Asylum by 8:30. A receptionist showed them into a waiting room.

"Sister Fitz will be with you shortly," they were told.

"Remember, dear," Michelle said. "Don't stare at the woman's uniform."

"Why would I stare?"

"Because they dress differently than women you're used to seeing; like me. They wear a special outfit that you might find odd. Just don't stare."

"All right, I won't stare."

It wasn't long before Sister Fitzgibbon entered the room.

Carl stared. *Her dress isn't all that different from those I've seen women around Lowell wear, Michelle, too. But what's that thing on her head? Not like any woman's hat I've ever seen.*

"Carl." Michelle squeezed his hand. "You promised."

"Welcome to our children's home," Sister Fitzgibbon greeted. "I hope your trip has been a pleasant one."

"Yes, it has, Sister," Michelle said. "It was very interesting to see so much of our nation that we never visited before. But it was especially exciting knowing that we were going to meet our new children."

Sister Fitzgibbon went right to business.

"I was very impressed with all the testimonials sent me by your neighbors and the Lowell Catholic priest. But I need you to tell me in your own words all about your home, your town's school, your Lutheran church, and especially why you want to adopt our two little children."

Michelle began. "The Lord only blessed us with one child. His name is Ethan. He joined Mr. Lincoln's army to fight for the Union. He was captured and is now a prisoner of the Confederate government. We believe he will be released soon.

"He is a fine young man and considered a leader in his military unit. We miss him a great deal and pray for him every day. We also miss all the activity he brought into our lives. We want to have all that back into our home. Your two little ones can revive us in a way that is impossible for us to do otherwise."

"Thank you, Mrs. Schock," Sister responded. "We have a lot of that activity around here, believe me. Some days I wish it wasn't so loud." Both she and Michelle chuckled at that.

"But what of you, Mr. Schock? Please tell me of your home and community."

"Well, Sister," he began. "We live in a small farm community. Our two-bedroom home is a few miles outside of Lowell. We have a school run by Mr. Clingman. I believe him to be an excellent teacher. He's a Catholic, by the way. Our Lutheran Church has about 50 members, including children. The little boy will attend Bible Study every Sunday while we have our service. The girl will join him when she is older.

"My wife and I attend every Sunday, and frequently we attend our church's Wednesday evening service, too. Everyone gathers after our Sunday service for a pot-luck dinner.

"We read from the bible in our home each night after supper. Actually, we're not much different from our neighbors, with the exception that we had only one child. We miss being parents.

"I am a farmer, Sister. My home is free of debt. What we don't grow or make, we can buy in town. Before he enlisted, my son helped me milk cows in the morning before he left for school. Last year, he helped Mr. Brady at his General Store on Saturdays. As my son grew, he spent time with school friends fishing and hunting when his daily chores were done.

"Frankly, I don't know what else to tell you except that we will give these little ones the love and education only parents can give; no offense intended."

"No offense taken, Mr. Schock," Sister Fitzgibbon responded as she stood. "Would you like to meet the children?"

"Very much, Sister," Michelle responded.

Sister Fitzgibbon rose to leave the room.

"Wait a minute, you two," Carl interrupted.

"What is it, Mr. Schock?"

"I didn't travel all this way just to meet a five-year-old boy and his infant sister. I want to know before we meet that they are going to be my children."

"I am so sorry, Mr. Schock," Sister Fitzgibbon said. "I did not mean to mislead you. I would be very disappointed if you didn't walk out of here this very day with your new family. Anything short of that would be cruel to both the children and you. Please, Mr. Schock, allow me to rephrase my invitation.

"Would you like to meet your new family now?"

"Yes, I would, Sister," Carl responded. "Right, Momma?" He reached out his hand to his wife.

"Yes, Papa." She smiled.

That's my Carl, direct and to the point; no pretense.

Sister Fitzgibbon left the room. She soon returned, walking with a small boy who clutched her hand. Another nun entered the room, too, carrying a sleeping infant.

"Joseph," she said, kneeling alongside the young boy. "I want you to meet your father and mother."

Michelle knelt in front of the boy and held out her arms. He looked up at Sister Fitzgibbon for approval. She nodded, and the boy walked into Michelle's arms.

"Joseph," she asked. "Would you like to live with me and Papa on our farm?"

The boy was silent. He looked back at Sister Fitzgibbon. She nodded again. He turned to Michelle and nodded to his new mother.

Michelle gave him a big hug. "This is Papa, your father, Joseph."

The little boy looked up at this tall suntanned man. He gripped Michelle's dress.

Carl knelt alongside the boy, reached out, took him in his arms and stood up.

"I'm so happy to have finally met you, Joseph," he said. "I want you to be my son. Would you like to help me with my cows and chickens and sheep?"

Little Joseph was silent, just looking down at the floor.

Little guy probably doesn't know what to say, I'm guessing. Be patient, Carl, be patient. He'll return your love eventually. Just be patient. Carl told himself.

ANDERSONVILLE PRISON

The day after the raid, George was resting with his men.

Unbeknownst to them, a Rebel guard detail opened the large gates and entered the camp. They were looking for John Ransom. They seemed to know just where to find him.

"Are you John Ransom?" the sergeant in charge of the guard detail asked.

"Yes, I am, Sergeant," John responded. "What do you want of me?"

"I have orders from Commandant Wirz to escort you to his office."

"That's fine, Sergeant," John responded.

What the hell? How could he know of my role in last night's raid so quickly? Whatever it is, I don't have much choice in the matter.

Thinking about it on his walk to the office of Captain Wirz, he decided that he shouldn't be all that surprised he had been identified so quickly. He was the only one of the attackers who had talked with all thirty-six men involved in last night's raid. One of them most likely traded information about the raid this morning for some extra food.

The guard closed the door behind him once John had entered the building. John stood at attention in front of Captain Wirz's desk in an otherwise sparsely furnished room.

Captain Wirz stood. "Please sit, Sergeant Ranson." He pointed to a straight-backed chair in front of his desk. John sat stiffly, his stomach in a knot, awaiting a judgment of some sort.

"Guards reported to me this morning that a group of prisoners attacked another group during the night," Wirz began. "I am also informed, Sergeant, that you planned and led the attack."

John had seen Wirz many times at the daily morning count of prisoners. About the same height as John, Wirz usually rode horseback around the prisoner formation. He was always in proper uniform and sat stiffly on his mount. He wasn't mustached and had his hair cut short.

John had heard him shout furiously when it became obvious that the prisoners had tried to increase the count of their particular group in an attempt to increase whatever ration would be given them that day. I was a game to the prisoners, a diversion. It seldom succeeded but earned the opposite result, the total loss or reduction of their rations as punishment.

There it is, John thought. *He knows.*

John felt his shoulders relax some as he sat back in his chair.

"Even if your information is correct, Captain Wirz, what do you intend to do about it?"

"I have hoped for some time that you prisoners would do what you did last night."

"Our survival depended on it, Captain. Your guards stood by and allowed the Raiders to prey on our weak fellow prisoners. We had to do it.

"What do you intend to do now, Captain?" John asked.

"The renegade prisoners who called themselves Raiders have gone too far with their violence. So, I intend to lead a patrol into the camp today, identify and arrest their leaders. At least I will arrest those who survived last night's raid."

"Why bother to tell me about it first, sir?"

"I'm telling you because I want you to set up a court-martial to decide the fate of these men," Wirz told John.

"Such a court will operate inside the prison and have the power to hear testimony and mete out punishment, even the death penalty. After you handle that, I need someone to organize the camp internally, draw up rules of conduct for the prisoners, and lead an enforcement team. Can you be that man, Sergeant?"

"I would be willing to lead such an effort, sir," John responded. "But only if we can actually be in charge of our own internal security, and only if you order your guards not to interfere with the enforcement of our rules.

"Nor can we tolerate the guards trading with prisoners. Your guards were in league with the Raiders, you know. They gave that rotten bunch free reign inside the camp in exchange for food, clothing, cash and other loot taken from other prisoners. If you want us to maintain order, it will be maintained. But you must keep the guards out of the camp."

"I can agree to that, Sergeant. All of it will be subject to my review of the rules you draw up and the enforcement procedures you want."

"That appears reasonable, Captain. But what of weapons? What will you allow us to have?"

"No firearms, Sergeant," Wirz responded quickly. "I would expect clubs would be sufficient. It was last night, wasn't it?"

John didn't respond.

Wirz went on. "I want you to draw up the rules of conduct you feel are necessary. I will decide if they are reasonable. Further, I want you to lay out an administrative structure to enforce your rules and include an appointed court to punish prisoners who break your rules. Once I approve your rules and administrative structure, I will order my guards to stay out of the prison proper and allow you enforcement authority. I will also forbid them to trade with the prisoners

"Lastly, Sergeant, I want you to set up a special court to judge the Raider leaders I intend to arrest today. This same court will determine the punishment these men should receive and carry it out."

* * *

John and Captain Wirz spent the next several hours working out a set of rules and an administrative structure for the internal administration of the camp.

"Of course," Wirz told him. "I will want you to be in charge of the security force inside the camp."

"I'm afraid I cannot do that, sir."

"Why can't you?"

"Anyone appointed by you would be suspected of being a turncoat. Actually, that man would most likely be killed the first day."

"Yes, I can see that," Wirz agreed. "Do you have a suggestion?"

"Yes, sir," John responded quickly. "Let the men in each of the ten camp districts you and I have identified in our plan select their own leader. We could call them Marshals. Then, allow the Marshals to select a Chief Marshal. Each man selected would have to be approved by you. Should any one of them not perform to your standard, you can replace that person with another Marshal selected by the men of his district."

"I will agree to that, Sergeant."

After a good deal of give and take, the structure was completed and approved by Commandant Wirz.

"Now, Sergeant Ransom," Wirz concluded. "I want you to set up a military court to try the Raider leaders. This court must be fully functioning tomorrow."

* * *

With their work finished, John was escorted back inside the camp.

Captain Wirz followed with thirty armed guards. They conducted a search for the surviving Raiders. Almost two hundred of those who survived Ransom's raid were arrested and marched out of the prison into a holding area, awaiting a trial.

Back in his mess area, John was greeted by Sam.

"We'd about given up on you, John," he commented. "I thought for sure Wirz was gonna put you into the stocks for leading our raid."

"Yeah," George joined in. "I thought so, too. But you look fine. What happened?"

"It turned out that Wirz thought the Raiders had corrupted his guards and were seriously disrupting the camp," John explained. "In fact, he felt that he needed to do something soon, or possibly he would lose control of the camp population. So, he was pleased we solved the Raider problem for him. I don't know if he knew about our raid before it happened, but for sure he knew that I had led it."

"But you were over there all morning, John," Phil observed. "It didn't take you that long to find out what you just told us, did it?"

"I haven't gotten to the rest," John responded. "Wirz wants us to set up an internal security force for the camp. He wanted me to head it up. But I told him whoever leads it should be elected by the prisoners, not appointed by him. I did work with him, though, on designing a security structure for inside the camp."

"Would we really be in charge of keeping order?" Sam asked. "And how would those who broke the rules be punished, if at all?"

Questions came at John fast and furiously from the five men. John stayed calm and answered each question. He watched their reaction because he was worried they might think him a turncoat or somehow disloyal for working with Wirz on this plan.

"He also wants us to set up a court-martial panel of judges to hear testimony and punish the leaders of the Raider group."

"Holy smoke, John," Sam exclaimed. "If that don't beat all. How are we gonna do that?"

"I'll talk to Pete McCullough about organizing a court," John responded. "He's a tough guy and seems to know about such things."

"By the way, Cory," John asked 'Doc' McElvain. "Any of the men need medical attention this morning?"

"Nothing serious, John," Cory reported. "I checked with each squad leader. They had me look at a couple of guys who were limping around this morning. Some others had bruises. Not much I could do for a sprain or a bruise. They'll all get over it on their own."

"Absolutely remarkable," John remarked. "Attacking over unfamiliar ground in the pitch dark and not taking any serious injuries; remarkable."

"Yep," Cory agreed. "The Lord was lookin' after us last night, John."

"Good thing too, Doc," John replied.

* * *

Later that day, John talked with Pete McCullough. Sure enough, 'Big Pete' agreed to be the Chief Judge for the trial of the Raiders. He recruited twenty-four men who had been sergeants in the Union Army and who were among recent arrivals to be jurors.

Consequently, each of the 200 Raiders arrested by Captain Wirz were tried by twelve jurors taken from the group of twenty-four sergeants. Each of the accused was allowed another prisoner to act as their attorney.

On the first day, almost all the Raiders were tried for various crimes. As they became aware of the seriousness of their situation, many sought immunity in exchange for information. Thus, the 'Ringleaders' were swiftly identified and a trial was ordered for them.

Six of these' Ringleaders' were found guilty and sentenced to hang. The leader of the Raiders was Charles Curtis, from Rhode Island. Once convicted and sentenced to hang, he boasted of personally bludgeoning over thirty fellow prisoners to death.

Five of the six men were of the Catholic faith. So, a priest, Father Whelan, visited the men often and administered the last rites before their execution.

The other Raiders were convicted of lesser crimes. Some had to run a gauntlet, others were flogged. All of them had their heads shaved and were released into the prison population.

"With their heads shaved," Sam observed, "we'll all know who they are."

"Makes it easier to target them for a revenge beating, don't ya think?" George added.

"Be my guess," Sam concluded.

"Couldn't happen to a more deserving bunch of guys," George decided.

"By the way, George," John asked. "How'd your knuckles get all skinned up?"

"It's like this, John. Remember when I got jumped by a couple of Raiders a few weeks back?"

"Ya, I remember you were pretty bruised up at the time. Took some time for you to get over the beating they gave you, too."

"Well," George continued, "I just happened to see a fellow who had a fresh haircut; completely shaven head, actually."

"Could he have been one of the Raiders who jumped you, George?" Sam asked, chuckling.

"Surely looked a lot like one of the fellows who beat me up, Sam. So, I had a brief conversation with him, just to be sure, don't ya know."

"A' course you wouldn't want to make a mistake about such a thing."

"'Course not," George agreed.

"So, what did you discover?"

"I convinced him to tell me how it was he had his head shaved."

"And that's how you got your knuckles skinned?"

"Not really," George told his tent mates. "His arm being twisted some got me that information. The condition of my knuckles was the result of his answer."

"You beat on him?" John asked.

"My fist ran into his head a few times. That's how my knuckles got skinned."

By this time, all the men in his tent were howling with laughter. Even John Ransom was holding his sides, laughing so hard.

Many of the other Raiders released into the prison population suffered revenge beatings from their fellow prisoners, too.

* * *

LeRoy Key, who had been one of Ransom's Squad Leaders, was in charge of the execution. He supervised the construction of the scaffold. Without a trap door, the condemned men were simply pushed off the platform.

After the execution, Big Pete asked John Ransom, "Now what, John?"

"You're going to continue to be the Chief Judge, Pete," John told him. "We need someone like you to come down hard on anyone who breaks our rules."

"What about Wirz? He going along with that?"

"He suggested it, Pete. He wants us to police ourselves within the camp and also punish those who break the rules. Makes life easier for him and his troops. And we don't have to depend on corrupt guards to maintain order in the camp. We all win with this arrangement. Are you up for that?"

JOHNSON'S ISLAND PRISON

Colonel Hoffman reviewed the list of local suppliers Secretary of War Cameron had given him. They were all located in Ohio, with most of them in the Sandusky area. But just to cover his moves, he arranged a meeting with the area's Congressman, James Mitchell Ashley. His Ohio Congressional District included Sandusky.

Colonel Hoffman walked into Ashley's Toledo, Ohio, office.

"Good morning, Colonel," Ashley's aide greeted. "The Congressman will be right with you."

It wasn't long before Ashley walked into the room.

"Good morning, Colonel," he said, extending his hand. "I understand you're looking to invest some money in my Congressional District."

"Yes, sir. That's true. We have identified and leased an island just off the coast at Sandusky as a prison location for Confederate officers."

"How can I be of help?"

Hoffman handed the congressman the list of merchants.

"At my recent meeting with Secretary of War Cameron, he gave me this list of merchants he recommended. He suggested I buy supplies from them for the construction and maintenance of the facility."

"So what do you want from me, Colonel?"

"It would be helpful if you would take a look at the list. I don't know any of these people. So, you can help me make the best selections and possibly add a name or two from your 5th District constituency."

Ashley looked at the list of names.

"I recognize a couple of names who live right here in Toledo. I know these men and can recommend them to you. As far as merchants in Sandusky are concerned, though, I must refer you to my office manager. He knows almost every good Republican in the district. Mind if I ask him to join us?"

"That would be fine, Congressman," Hoffman quickly agreed.

Ashley picked up a bell from his desk and rang it.

Almost before the sound of the bell had faded, the door to the office opened.

"You called, Congressman?"

"Yes, Billie, I did. Take a gander at the list of merchants and tell me if there are any from the Sandusky area who are good Republicans."

Billie took the list and glanced at it.

"Yes, sir," he said. "There are several on this list who fit that description. I can't vouch for the quality of their work, but I can identify several good Republicans in the Sandusky area whose names are on this list."

Ashley interrupted his aide. "Billie will check off those he recommends. I will do the same for those in the Toledo area."

"Thank you, Congressman," Hoffman said.

"Colonel," Ashley asked. "Can I notify these merchants of your interest in them as a supplier for your new prison?"

"Of course, you can, Congressman."

"And can I tell each merchant that I recommended him to you?"

"Absolutely, sir."

Congressman Ashley stood and said, "I believe we're off to a good start, Colonel. Please feel free to call upon me personally or Billie here should you need our assistance on anything else. In the meantime, I will tell Secretary Cameron and President Lincoln that you called upon me for advice and how pleased I am to be working with you on this project."

"That would be most appreciated, sir," Hoffman said, shaking the congressman's hand.

SANDUSKY, OHIO

Colonel Hoffman was looking for Mayor O.C. McLouth. After several inquiries, he found the portly elected official having lunch at a local tavern.

"You've been lookin' fer me, have you? Now that ya have found me, take a seat, Colonel, and join me in a portion of stew. Best in town, don't ya know. Hey, Mary," he shouted to the waitress. "Bring this fella a bowl of stew, some hot bread and a beer fer the both of us, too."

"Thank you, Mayor," Hoffman responded. "Don't mind if I do."

"While we're waiting for your lunch, tell me why you've been lookin fer me."

"I'm in charge of prisons for the Union Army, Mayor. I just leased Johnson Island out in Sandusky Bay as the site for a new prison."

"What do ya need from me, sonny?" he asked between spoons of stew.

"I need help in finding several contractors who'd like to bid on the contract for the construction of buildings on that site. Know any men who could handle that kind of work?"

"Are you talkin' about carpenters or men who can manage the whole project, like a general contractor?"

"I'd rather find a man to manage the whole project, Mayor."

"I get ya now. You want a general contractor."

"Right," Hoffman confirmed. "But they also have ta be Lincoln supporters. I can't have any Copperheads or Democrats who are shaky about supporting the war effort."

"What leads ya to thinkin I'm a good Republican?"

"Congressman Ashley told me you were one of his supporters; one of the good guys."

"As it happens, Colonel, he's got that right. You have the specifications for that project with ya, by chance?"

Hoffman took a folder out of his haversack and handed it across the table to the mayor.

"Here's yer food, sonny. While I look this over, just dig in. Don't hesitate to dip that good bread inta yer bowl; gravy is great. Beer is pretty tasty, too."

While Hoffman ate, Mayor McLeouth went through the document. In the darkened room, he held the pages close to the table candle as he reviewed the pages.

"Ya say the land fer the prison's been cleared, I see. Can the timber jus lying about be cut and used for construction of the thirteen-two-story barracks you want?

Hoffman swallowed a mouthful of stew and answered, "No. We had hoped to use that wood for fuel this winter."

"Seems a waste ta me," McLouth told him. "Save a lot a' money if we can use it fer beams and siding. You plannin' ta' run a rest home or a prison, Colonel?"

"What are you getting at, Mayor?"

"Let the prisoners forage on the other half of the island fer their wood fer burning. Give em something ta do, don't ya know. Wood details outside the walls be good fer em, don't ya think? But if ya got a big budget for wood beams an such, I got a couple a' lumber yards willin' ta charge the pants off'en ya. That what you want, sonny?"

"You're sounding more like a general contractor all the time, Mayor," Hoffman said with a smile.

"Now you're catchin' on, laddy. If'n ya leave it ta me, you'll get this project done early and within yer budget."

"How soon, Mayor?"

"How does Christmas sound to you, Colonel?"

"That would be a great present, Mayor."

The two men were ferried out to the island a few days later. Hoffman noted that within a week, the site had been cleared, a sawmill put in place and the timber converted to usable lumber. Tents were also erected to house the workers. And they were already setting up the flooring for the first floor of one of the three two-story buildings.

Hoffman also noticed that several men seemed to be supervising the workers holding clubs in their hands. And, each of these supervisors carried a holstered pistol.

Surprised at this observation, Hoffman asked, "Are you using county prisoners as laborers, Mayor?"

"Seems ta me you're either just unaware of how we do things around here in war-time or just plain dense, Colonel. Fer the sake of the Union, I'll assume you're just unaware. So, let me inform ya.

"These men would just be sittin' around in a prison cell moochin' off'n the taxpayers otherwise. In the first place, working outside is good fer 'em. And secondly, since the Army don't want criminal types like them, these men can contribute to our 'cause' by helping out in this way.

"Anyways, with the war an' all, we're sort 'a short of carpenters around here. And lastly, using these prisoners keeps the cost down.

"Are you doubting your General Contractor, Colonel?"

"No. Just surprised, that's all."

"Sonny," McLouth continued irritably. "Havin' you underfoot like this ain't gonna work. I'll get the job done on schedule; don't you worry none. But it'd be best if you go away fer a couple a' weeks; no, make it a month. Then meet me back at the tavern fer lunch, an' I'll bring ya out here to inspect our progress. What da ya say?"

Hoffman thought of the request for a moment.

There is no way I could get this work done without Mayor McLouth. He's got the whole town sewed up. Might as well let him do it his way.

Hoffman left town.

LOWELL

A few days after arriving home from their trip to New York City, the Schock family entered St. John's Lutheran Church. It was Sunday, a few minutes before the ten o'clock service. As usual, they went directly toward the pew they always occupied for the service.

But this Sunday, Carl Schock walked alongside his newly adopted five-year-old son, Joseph. And his wife, Michelle, carried her adopted daughter, Mary.

Reverend Zimmerman greeted them and then led them to the baptismal font to the left of the sanctuary. Mr. & Mrs. Petzold, the godparents, joined them.

"Good morning, Joseph," the minister greeted. "Are you ready to be baptized?"

Joseph looked up at his father. Carl nodded, and Joseph said, "Yes."

The minister asked the Petzolds, who were to be the godparents, if the infant Mary was prepared to be baptized.

They answered, "Yes, she is, Reverend."

The Petzolds spoke for both children during the ceremony. That morning, both Joseph and Mary were baptized as members of St. Paul's Lutheran church.

After the service, most of the congregation attended the church potluck dinner. The men cleared the pews against the walls and set up tables. The women brought food and jugs of milk, cider and water from their wagons.

After the meal, the men cleaned things up, lit their pipes and talked of the war. The ladies of the church had something else on their minds.

Michelle Schock and her two adopted children held their attention that day.

They wanted to hear about the Schocks' trip to New York and the story about Joseph and Mary.

Some just were anxious to know about New York.

"What was it like in New York? Was it busy, noisy and dirty? Was your hotel comfortable? How about the food? Did it cost a lot?"

"We thoroughly enjoyed ourselves. We stayed overnight in Cleveland the first night of the trip, then New York the second night," Michelle told the ladies. "It was so exciting. I bought a new dress in a store just for women and had my hair done at what they call a salon. I even had a hot bath in what they call a bathroom, right in our hotel room. All the food we were served was excellent; I think even Carl enjoyed it. Being waited upon was a special treat for me.

"Having wine with our meal was a new experience, too. Our waiter brought me white because I ordered fish. Carl had a red wine because he had beef. Congressman Kellogg's office people arranged everything for us."

But others were more interested in Michelle's adopted children.

"They're actually brother and sister?" one person asked.

"Yes, isn't that fortunate?" Michelle answered cheerfully.

"You were allowed to adopt them even though the Catholics who ran the orphanage knew you were going to raise them as Lutheran?" another wondered.

"The good people who run the orphanage only wanted to be sure that the children would be raised in a good Christian home," she continued.

"Won't it be a problem when they're older, you know, when they realize they're adopted?"

"We're not worried about that now. For now, we're determined that every day we will be sure the children know, without any doubt, that we love them with all our hearts," she countered the negative suggestion.

Michelle was very patient with her neighbors. But after someone asked her why in the world they opened their home to orphans, foundlings from the streets of New York, she did become exasperated some.

"It made no difference to us where they had been abandoned. Carl and I wanted to answer God's invitation to provide the love and care these innocent children need. It's as simple as that. Is that so hard to understand?"

No one asked any more questions of her.

Charleston

At the Pope home, Mary Jacqueline was kept busy caring for her newborn son. She had recovered nicely from the childbirth experience, and her son, Charles, seemed healthy and alert. Her personal slave, Helen, seemed to be always by her side and ready to help, too.

"You listen to Helen, chile," Helen was fond of saying. "I ben around infants a'fore. I know what dey need. Right now, your son Charles needs a lot of holdin and as much breast milk as you can supply.

"Don't you worry, I'll be takin care of cleaning his bottom, but you gotta keep strong an full a' milk fer him."

"I hear you, Helen."

"You might hear, but are you listenin'?"

"Yes, Helen, I'm listening," Mary Jacqueline said, somewhat exasperated. "How can I not? You've been saying these things to me over and over. Honestly, I'm tired of hearing it."

"Jus makin sure you don' forget, chile. Dat's all.

"I don' want Master Charles hollerin at me if'n you come down sick. An' you gotta 'member that babies can gets peak-id an' die. Happens all da time. No, sir, dat won't be my fault, no way. I don' want ta be sold down da river."

"That's never going to happen, Helen," Mary Jacqueline assured her. "At least not as long as I draw air."

"Jus da same," Helen mumbled under her breath. 'I'm jus' saying."

"I just hope Master Charles gets home in time for the baptism. The ceremony is only a week from now, and I haven't heard from him if he's even going to be here," Mary Jacqueline confessed.

* * *

At supper that evening, Colonel Pope and Mary Jacqueline were sitting alone at the dining room table. Pope's wife seldom joined them, preferring to be served meals in her room.

"Thank you for allowing me to hold baby Charles this afternoon," he told his daughter-in-law. "Mrs. Pope never allowed me to be that close to any of my sons when they were infants. In fact, she kept them in the nursery with a wet nurse most of the time. For that matter, I don't think I ever saw her hold any of them either, except her youngest son, David.

"She's kept that poor boy tied to her apron strings since he was an infant. He never did learn to stand on his own. Much to my regret, I never interfered. I should have, but I let her have her way. He's turned out to be a spoiled and lazy. She raised him filled with hate for his brothers and me."

Mary Jacqueline agreed. "That's very sad, Grandfather.

"When you go off to join your military unit, Grandfather," she told him, "I'll be all alone here. Your son has made horrid comments to me since Charles left for Richmond. He looks at me with that wicked grin of his. I'm afraid of him."

"I don't blame you, my dear," the colonel responded. "For that reason, I'm giving you a small pistol to carry. I also want you to keep a shotgun by your bed. Do not hesitate to use either if he or any of his evil friends should bother you in my absence."

"I can't imagine using either of those awful things, Grandfather."

"You've a little boy to protect now, young lady," Pope reminded her. "Believe me, you'll use the weapon should the need arise."

"Can I change the subject, Grandfather?" she asked.

"Of course, my dear," he responded. "What is it?"

"Why is it taking so long for Charles to obtain leave from his duties in Richmond?"

"I must confess that his delay puzzles me, too.

"The last communication I received from the War Office there was that Charles couldn't be spared because of some battles going on down near Williamsburg. It seems the Yankees are determined to capture our capitol. So, his Richmond hospital has been swamped with casualties from the battles being fought on the peninsula between the capital and Chesapeake Bay.

"Even our commander, General Johnston, was seriously wounded recently. General Robert E. Lee has taken over command of the Army of Northern Virginia. And I'm told that the attacks are expected to continue."

"So, you're saying that Charles could likely not get a pass to visit our son?"

"That's how I read the latest telegram I received. He appears to be safe, but very much needed at the military hospital in Richmond."

"If only I were with him there," Mary Jacqueline mused aloud.

"With the fighting right at their doorstep, it's too dangerous, my dear," Pope reminded her. "Charles and I want you and baby Charles safe, here in Charleston."

"I know," she revealed. "I'd give anything to be with him in Richmond, though. Every time I've suggested it, he tells me the same thing."

"He's right, my dear," her father-in-law told her gently. "Now finish your dinner. Must keep your strength up, you know."

Mary Jacqueline smiled. "Helen keeps telling me that, too."

"She's right. Now eat up and finish your wine. That's good for you as well."

"Yes, Grandfather."

THE WAY HOME

Several thousand Union soldiers at Camp Chase were ordered to line up.

Outfitted in their new blue uniforms and shoes, they made a smart looking formation.

"At ease, men," a Union sergeant ordered. "You have been patient the past weeks while we sorted out all the issues of getting you fed and clothed properly. While that was going on, we were also organizing the matter of getting you to your homes for an extended leave.

"You will be pleased to know we believe that problem has been solved. Today, you will board trains that will take you home for an extended leave."

Cheering broke out everywhere.

After indulging the excitement of the men, the sergeant ordered the men to attention once again.

"This time you will not be jammed into cattle cars. Each of you will have a seat on a Pullman passenger car. It's not first class, but it's a hell-of-a-lot better than how you got here."

Cheers broke out again.

"Listen carefully," the sergeant warned. "Cooperate, and this operation will be accomplished quickly. Any group causing trouble will be moved to the end of the line. Refusal to cooperate will mean you will stay here until the next train is available. Do not test me on this. So, be quiet listen up. I don't want to have to say this a second time."

He paused until everyone was quiet.

"We will move, one platoon at a time, toward the railroad cars to your right. When you are ordered to halt, look for you mess number on the railroad cars. Upon dismissal, go line up single file by that car. Do not board until ordered to do so.

"First platoon!" he shouted. "Right face. Forward march!"

Every few minutes, he ordered another platoon to proceed. The non-commissioned officer who was in charge of each body of men moved them to the train and boarded them, one platoon at a time.

The operation was complete by noon. Before the trains left, a hearty meal was served. Alongside the trains, tables loaded with food were set up. Men filed past them, picking up their food. Each man was given a canteen filled with water to take on the train.

By two in the afternoon, all the men had been fed and the area picked up. The former prisoners were even given a chance to relieve themselves before they boarded the train.

"Where are we going, Ethan?"

"We're going home, my friend."

"Are Tom and Kelly going to our town, too?"

"No, Willie," Tom told him. "Kelly and I live in a different town, Detroit. This train has to go through that city to get to yours. It will stop and let us off."

"Will I ever see you again?" Willie asked.

"How about we come visit you, big guy?" Kelly said.

"That would be nice, wouldn't it Ethan?"

"Sure would," Ethan agreed. "We could teach them how to milk cows an' such."

"I can hardly wait," Kelly said.

* * *

It was after dark when their train pulled into Detroit.

The train station was full of people. As the engine inched its way under the covered tracks at the main Detroit station, a loud cheer went up for the crowd. The men in the cars began to clap and cheer as well.

The men of Ethan's squad hugged and promised to see one another soon.

"Will we ever see them again?" Willie wanted to know.

"I don't know," Ethan admitted. "But I have their addresses. I'll write them soon. So, we'll see."

Maybe they'll visit us in Lowell during our leave. I know I'll join them when we have to report to our unit this January. I don't think you'll see an Army camp any time soon, Willie. I think you're home for good.

Later that day, the train stopped for fuel. The men were given food and an opportunity to visit the lavatory at the station. As they traveled northwest during the night, the train stopped from time to time to drop men off. Despite the hour, crowds greeted them at every stop. In Lansing, Michigan's capital city, a band was on hand, too. The crowd also brought food for those going further west.

"We're almost to Grand Rapids, Willie!" Ethan told his friend.

"Is that where our house is, Ethan?"

"No, but that's where our families will be waiting for us."

"I don't understand."

"It's like this," Ethan patiently explained. "Remember when we dropped off Tom and Kelly back in Detroit?"

"Ya."

"Well, Grand Rapids has a train station just like that one. Our families will meet us there. Then they will take us to our houses in the nearby town of Lowell. OK?"

"OK."

It was midnight when their train pulled into the Grand Rapids station. Just as Ethan had promised, several families were waiting, theirs included.

The two friends were greeted with hugs and tears.

Willie's father hugged Ethan. "Thank you so much for looking after my son. God bless you."

"You're welcome, sir," Ethan responded, shaking Mr. Petzold's hand. "I'm sure he would have done the same for me."

"Is there anything you need to tell us about his injury?"

"Yes, sir. I think there is. Would it be all right if I come over tomorrow after chores for a talk with you and Mrs. Petzold?"

"Please do, Ethan. Can we expect you right after breakfast?"

"Yes, sir. That will be fine. Now excuse me, I must go with my parents."

Before he could, though, Willie called to him.

"Ethan, where are you going?"

Ethan told his parents, "Give me a minute with Willie, please."

"I am going to my parents' house, Willie. You are going with your sisters and parents to your house. You need to sleep there tonight."

"We're not going to be together anymore?"

"I am coming to your house in the morning, right after chores. We'll talk then. Right now though, you go with your family to their house for tonight. OK?"

"OK, Ethan."

Willie was disturbed. But he joined his family in their wagon for the trip their Lowell home, because Ethan said so.

Talking in their wagon, Ethan's father asked, "Is Willie going to be all right, son?"

"I don't know, Papa. He and I have been together since I found him in the prison at Richmond. He's hardly been out of my sight since then. He's pretty dependent. I expect it's going to take him a while to settle in.

"Momma, what's this great news you have for me?"

"Wait till you get home. You'll see."

"Why do I have to wait? Can't you just tell me?"

"Just wait, son. Then you'll see."

* * *

As Carl Schock pulled his wagon into his yard, Ethan noticed lights still on in the house.

"Papa," he asked, "why would you ever leave lights on?"

"You'll see, son."

"What is this all about, you two?'

"I want you to help me in the barn for a few minutes. Momma, you go ahead into the house."

"You two are so mysterious. I never." Ethan chuckled in dismay.

When he and his father did enter the house, Susan Drieborg and Ann Drieborg greeted him with hugs.

"Welcome home, Ethan," they gushed.

"What are you two doing here?" he asked.

I don't remember them being so grown-up looking; and pretty, too, Ethan thought.

"They volunteered to babysit while we went to pick you up."

"Babysit? What's that all about, Momma?"

The two Drieborg girls giggled.

"Papa, would you take the girls home, please?" Ethan's mother asked.

"See you later, Ethan," Susan Drieborg told him.

"Goodnight, Ethan," Ann Drieborg said as she followed Carl Schock out the door.

"Hey!" he shouted after them. "How's Mike?"

"Tell you later," Ann shouted back.

"I am totally confused with all of this, Momma. What is going on?"

"Let me warm some food for you, and I'll tell you."

While his mother was warming up leftovers and fixing some fresh coffee, they talked.

"So, you and Papa decided you wanted to have a baby?" Ethan asked.

"Yes, and no."

"What does that mean? Either you're going to have a baby or you're not."

"Your father and I know how to make a baby, son. After all, we had you."

A little embarrassed, Ethan said, "I understand that, Momma."

"We wanted another child. But in all the years of trying, we just figured it wasn't God's will that we have another child the natural way."

"All right. So?"

"But we agreed that our house was lonely without you in it. So, we decided to adopt a child."

There it was. She told him.

She was quiet as she served him his meal and poured some coffee for herself.

"Oh, that smells good," Ethan gushed. He dug right in. "This is great, Momma," Ethan told her. "I haven't had roast beef with mash potatoes and gravy since I left home for the Army."

It didn't take him long before he was mopping up the last of the gravy with a piece of his mother's bread.

"Give me your plate, son." She reached for his plate. "I'll give you seconds."

"Thanks, but I can't eat another mouthful, Momma."

"But you're so thin, son."

"That's what months of prison food, or lack of it, will do, Momma. But I think my stomach has shrunk. I'm so full right now, I can't even touch that peach pie you set in front of me."

"Well, my word," his mom responded. "I'll take care of that, believe me. You'll be asking for seconds before you know it."

"I hope you continue to spoil me like this, Momma. If the Drieborg girls were babysitting tonight, you must have already adopted a child. Right?" Ethan decided. "They were watching the baby while you came to get me. Right?"

"Yes, we did," his mother told him. "That's why they were here. But there's more."

"Oh, my Lord!" Ethan almost choked on his mouthful of food. "What else?"

"We adopted two children; a boy and a girl."

Ethan sat back in his chair and started laughing.

"What's so funny?" his mother asked him.

"I'm not sure, Momma," he answered. "I don't mean to disrespect your decision, but I guess it's because it strikes me funny that as soon as I leave, you go out and adopt two children.

"It's like, wow. I come home to find I have a brother and a sister, ready-made."

"Are you angry with us, son?"

"Absolutely not, Momma," he assured her. With that, he rose and embraced his mother. "I'm excited for you and Papa; and for myself."

"I'm so relieved, son."

"Momma," Ethan told him mother. "You and Papa gave me a great home with lots of love. I remember our home as always a happy place for me. If I am anyone of value in this world, it's what you and Papa made me.

"So, it seems to me that the children you adopted are lucky to have you as parents. And if it makes you happy to have children around your home, it makes me happy, too."

"Thank you for understanding, son," Michelle told him. "I'm sure you will love your new brother and sister, son."

"I have no doubt, Momma. What are their names?"

"Your brother's name is Joseph. Your sister's name is Mary."

"Tell me all about how this happened and where the children came from, everything."

"Let's wait until your father returns. I want him to be part of that conversation, too. You know your father. I didn't do this on my own. "

Ethan chuckled. "I never had a doubt about that, Momma."

It wasn't long before Carl walked in the door.

"Well, Momma," he asked. "Did you break the news to Ethan?"

"Momma did, Papa," Ethan interrupted. "Please tell me all about this great adventure you and Momma have started with Joseph and Mary."

"Ya, it is an adventure all right." His father chuckled. "Since you left for the Army, we, Momma and I, realized two things. First, how much we missed you and your just being around home. We didn't like that it was so lonely for us. And we realized that we still had a lot of love to give a child. So, we decided that we wanted to share that love and our home with children who had none of either."

"Where did you find the children, Momma?"

"We read a story in the Grand Rapids paper about a New York orphanage. It seems that they took New York orphans out of that city to families all over the country, right here in Michigan, too. They traveled west on what was called 'The Orphan Train.'"

His father joined this conversation. "Because of the war, the train has stopped. But we also read of the New York Foundling Asylum. This is a Catholic facility run by the Sisters of Charity. It provides a place for young girls in a family way who have no place to go. They provide everything for the young ladies and then place their children in good homes. So, we contacted Sister Fitzgibbon, who is in charge."

After we were approved by the Sisters, we traveled to New York City to meet Sister Fitzgibbon and pick up the children."

"How did you end up with two children?"

"Joseph and Mary are brother and sister, son. It's sort of funny that Papa wanted a boy and I wanted a girl. It was perfect. Sister Fitzgibbon didn't want to split them up. We couldn't bring ourselves to do that either."

"How did you convince a Catholic orphanage to give the children to a Lutheran family?"

"All our Catholic friends, even their priest here in Lowell, vouched for us. That's how," Carl said proudly.

Michelle added, "Sister Fitzgibbon impressed me as a special person. She knows we will raise the children as Lutherans. But she believes that being raised in a good Christian home was more important than just a Catholic one. And she told us that our Catholic neighbors had convinced her that your father and I are the kind of parents who would provide the right kind of home for her two orphans."

"I could have told her that."

"Thank you, son," his mother said.

"Well, you two," Carl suddenly said. "Do you realize that it's almost time to milk the cows? We'll talk again tomorrow, all right? Let's get to bed."

"And don't forget, baby Mary will want her early morning feeding, too," Michelle reminded everyone.

"Ya, I almost forgot," Carl joked. "I'll take care of the cows, you take care of Mary. OK, Momma?"

"Good night, son," his father said, giving him a hug. "It's good to have you home."

"It's great to be here with you," Ethan said. "I want to help you in the morning, Papa. Wake me up when you get up, will you?"

"I won't turn down good help. Are you still up to milking and chores, son?"

"Get me up in the morning and see for yourself, Papa."

"With the children in my old bedroom, I suppose I need to sleep in the loft."

"I hope you don't mind, son," his mother inquired.

"Not at all, Momma. See you in a couple of hours, Papa."

JOHNSON ISLAND PRISON

Back in Sandusky, Ohio Colonel Hoffman was anxious to see the progress made on the construction of barracks on Johnson Island.

He walked into the tavern frequented by Mayor McLouth.

"Good morning, sonny," the mayor greeted from his seated position. "Back to check on my progress?"

"As you instructed, Mayor," Hoffman spat back.

I don't like this guy much. But I'm stuck with him.

"As soon as I finish my lunch, we'll go out to the site," McLouth promised. "You might as well have a bite. Be a long time a'fore supper for both of us."

As much as I don't want to admit that he's right; he's right.

"I'll have whatever you're having, Mayor."

With both of them finished, the boarded the long-boat to Johnson Island.

Hoffman was astonished with the progress he saw on the prison site.

"My Lord, Mayor," he exclaimed. "How did you erect three of the barracks in only a month?"

"I have three crews working on construction here," McLouth explained. "They're in competition for extra food and a liquor ration. First crew to complete their building gets the rewards. Works every time."

"I'd like to inspect the buildings, if ya don't mind, Mayor."

"Suit yourself, Colonel."

Hoffman got out his designs and walked the buildings.

Damn! This is amazing. He's working with unskilled prisoners and accomplishes this in record time. I can't fault the construction, he judged. *These buildings meet the specifications exactly.*

"Surprised, aren't ya, sonny?"

"How soon can I move men into these buildings, Mayor?"

"Hows about tomorrow, Colonel?" McLouth chuckled.

"We got some pickin' up ta do. But the buildings themselves are ready. Each building has its own cooking area an' mess, as you required. Your people can use our sinkholes fer their waste.

"So, as long as you can keep yer prisoners outta' the way of my crews, I got no problem with you bringin' prisoners here now."

"Tell you what, Mayor," Hoffman decided. "I'll bring my prisoners here in groups of 250. We'll settle them in and bring in another batch each week. The first group will arrive in one week. Will that work?"

"Sure will, Colonel. That'll give me three weeks to have the next building up an' ready," Mclouth calculated. "That should work.

"Gonna bring guards with 'em, aren't ya?"

"Yes, of course."

"Ya need a building ta house them, don't ya?"

"Right," Hoffman responded. "I'll house them in the second building here. Can you have one a' your crews put up a building outside the prison for them? Can you do that in the next week?"

"Sure can. In the meanwhile, my crews will keep a barracks or two ahead a' your arriving prisoners. We'll get er' done a'fore the first snows. You can count on that."

"How are ya doing on lumber an' such, Mayor?"

"We run out a' timber we cut on the island. But as long as you keep the cash flowing, the locals are happy to supply our needs."

"Let's go back to that tavern of yours, Mayor," Hoffman suggested. "I need to look at all the invoices you signed for deliveries and compare them to the bills I've been paying."

"That's another thing I like about you, sonny," McLouth said, slapping Hoffman on the back. "You're so careful with the government's money. Love it, love it."

CAMP DOUGLAS

Several hundred Confederate officers were standing in formation.

"Listen up, now!" Colonel Joseph Tucker, the camp commander, ordered.

 "I've just received a telegram from the war office in Washington City. You're to be moved to another prison facility. The details will be announced as soon as travel arrangements have been made.

"Colonel McGavock," he ordered. "Report to my office after I dismiss the formation."

Once the men of the formation were ordered to attention, the Confederate officer shouted, "Formation, dismissed!"

Back in their barracks, the officers congregated.

"Try to get us a plush Pullman along with a dining car attached, will you, Colonel?" Richard Pope jokingly urged.

As the most senior officer among the prisoners in Camp Douglas, McGavock was the customary conduit for information to be shared with his officers.

"Surly will, Major Pope," he responded. "I'm sure the Yanks will grant your request just as soon as your Pope becomes a Protestant."

"Oh! That's funny, sir," Pope joked.

Another Confederate officer quipped, "If that's the case, Colonel, I suggest he just lets us disappear into the Chicago population, like so many of the enlisted men do."

"Any more bright ideas?" McGavock asked. "Come on, now. I'm due at Tucker's office."

"There is one thing, Colonel," another Confederate officer added. "'Tis getting colder with winter coming on, don't ya know. Most a' us had our overcoats an such taken from us back at Fort Donelson. We could do with another blanket, too."

"If given the opportunity, I'll mention that. Anything else, gentlemen?"

* * *

"Come in, Colonel," the camp commander suggested. "I want to go over the move with you."

"Good idea," McGavock said. "My men are full of questions. So am I, for that matter."

"I don't know much myself, actually; especially how soon it will be. But I still think it's best to be clear about what your men can take with them."

"What did you have in mind, Colonel?" McGavock asked.

"They'll be allowed to keep their clothing and head covers, of course. I'm inclined to have them take one blanket each as well."

"That seems reasonable," McGavock agreed. "What about their cooking utensils? Will that type of thing be supplied when we arrive at this officer's prison camp, or should we take what we've been using here with us?"

"Good question, Colonel. I don't know the answer to that right now. I'll put that on my list of questions of the Quartermaster in charge of prisons. I spent a whole lot of good will getting that stuff for your men. So, I'm reluctant to let it go."

"I understand your concern, sir. But I'd hate to show up at the new camp and them not have cooking gear waiting for us. Please let us know."

"Anything else you can think of, Colonel?"

"One of my men requested a plush Pullman along with a dining car. Any chance a' that?"

"I don't travel that well. I'm sure as hell not arranging such comfortable travel for your men. But I'll get word to you on the other matters you raised as soon as I know the particulars. In the meantime, have your men ready to move quickly."

"Yes, sir," McGavock said.

JOHNSON ISLAND PRISON

"You got that first building ready for my prisoners, Mayor?" Hoffman asked.

"The cooking room got finished yesterday, Colonel," Mayor McLouth told him. "Just like I promised.

"The second building will be ready next week, an' so on an' so on. You keep them Reb officers coming, and I'll have the buildings ready."

"Good," Hoffman assured him.

"Jus' you keep tha payments coming as well, sonny," McLouth warned. "I ain't a bank, don't ya know."

"Have I been late with your money yet, Mayor?"

"Nope. Gotta give ya that. Ya been right on time every week; jus' like my workers have.

"When can we expect the first batch of your slavers?"

"I'll telegraph my people in Chicago today. We should see the first trainload in three days."

"We'll be ready."

* * *

Sure enough, by the end of the week an Illinois–Central railroad company locomotive pulling several boxcars pulled into Sandusky, Ohio. Word had spread in the small community about the expected arrival, and quite a crowd of local citizens had gathered to take their first look at men they believed to all be slave owners.

"Why did so many people turn out for the arrival of my prisoners, Mayor?" Hoffman asked.

"None of us ever laid eyes on rebs a'fore, Colonel. We only read about em. 'Sides, a good number of boys from our town have gotten killed and others shot up since Jeff Davis started this war."

"Are they angry?" Hoffman asked.

"Wouldn't you be if'n your son lost an arm or came home in a coffin?" McLouth snapped. "I sure would be."

"I suppose so," Hoffman agreed.

"Would seem strange ta me, if'n they weren't mad as hornets."

Prison guards opened the boxcar doors and ordered the prisoners to jump down and form up.

"All right," a Union sergeant hollered. "Get in formation, now. The sooner ya do, the sooner ya get fed. The longer ya take, the longer you don't eat."

There was some jostling around, but order was restored quickly and over two hundred Confederate officers stood at attention.

"Right face!" the sergeant shouted. "Forward, March!"

The column moved to the main street of the city. "Column, left!"

Monroe Avenue was the main street in Sandusky.

"My lord," Richard Pope said to the man next to him. "I thought the people in Chicago were a curious bunch. But this little town is just as inquisitive."

"Yep," the man marching to his left responded. "'Least they ain't throwing rocks and lumps of dirt at us, like back in Chicago."

"There's that, I suppose," another of the marchers added. "They still look angry ta me, though."

Lake Erie was on the north side of the city. The column reached a dock there in just a few minutes of marching.

"Column, halt!" the Union sergeant shouted. "Is there a Colonel McGavock here?" he asked.

"Right here, Sergeant."

"Front an' center, Colonel.

"I want yas to order the prisoners to take a seat on the ground. Organize them in groups a' thirty, Colonel. March your first group to the barge on the right side of the pier. As soon as that barge is on its way to Johnson's Island, we'll load the second barge.

"Got that, Colonel?"

"Yes, Sergeant," Colonel McGavock answered. "I think we can handle that."

"Good. Get to it then, Colonel. You can tell yer men food is waiting for them on the island. The longer it takes you to organize things, the longer they go without food."

It took the better part of the afternoon to transport the almost two-hundred-fifty men to Johnson's Island. Richard Pope was one of the last to reach the island prison. The plate of food he received on arrival was no longer hot; it was stone cold.

"At least the coffee's not cold," one officer commented. "I can hardly hold the tin cup, it's so hot."

"Maybe so," another chimed in. "But did you taste the stuff? I could stand up my spoon in my cup, the stuff is so strong."

"That's what we get fer being last in line. The Yanks have reheated this stuff for so long today, all that's left is the caffeine."

"Probably be better tomorrow."

"Maybe. We'll see how it all works out."

By nightfall, all the Confederate officers were in the new building, sleeping two to a bunk.

LOWELL

The two Schock men were each sitting on a three-legged stool in side-by-side stalls. In the silence, you could hear the hiss of the milk as it was squeezed into a pail.

"How's it going, son?" Carl asked his son.

"Didn't take long, Papa," Ethan answered. "The cow didn't seem to mind a strange pair of hands milking her."

They were soon done, and the milk taken into the house.

"I'll milk the goat," Carl told his son. "Why don't you get the feed around for our animals? We've added some sheep, too. Just let them out in back of the barn. They pretty much take care of themselves out in the pasture."

"Momma wrote me about you getting sheep," Ethan reminded his father. "How's that going?"

"Rather well," Carl said. "As I told you while we were milking, sheep are easy to care for, their meat tastes good and there's a great market for wool right now. I started with two, and now we have over a dozen."

"Sounds like a good investment."

"Most of the farmers around here have small flocks like ours. With the war's demand for wool, the sheep provide us small farmers with another annual cash crop."

"Maybe my wool uniform came from your wool, Papa."

"That would be interesting, wouldn't it?"

It didn't take the two men long to finish the rest of the morning's chores.

"We best get washed up and into the house, son. Your Momma will not appreciate our being late for her breakfast."

Ethan laughed. "Some things never change, do they Papa?"

"You have that right, son."

* * *

When Ethan entered the house, they saw a little boy standing beside his mother.

"Look who's here, Joseph," she told the little fella clutching her skirt. "This is your older brother, Ethan."

Ethan could see that Joseph was shy and probably afraid of this new person in his life. So, he took a chair and greeted the young fellow.

"Good morning, Joseph. Momma has told me a lot about you. I was out in the barn working with Papa. Maybe this afternoon you would like to join us when we do the afternoon chores, eh?"

Carl Schock said, "I don't know about you two, but I'm a hungry dude. How about you, Joseph? Would you like some of the food Momma fixed for us?"

"How about it, Joseph?" Michelle said to him. "Here, let me help you into your high chair."

"I used to sit in that chair, Joseph," Ethan told him. "I'm too big for it now, so you can use it."

"I think these two men are forgetting something, Joseph," Michelle said. "In the Schock household, we thank God for our food before we eat. Remember, you two?"

"Oops! Momma is right," Carl admitted. "Would you say grace, Ethan?"

"Sure, Papa.

"Thank you, Lord, for the food on our table.

Thank you for bringing me home from the war safely.

And thank you for giving me my brother, Joseph, and for my sister Mary.

Amen."

"Now, can we eat, Momma?" Carl asked.

"Yes, Papa," she responded. "Now you can eat."

It was silent for a bit as the dishes were passed and everyone's plate filled with fried eggs, potatoes and stripes of bacon. Hot coffee was poured with cream and sugar added as well.

"I don't remember you drinking coffee, son," Ethan's mother observed.

"You're right, Momma. I used to think it was too bitter.

"But that's all we had to drink in the Army," he told her. When we'd get a few minutes when on the march, someone in my platoon would break out some coffee beans, another soldier would start a fire and we'd have a quick cup of coffee. Sometimes we even had cream and sugar with it. In fact, Momma," Ethan continued, "the Army came out with a powdered coffee just before I got captured. They called it, instant coffee. It had the cream included, even."

"Well, I never," Michell exclaimed. "Did you hear about that, Papa?"

"No, I haven't. Does it make good coffee, son?"

"I couldn't tell, Papa. Remember, I never drank the stuff before I left for the Army, so I didn't have anything to compare the instant stuff to. But it was hot and helped the guys stay awake on guard duty or a long night march.

"But I got used to the taste. I had some a couple of days ago, at Camp Chase. I think yours has more body to it, Momma. Your cream is better tasting, too."

"What will they think of next?" Michelle commented.

"By the way," Ethan said. "I promised Willie Petzold I'd check on him after we got home. So, I'm going to ride over to his place this morning."

"Why do you have to do that, son?" Ethan's mother asked.

"Remember when I wrote you about Willie's injury?"

"Yes, I do, son," Carl told him. "What about it?"

"Before he was captured, Willie was hurt at the Battle of Shiloh; he seems all right physically now, but something happened inside his head, it seems.

"He's just not the same."

Then Ethan told his parents about how close he and Willie had become and how nervous Willie had become about going home without Ethan.

"Go ahead, son" his mother told him. "It's good that he has had you to help him through this injury. I will fix dinner like always. So, whenever you get back, I'll have something to heat up for you if you don't eat at the Petzolds'."

"That would be fine, Momma. Think I did all right this morning, Papa?"

"You haven't lost your touch with the cows, Ethan."

"I should be back in time for the afternoon milking, Papa."

"I'll see you later, Joseph," Ethan said as he headed for the door.

After he left, Michelle freshened up her husband's coffee and began to clear the table.

Carl lit his pipe and then walked over to Joseph, still in his high chair. He picked the boy up and set him on his feet.

"Let's go out in the barn, Joseph," he told his son. "I've got to check on a few things, and you can help me."

Joseph nodded and took his father's hand.

"We'll see you later, Momma," Carl said. "We men have work to do in the barn."

Carl and Joseph walked out of the house.

Elmira Prison

Located in southwestern New York state, Elmira was home to a little over 8,682 citizens. It was known for its productive farmland, beautiful countryside and very cold winters. Early in the war, a training camp was set up outside of town. Barracks were constructed and a parade ground was set up to train Union recruits. As the war wound down, so did the number of recruits sent to train there.

In May of 1864, Colonel Seth Eastman, in command of the training facility, directed a telegrapher to send the following message:

"This is in response to your recent request for information about this facility. At this time, I have barracks available to accommodate up to

5,000 men. However, our mess hall facility is limited and the grounds are not yet set up to accommodate prisoners of war." Col. Eastman: Commandant Elmira Training Camp.

Commissary General William Hoffman responded from his Washington City office:

"Col. Eastman: You are hereby instructed to arrange for housing up to 10,000 Confederate prisoners of war. Expect arrival mid to late June. You are authorized to spend up to $2,000 on any barrack renovation and the construction of a twelve-foot-high wall surrounding the prison area. Four feet from the top of said wall construct a guard walk. Respond, soonest."

Eastman read the message and handed it to his aide, Captain Benjamin Moore.

"These Washington desk jockeys either can't read or just don't care. I told Hoffman we could handle 5,000 prisoners and he demands double that."

"What do you want to do, colonel?" Munger asked.

"You check out the barracks and give me a report on what you need done there. Also, see what our situation is with our food services. Let's meet again first thing tomorrow. I'll arrange for a couple of builders to meet with us tomorrow afternoon about the wall Hoffman wants."

"Yes, sir." Munger said. "Want me to get Dr. Sanger in here to tell us about what he will need in the infirmary?"

"Good," Eastman said. "Have him here, too. But, be sure to tell him today to be prepared tomorrow to tell us what he needs to service 5,000 plus prisoners."

"I'll do that right away, Colonel."

"I want that report in writing, Captain."

"Got-it, sir."

CHARLESTON

Colonel Pope had left the day before and headed toward Richmond. There, he would join General Robert E. Lee's Army of Northern Virginia. He would command a regiment in Stonewall Jackson's Brigade.

So, his daughter-in-law, Mary Jacqueline, was home in Charleston, alone.

Helen answered the knocking on the front door.

She opened the door and saw Dr. Charles Pope standing on the porch

"My Lord in heaven, Doctor Charles, as I live and breathe. Ain't you a sight for these sore eyes. Come on in now, you hear! Standing out der like a peddler.

"Your wife be upstairs with baby Charles. I'll get her down here directly."

"No, Helen," Charles told her. "Let me surprise her."

"You showin' up like dis, you do dat fer sure," Helen chuckled. "But you might jus' scare her into a faint. You best be gentle, sir."

"I'll be gentle, Helen." So, up the stairway he went quietly.

Charles slowly opened the door to the nursery. Mary Jacqueline sat in the morning light of the window. She was slowly rocking his son. Hoping not to startle her, he knocked on the door frame.

His wife looked up at the sound. Then he saw a strange thing. Mary Jacqueline reached for a revolver which was lying on the floor beside the rocking chair.

"Oh, my Lord!" she exclaimed. "Charles!" She dropped the revolver.

He covered the few feet between them quickly, knelt and held his wife and son.

"I think I will always remember the sight of you sitting here in the morning sunlight holding our son."

"Kiss me, darling," Mary Jacqueline asked. Her husband leaned across his son and did just that.

Charles settled back and looked at his son. "Can I hold him?"

"Of course, you can," Mary Jacqueline told him. "He's been waiting for you."

With his son in his arms, Charles stood and looked into his face.

"He's so beautiful," he whispered. "Looks a lot like you, sweetheart."

"He is beautiful," his wife agreed.

"I'm sorry I missed the baptism. Who were the godparents?"

"Your father stood in for your brother, Richard. And would you believe it, my mother was the godmother."

"How did she ever travel from Philadelphia with the war going on?"

"You can ask her yourself," Mary Jacqueline told her surprised husband. "She's still here. I'm surprised you didn't find her holding baby Charles. Seems like she is always in here, rocking him or changing his diaper or just talking to him."

"Where is she now?"

"She went with cook to the market, downtown. She wouldn't hear of me going."

"My Lord," Charles chuckled. "What a stir she'll create with that Yankee accent of hers."

"I warned her to let cook do all the talking," Mary Jacqueline told him. "But you know my mother. She'll probably shock the heck out of the vendors at the market, and get away with it, ta boot."

"That's your mother, for sure."

"By the way, dear," his wife reminded him. "I've told you this before, those of us from Philadelphia don't believe we have an accent. It's you South Carolinians who have the accent."

"Oh, ya, I forgot."

"You probably traveled most of the night," his wife said. "Have you had any breakfast?"

"What I really need, young woman, is you. Can you somehow arrange that sometime for me in the next five minutes?"

"Give me little Charles, dear. Helen will take him for a while. You go to our bedroom and dust yourself off. I'll be right back."

A few minutes later, Mary Jacqueline entered the bedroom. Her husband had hardly taken off his boots and was sitting on the bed unbuttoning his grey blouse when she came in. She rushed over to the bed and pushed him back on the mattress.

"Whoa!" he said. "Give a guy a chance here."

"I thought you were famished, Major Pope," she teased. "What do you really want, food or me?"

Charles rolled his wife over and looked down at her beautiful face.

"I can always have food, but you're the one I need the most; and right now,"

"That's what I wanted to hear, mister. Help me take off all this clothing."

"My pleasure, young lady. Definitely my pleasure."

Charles slid off the bed and locked the door. As he returned to the bed, he slipped out of his trousers and shirt. Then he helped his wife with her shoes and such.

Much later, they were lying in one another's arms.

"You can't imagine how I longed for this, sweetheart," he told his wife.

"It may shock you to hear me say it, Charles, but I've missed our lovemaking, too."

"You're right, it's not lady-like to admit you enjoy a good romp in the hay. At least not in Charleston. But it is an immense turn-on for me to hear you say it."

His left arm was under his wife's head, so he began to caress her with his right. She closed her eyes and enjoyed the sensations he caused with his fingers.

"Oh, that feels so good, Charles. Don't stop."

Mary Jacqueline turned in his arms and ran her hand down his torso. When she reached his midsection, she smiled and said, "Oh, my! Does this mean you want more of me? So soon?"

"I want you all the time, sweetheart."

"Well, then," she teased. "Stop talking and show me."

It was some time before they rested again.

Mary Jacqueline looked into her husband's eyes. It seemed to her that he could hardly keep them open.

"Darling," she whispered. "I need to feed our son. Why don't you get some sleep? I'll wake you for dinner. All right?"

* * *

Shortly before noon, Charles walked into the inside kitchen.

"Can a famished soldier get some dinner around here?" he asked the collection of women he found there.

Cook responded first. "Ya sir, master Charles. It's cooking in the outside kitchen right now. You get yourself to da table with da ladies, and I'll bring y'all dinner directly."

Charles went into the dining room to find his wife and mother-in-law having a cup of tea. His wife was breastfeeding his son as well. First, he gave her a kiss and then went to Mary Jacqueline's mother.

"Mother Murphy," he began. "It's so good to see you."

The two exchanged kisses before Charles sat down on a chair alongside her.

"It has been a while, Charles," Judy Murphy responded. "The day after you two were married was the last time I saw you. And then this damned war started."

"That didn't seem to stop you from traveling here," Charles reminded her.

"Just because my Mr. Lincoln and your Mr. Davis got us into this war, doesn't mean that I'm going to let those two rascals keep me from seeing you two, and my new grandson."

"How did you ever finagle all the passes you needed to get here?" Charles asked.

"Dr. Miles Murphy, your father-in-law, is not one to be put off by a little war, either. You should know him, Charles. He was your teacher in medical school, after all."

"I remember him, mother Murphy, I remember him well," Charles related. "I didn't think he would agree to allow his daughter to marry me, much less let me take her to live in the South. So, he arranged for your travel, did he?"

"Yes, he did, Charles," Judy Murphy revealed.

"And he wanted me to be sure to give you his best wishes. By the way, you two," Judy Murphy went on, "I want us to go to one of those places that takes photographs, whatever they call them. He wants a picture of his grandson and both of you as well."

"As I recall, mother Murphy," Charles said, "there's a fellow in downtown Charleston who does that sort of thing. I'll see him tomorrow and arrange for the process before I go back to Richmond. I'd like a photo of us, too."

"I thought you were going to wake me up, sweetheart?" he reminded his wife.

"Charles, you were sleeping so soundly, you didn't even respond when I tried to wake you."

"That's strange," Charles told his wife. "I slept on the train getting here from Richmond. I wonder what made me go into such a deep sleep?"

"I wonder?" Mary Jacqueline said with a smile. Her son was still feeding on her breast when their food was brought from the kitchen.

"Your son likes to take his food this way," she said. "So does his father."

JOHNSON ISLAND PRISON

The Confederate officers were walking around the grounds outside their barracks.

"What do you think of this place?" Richard Pope asked his bunkmate and fellow prisoner. He coughed continuously while he talked.

"Pretty scenic, actually," Jim Mackey responded. "But I never seen so much water. At Camp Douglas, a person could see water clear to the horizon. Now, Lake Erie is so big we can't even see Canada off to our North.

"I'm from upriver in Alabama, don't ya know. Never seen the like."

"I've spent my whole life lookin' at the Atlantic Ocean," Pope told him. "So, this is a puddle to me. I love the breeze coming off the water. Nice an' cool. Keeps the bugs away, too." Pope continued to cough.

"Breeze seems cold ta me. But I get what yer saying about those pesky bugs. We got 'em so big back home, ya gotta keep the kids indoors sometimes, lest they get carried off by the damn things."

Pope laughed, and that triggered more coughing.

"Don't ya think you'd better see the Yankee doctor?"

"It's just a cold that settled in my chest," he responded. "It should be all right in a few days."

"All right, men," a Union Sergeant shouted. "Form up in yer platoons."

"Welcome ta Johnson's Island. This island used ta be a place for Sunday picnics an' such. But lest ya get the idea that our stay here will be a picnic, I gotta tell yas we've got some policing ta do around here."

"I just want to know when we're going ta get our morning chow," Mackey whispered to Richard Pope.

"Some hot coffee would help me with this damn cold."

"Just stop coughing on me, will ya?" Mackey urged. "Bad enough I gotta sleep next to ya. Turn yer head the other way when you feel a cough or a sneeze coming on."

"So much for sympathy," Pope said. "Thanks for caring."

"A guy's gotta look after himself, don't ya know."

"First Platoon!" the sergeant shouted. "Attention."

Then he told the Platoon Leader to take his men and pick up all the lose lumber lying on the ground in back of their barracks.

"Second Platoon!" he continued. "Attention!"

Then he told the Platoon Leader of the second squad to take his men into the barracks and get a fire going for morning chow. The men of this platoon would be in charge of cooking the meals for all the men today.

He continued to give out assignments to the other platoons. Finally, he ordered, "Dismissed, to yer Platoon Leaders.

"You men in first platoon," he directed. "Take all the wood ya pick up into the barrack kitchen. They'll need it for the breakfast fire. The longer it takes ya, the longer you'll have ta wait for morning chow."

"You there," he shouted. "You, the man doin' all the coughing." He pointed at Richard Pope. "I want ta see you at the surgeon's tent immediately. Can't have ya spreading that cough a' yours around. Get on with ya, now."

* * *

Pope stood at attention in front of the doctor's tent. He was in line with several other prisoners. It wasn't long before he was next.

"Come in here, whoever's next," Pope heard.

He parted the tent flap and entered the doctor's tent.

"Are you the one doing all the coughing?" he was asked.

"Yes, Doc, that's me," Pope answered.

"Come over here and sit down. I won't bite ya," Pope was ordered. "Open your blouse so I can listen to your lungs."

After a few minutes listening with his stethoscope and looking down his throat with a stick on his tongue, the doctor told him, "You got one hell of a inflamed throat an' a lot of congestion in your lungs, ta boot.

"I haven't got much for ya in the way of medicine except this cough syrup. Take a swallow a' this when the coughing gets bad. While yer cold is working its way out, keep warm and drink a lot of water. Remember ya need ta feed a cold. So, eat even if ya don't have an appetite.

"Ya waited too long ta see me as it tis. So, come back to see me in a week."

"Yes, sir."

"Off with ya, now. I got more men sicker 'in you ta see."

Pope was hungry. So, he had no difficulty cleaning his bowl of oatmeal or whatever it was he was served. He even had a second helping.

"The doc say you're probably going ta survive, did he?" Mackey asked.

"He wouldn't go that far, actually," Pope told his bunkmate. "He did tell me not to go near water for a week. I think that meant he doesn't want me to wash. Make sense to you?"

"I think I'm going ta ask for a new bunkmate, Pope." Mackey laughed. "You're no beauty as it is. Now, if ya smell worse than ya do now, it will be pure torture ta be around ya."

"Oh, ya think he just meant no swimming in the lake?" Pope asked.

"I hope that's all he meant, or I'm in for a rough time breathing during the night. Maybe I'll just sleep outdoors for the next week an keep away from all that coughing a' yours."

"Suit yourself, buddy."

ANDERSONVILLE PRISON

Several of the Confederate guards worked their way through the makeshift sleeping areas.

They stopped at Sgt. Ransom's area.

"Sgt. Ransom?" one of them inquired. "Captain Wirz wants to see you."

Ransom walked with them toward the main gate of the prison.

He was led to the building used by the camp commandant.

"You ordered me here, Captain?"

"Yes, Sergeant, I did," Wirz acknowledged. "I've just been ordered to move several thousand men to other prison sites."

"Just when you have this prison set up so comfortably for us," Ransom quipped.

"I see your point, Sergeant." Even Wirz had to smile at the black humor. "Nevertheless, the move could be handled much more smoothly if you and your team of deputies were to help manage it."

"What do you have in mind, Captain?"

"Trains will begin arriving here the first of next week," Wirz revealed. "If the schedule I've been given is actually followed, I've been ordered to have a detachment of a thousand men ready to board trains each day."

"You and your deputies could help me make that happen in an orderly manner."

"Food and clean water, Captain Wirz," Ransom said.

"Excuse me, Sergeant?" Wirz asked, puzzled. "What the hell does that have to do with my problem?"

"The men will do most anything for food and a drink of clean water, sir," Ransom said again. "I suggest you allow me to promise the men extra rations and clean water for their cooperation."

"Simple as that, eh?"

"I believe so, sir," Ransom said. "Food and a drink of clean water."

"All right, Sgt. Ransom," Wirz concluded. "During roll-call tomorrow morning, I'll identify a detachment of 1,000 men and promise them just that if they sit quietly and wait for your deputies to board them on the trains. Each morning thereafter, we'll do the same for as many days as transportation is provided."

"Sounds like a plan to me, sir," Ransom agreed.

"Thank you, Sergeant," Wirz concluded. "You and your deputies report to me at roll-call tomorrow morning."

"Yes, sir." With that, Wirz dismissed Ransom and he was escorted back into the prison.

LOWELL

"Momma," Ethan asked, "I'm going to take a ride over to the Petzold farm again. I promised Willie that I would check in with him today. Would it be all right if I took Joseph with me?"

"Get the horse hitched and bring it around the front of the house, Ethan," she responded. "Joseph might be a little hesitant to go with you just now. So, let's have Papa go with the two of you. How about that?"

"Good idea," Ethan agreed. "I'll bring the wagon around in a few minutes."

"Joseph loves to ride with me in the wagon," Carl told Ethan.

"Don't you, Joseph?"

"Yes, Papa," the little boy answered.

"I used to love it, too, Joseph," Ethan told his new brother.

Joseph sat between Ethan and his father. Ethan had the reigns, and Carl had his arm around Joseph.

It only took a few minutes to reach the Petzold farmhouse.

"Here we are, Joseph," Carl told him. "Let me help you down, son."

Ethan tied the reigns to a post and walked to the door of his friend's house and knocked.

Willie's sister, Mary, opened the door.

"Well, I'll be. Look who's here, Willie," she said. "I'll bet he's here to see you."

Quickly, a figure was behind her in the doorway.

"Ethan!" Willie exclaimed. He sorta pushed his sister out of the way and embraced his friend, Ethan.

"Easy, big fella," Ethan groaned. "You're squeezing me to death here."

"Sorry, Ethan."

"Can I come in, Willie?" Ethan asked.

"Ya, sure. You got someone with you?"

"Yes, I do, Willie. This is my father. And this tyke is my new brother, Joseph."

Carl stepped forward and extended his hand to Willie.

"Welcome home, son. It is good to see you," Carl said.

"Joseph, say hi to Willie."

"Hello, Willie," Joseph said as he grabbed Carl's leg.

"Hello, everyone," Carl greeted everyone.

Mary Petzold asked, "Can I give Joseph a piece of hard candy, Mr. Schock?"

"What do you think, Joseph?" Carl asked. "Would you like Mary to give you some candy?"

Joseph just whispered, "Yes."

"What do you say to Mary, Joseph?"

"Thank you, Mary."

"Hey, Willie," Ethan said, slapping his friend on the back. "Let's go for a little walk. What ya say?"

"Sure, Ethan."

"Nice to see you, everyone," Ethan said to the Petzolds.

Mrs. Petzold responded, "Nice to see you, too, Ethan. Can you join us for supper tonight?"

"That would be great. How about that, Willie? Would you like me to come over for supper tonight?"

"Sure, Ethan," Willie responded quickly. "Can we go for that walk now?"

Before they left the house, Mr. Petzold walked over to Ethan and gave him a hug.

"Thank you for taking care of my son, Ethan," he said. "I think he would have suffered a lot or even died if it wasn't for you."

"Willie's my friend, sir," Ethan explained. "Besides, he would have done the same for me if our positions had been reversed."

"Thank you, Ethan, just the same."

LIBBY PRISON

Mike headed for the other side of the room. On the way, he turned to Major Hamilton and asked, "Major, is there a Lieutenant Blanchard here?"

"Yes, there is. Captain. Lt. Blanchard is assigned to floor three, just above us."

"Would it be all right if I went up there to talk with him?"

"Not a problem, Captain. Just remember to return to this room afterwards. The rebs get mighty nervous when prisoners wander about the building."

"Got it, sir."

Mike went to the fourth floor and asked the first prisoner he saw about Lt. Blanchard.

"Ya, he's up here somewheres. Try over that way."

Asking as he walked along, Mike finally saw his friend from the Michigan Brigade.

"Hey, Drieborg," Blanchard shouted as he greeted Mike with a hug and a hearty slap on the back.

"So," Blanchard said. "You were captured, too?"

"Afraid so, my friend. I just arrived, as a matter of fact. The rest of my troop should be back across the Rapidan River by now. I wish I was with them."

Another prisoner seated nearby said, "We've been expecting you fellows for at least the last week."

"What?" Mike responded in astonishment. "How would you know we were coming on a raid?"

"Don't look so surprised soldier," the other prisoner urged. "News about your raid was in the Richmond newspapers two weeks ago. The rebs were waiting for you."

"Don't get me wrong," the man continued. "I wish that you had succeeded in freeing us and the enlisted men out on Belle Island, but believe me, you had no chance."

"Damn it all to hell!" Mike spat.

* * *

So far in his life, Mike had never just sat around like he was forced to do at Libby Prison. Living on a farm, doing nothing had never been an option for him. In captivity, doing nothing simply had to be endured.

However, Mike heard a rumor that someone was doing something. That someone was Colonel Rose.

He approached the colonel. "Colonel, my name is Michael Drieborg. Can I speak with you privately, sir?"

"You're one of the new arrivals, aren't you, Captain?"

"Yes, sir."

"Follow me," Rose directed.

He led Mike to an empty corner of the second floor. Mike assumed that this was the colonel's private area, since a guard kept other prisoners away while the two men talked.

"Now, what's on your mind, Captain?"

"Sir, I heard your aide talking to one of the men who's on my Room Committee," Mike began. "He told the other man about a shift schedule. It seemed to me that they were talking about digging.

"I gotta tell you, Colonel Rose, this sitting around is killing me. I am a healthy and strong fellow. Whatever it is you're digging, I can help. Will you let me, Colonel?"

"Drieborg," Colonel Rose began. "Let me be very clear right now about the conversation we are about to have. If I hear that you talked to anyone about our conversation, you will not survive to see another day. Do you understand me?"

"Look, sir. I only want to get back to my troop and back to the war. If I can accomplish that by helping you dig, I have no problem keeping quiet about it. Besides, my wife is having our first child. I have no death wish."

Rose continued to question Mike. He asked about life on the farm, the circumstances of his enlistment, being wounded at Gettysburg, recovery and his recent marriage. The conversation lasted over two hours. Mike's experiences in Washington seemed of special interest to the colonel.

"Tell you what, Mike," Rose told him. "Let me think about it. I'll get back to you with my decision. Remember what I told you. Talk about this to anyone, and you will never see your child."

"Yes, sir. I understand."

Within a few days, Colonel Rose had accepted Mike's offer. As the colonel had explained it, the lowest floor of the building was on the river side of the prison. In that space, there was an unused basement room called the Rat Cellar. The prisoners knew about it because they were sometimes allowed to cook food on the stoves in that area. In one corner of the room was an unused fireplace. It had a chimney that ran through the ceiling of that room and through all three of the upper floors of the prison. Colonel Rose saw this chimney as an ideal hidden entrance to the Rat Cellar from the upper floors.

It was there, in the Rat Cellar, that Colonel Rose and his handpicked men had begun digging an escape tunnel. The tunnel was headed toward a shed located a good thirty yards to the northeast of the prison building.

On his first night, Mike was given his assignment.

"Follow me down this rope ladder, Mike," the colonel told him. Once in the Rat Cellar, Mike could see the tunnel opening on the north wall. He noticed that the opening was pretty small.

"Colonel," he said. "I don't think I can work in such a small space."

"Just give it a try, Mike."

Mike obeyed. But after pulling himself completely into the tunnel, he found the dark passage frightening.

I can't stand this. I have to get out of here.

He hurriedly pushed himself out and sat by the entrance, sweating and gasping for air.

"Mike," Colonel Rose assured him. "Don't worry about it. We have other things that need to be done down here."

Mike still had a four-hour work shift on his digging team. So, he was assigned to pull out each bucket of dirt when a digger had filled it. Then he spread the dirt on the floor of the cellar end eventually covered it with straw. He also operated a billow fan to push air into the tunnel entrance, to help the diggers.

The nightly effort was not without its dangers. Even though guards did not venture into the rat-infested cellar, one might stumble on their chimney entrance, or a guard might notice fresh dirt on the knees of one of the conspirators. A fellow prisoner might even tell a guard about the project in hopes of special privileges or food.

The dirt ceiling of the tunnel was a potential danger, too. On the first attempt, the men had dug almost ten yards when the ceiling of the tunnel caved in. They feared guards might notice the depression in the ground. After a few days of waiting, they began again. When the second tunnel had gone over twenty yards, they decided to poke through to the ground above. It was discovered that they had been digging on an angle and were still seven or eight yards away from their shed objective. They had to start again. It took another week, but finally one of the diggers poked his head through the ground inside the shed. The conspirators were almost ready.

* * *

One moonless March night, all the men involved in the digging project successfully escaped through the tunnel and into the city.

Unfortunately, that same night some other prisoners discovered the chimney opening and followed Mike's group through the tunnel. By dawn, one hundred and nine men had managed to escape. At the morning count, the jailers could not overlook that many missing men.

On the contrary, they noticed. The Confederates immediately began an intensive search of the prison. Sure enough, after morning count the guards found the chimney opening, which led them to the Rat Cellar and the tunnel.

This was the first escape of the war from Libby Prison. The commandant was outraged, and he was determined to catch every single escaped Union officer. He alerted the Richmond authorities and the commander of the Confederate military in the city. Cavalrymen, together with units of the Home Guard began searching the city and, in ever widening circles, the local countryside.

* * *

Earlier that first day, while the general population slept and before the prison authorities were aware of the escape, Mike made his way through the quiet city. It was around midnight. He and the other escapees figured that they had five hours before their absence was discovered.

He had traveled a good number of miles northeast of the city, following the tracks of the Richmond and York railroad. It was almost dawn when he reached the Chickahominy River Bridge.

Damn! he thought.

He figured that the bridge would be guarded, but he had hoped that he would find the guards still sleeping. Instead, they were awake and cooking their morning meal. So, he moved back into the woods at the southern bridge approach, hid in some shrubbery, and slept.

He awoke at dusk and moved further east in hopes of finding some shallows to cross the river. When he tried, he slipped, thoroughly soaking his clothing and shoes. On the other side, he was shivering from the bitter night's cold but continued to move northeast through the Virginia countryside.

For a second time, he hid himself during the daylight hours. He moved only after dark. He was able to spot Confederate patrols during the night by the campfires. By the next dawn, he had reached the New Kent Courthouse, some twenty miles northeast of Richmond. According to the crude map each of the escapees had been given, Mike believed he was close to the Union lines at Williamsburg.

On the third day, he took a chance and crossed an open field in broad daylight. On a ridge, several hundred yards to the east, he saw some Union cavalrymen.

My Lord, he thought. *Those are my guys up there. I made it!*

He moved further into the snow-covered field. Unexpectedly, a group of Confederate cavalrymen rode into the field.

"Pull up there, Yank," one of the riders shouted. "Or you're dead in your tracks."

Mike stopped. He could still see the Union cavalrymen on the ridge ahead. But the Confederates were closer.

Damn.

Elmira Prison

Colonel Eastman met with his aide Captain Munger and the camp's surgeon Dr. E.L. Savage.

"Let me start with you, Ben." He said. "Do the barracks need much attention to be ready for the prisoners?"

"As you can see in my report, I noted three problems. The roofs need a good deal of repair. They leak badly. In addition, when winter comes there are no stoves to heat the barracks. Other than these two concerns, the barracks are ready for occupancy.

"And third, the mess facility is inadequate. We can accommodate only about 150 prisoners at a time. So, to feed 5,000 men even twice a day it will take until almost noon to serve the morning meal and eighteen hundred hours to manage the second meal."

Eastman responded. "This afternoon several builders from Emira will meet us about the prison wall contract. We best have them look at the roofs. too."

"Possibly they can enlarge the cooking facility while they're at it, sir?"

"We'll see about that, Captain. We've only been allotted $2,000 for the prison wall. I doubt if much will remain for anything else. Remember the War Department has been pretty stingy while we've been training our own recruits here. I can imagine their attitude about spending a lot of money on prisoners.

"We'll have to see what the builders have to say this afternoon."

"I understand, sir." Captain Munger said.

Eastman turned his attention to the infirmary issue.
"And your infirmary, doctor?" Eastman asked. "How many ill prisoners can you accommodate?"

Sanger smiled. "To serve the needs of healthy prisoners, I expect to be able to handle a few dozen at a time. If we receive sickly ones, the best I could do is ten or so bed patients and a daily sick call of twenty or thirty. Remember Colonel, I am the only doctor here and I have one medical aide."

Eastman reminded Dr. Sanger, "We are expecting in excess of 5,000 prisoners transferred from other prisons. Some of them will probably be sickly, as you put it. So, what do you need?"

"Remember, colonel," Dr. Sanger responded. "We're dealing with traitors here. How concerned must we be, after all?"

"These men will be in our care, many of them in your care, doctor. I expect we will all do our best to tend to their needs."

"Colonel Eastman" the doctor responded. "Have you seen the recent edition of Leslie's Illustrated Magazine?"

"No, I have not."

"Here, take a look at photographs of some of our boys who've spent time at Andersonville Prison."

Colonel Eastman looked over the magazine and the photographs of the prisoners from Andersonville Prison.

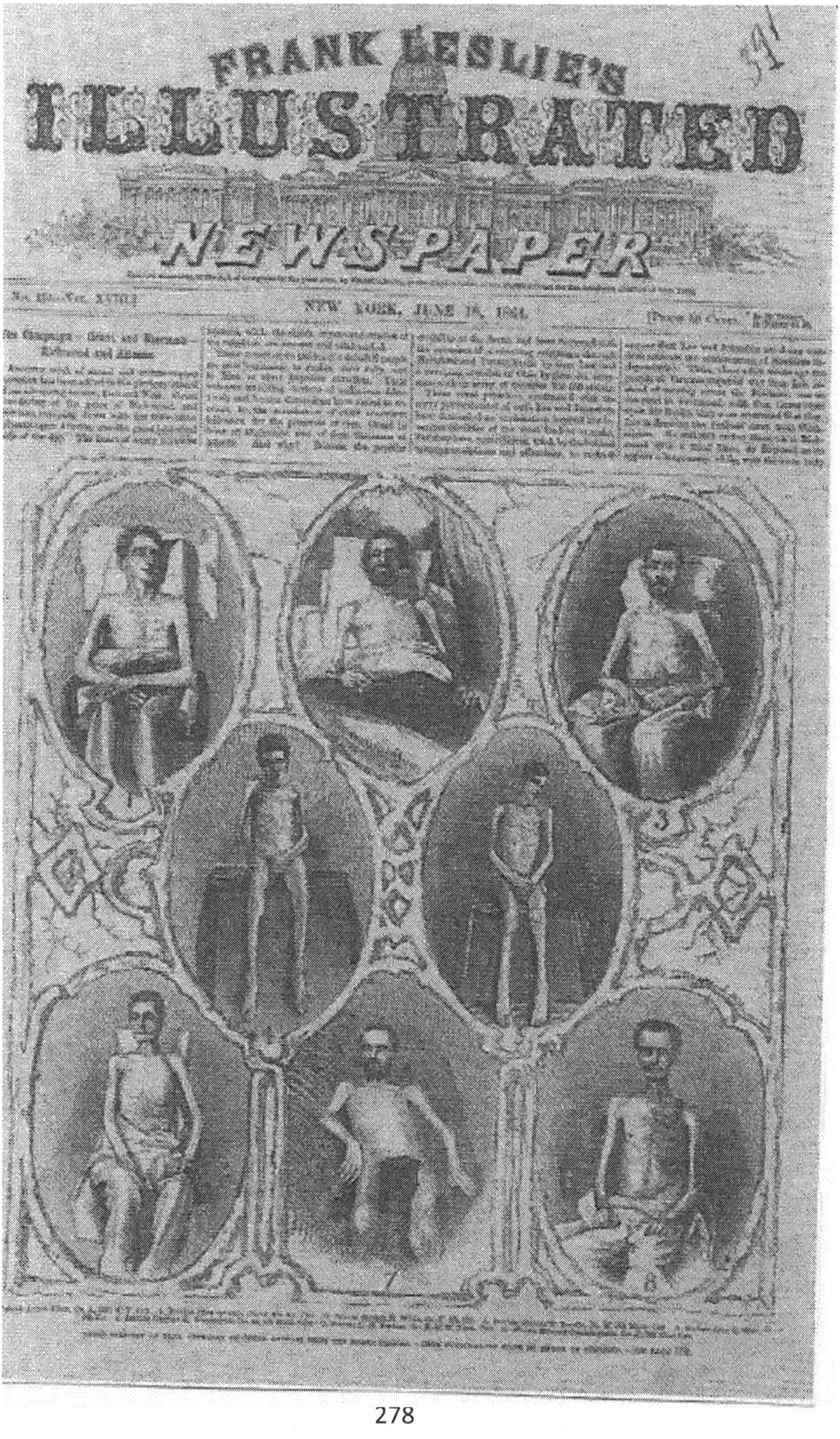
FRANK LESLIE'S ILLUSTRATED NEWSPAPER

NEW YORK, JUNE 18, 1864.

"Sweet Jesus." He exclaimed. "How could the Rebs allow this to happen, doctor?"

He handed the magazine to his aide, Captain Munger.

"This is barbaric," Munger exclaimed. "Are you sure these are authentic photographs?"

"As I understand it," Dr. Sanger told the stunned officers. "The reporters who were invited to go to Andersonville and talk with Union prisoners there could have taken hundreds, if not several thousand pictures just like the one you see published on the cover of this magazine.

"So, we're just seeing a sampling?" Munger asked

"It would appear so, Captain." Doctor Sanger informed him.

Munger commented to no one in particular.

"Seems strange to me that the Reb government would allow photos like these to be taken. They had to know the northern public would be outraged; maybe even see our government take it out on their soldiers held in northern prisons, too."

Doctor Sanger responded. "My information is that the reb government allowed photos like these to be taken in an attempt to get the northern public angry enough force Lincoln's people to reopen the prisoner exchange cartel. "

Eastman commented, "From what I can tell, they failed in that goal. Our people in Washington have not even reopened discussions to exchange prisoners In fact, Secretary of War, Stanton and his generals are opposed to reopening the exchange cartel; and President Lincoln appears to support that position as well."

"Getting back to my earlier point to you, Colonel," Sanger interrupted. "Is that seeing this type of treatment our boys are receiving makes me want to do the same to their troops in our care."

"It is certainly a temptation, doctor. But, not on my watch," Eastman stated firmly. "The order General Halleck's issued two years ago directing us to treat prisoners as though they were our own still stands. It has not been rescinded.

"So, doctor. We will treat the prisoners in our care in accordance with our orders; as though they were our own troops. Is that clear, gentlemen?"

"Yes, sir." Captain Munger responded.

Eastman pressed Dr. Sanger for a response. "Doctor?"

"I will follow your orders, Colonel."

"Good," Eastman concluded. "Now, doctor, I need you to get me a list of the medicines you believe you will need to treat up to 5,000 prisoners.

"I also need from you, doctor, a plan to deal with all the human waste and garbage that will be generated by that large a group."

"When do you want list of medical supplies and my suggestion on the human waste issue, Colonel?"

"Today is Wednesday, gentlemen," Eastman reminded them. "And, we need to get moving on our preparations. So, we will meet this Friday right after morning chow."

With that, the two men stood, saluted and left Colonel Eastman's office.

LOWELL

"Let's walk over to the pond where we used to fish," Ethan suggested.

"Sure, Ethan."

They talked as they walked the familiar path to the pond where they and their friend, Michael Drieborg, used to fish and swim.

"How are you doing, Willie?" Ethan asked.

"I miss Tom and Kelly, Ethan. When are we going to see them?"

"When we get back to your house, let's write them each a letter. We can mail it when we go into town on Saturday. Good idea?"

"Think they'll come visit us, Ethan?"

"We'll ask them in the letter, all right?"

"Sure, Ethan."

"So, my friend, are you getting enough to eat?"

"Oh, my, yes," Willie told him. "My mother and my sisters keep filling up my plate with food. I feel stuffed all the time."

"You've only been home a couple of days, but I figure we'll both put on the weight we lost in prison camp."

"I've got nothing to do all day, Ethan," Willie complained. "Papa works in the barn, and my sisters help Momma in the kitchen and in the garden. But there doesn't seem to be anything for me to do.

"At least you and I played catch or took walks around the prison. Here, I've got nothing to do."

"Do you remember how to milk a cow, Willie?"

"I don't know, Ethan. I haven't tried."

"Have you helped your father with the other chores, like filling the wood-box or cleaning out the stalls in the barn?"

"No."

"Who takes out the chamber pot?"

"I don't know."

"How about when we get back to your house, we'll have a talk with your family?"

"What about, Ethan?"

"They probably think you want to rest and not be bothered with chores. How about we tell them you want to help with chores an' such?"

"Will you help me, Ethan?"

"Sure. But I think you'll find that once you do them a few times, you'll remember how to do it."

Back at the Petzolds' home, Ethan asked if he could speak with the family.

They sat around the table; Willie, too.

"Thank you for allowing me to speak with you," Ethan began.

"If you think I'm sticking my nose in where it's not welcome, please tell me."

Willie's mother spoke up. "Not at all, Ethan. You rescued our son and looked after him in prison. He came back to us because of you. Now that he is home, please tell us how we can help him."

"Willie needs to feel needed," Ethan began. "He needs to be included in the daily work of the farm. He needs you to treat him just like he is normal in every way. You may have to show him how to milk the cow or the goats, Mr. Petzold. Willie may have forgotten how to do that.

"But he can learn, believe me. I know he can learn to help with any of the farm work if it is explained patiently and repeatedly."

"We just wanted Willie to get his strength back, Ethan," Mrs. Petzold said.

"He wants to be needed. The worst thing for him is for you to just have him sitting around. Don't worry about his strength, Mrs. Petzold. He is strong as a bull, believe me. No one in prison camp fooled around with the guys in our mess. Willie made sure of that.

"But he does need direction, some. And he needs your patience.

"Mr. Petzold, when I come over for supper tonight, can I come a bit early? Say, during your milking time?"

"Certainly, Ethan" Mr. Petzold said. "Why?"

"Here is my suggestion," Ethan began. "You and I will go out into the barn after we're done here. Under your direction, Willie will clean out a stall or two. Later, during milking time, we will show him how to milk one of your cows.

"It would be best if you do the teaching, Mr. Petzold. I'll be there just to give Willie some assurance if he needs it. Believe me, he's a quick learner. Just have patience with him, because it may take him a few times to get it right. Once he does, it will be fine. He won't forget. Would you mind doing that, sir?"

"Certainly not, Ethan. You have helped my son survive his injury and prison camp, too. Now, I would be grateful if you helped me, help my son."

"What about us, Ethan?" Willie's sister, Mary, asked. "Is there anything we can do to help?"

"You can stop waiting on him so much," Ethan told them. "Invite him to help you with the chickens, your flock of sheep and in the garden. Take him to town with you on market day. He's healthy and can help you with your packages an' such.

"You see, he's physically strong but a bit challenged in expressing himself," Ethan continued. "Rather than anticipate what you think he is trying to say and finish his sentences, be patient and allow him to find the words.

"He'll get there," Ethan assured them, "but he takes more time to do things. You're just not used to seeing him struggle."

"Phew! You've given us a lot to think about, Ethan," Mrs. Petzold said. "Looking back on the past couple of days, I can see exactly what you're talking about, though. The Willie who has come home to us is different than the one we sent off to the Army.

"Thank you for helping us help our Willie," she said. Tears were rolling down her cheeks. "We'll try not to intrude on the time you need to spend with your family. But can we talk with you from time to time about these things?"

"Of course, Mrs. Petzold," Ethan assured her.

All during this conversation, Willie sat without saying a word.

"Hey, big guy," Ethan said to him. "Want to go to the barn with me and your Papa?"

"Sure, Ethan."

*   *   *

Back in the house, one of Willie's sisters asked.

"Momma," Mary asked. "Why doesn't Willie talk very much?"

"It has something to do with the head injury he got at the Shiloh battle, I think."

"He's so quiet," his sister went on. "He used to joke around with us an' all. Now he just sits there, no matter what we say."

"I know, dear," Mrs. Petzold agreed. "But we must be patient. Remember, Ethan told us Willie is much better than when he first found him at Belle Island prison in Virginia."

"So, we talk to him and treat him just like everything is normal. Is that it, Momma?"

"Yes," she responded. "And when we are in the garden or collecting eggs, anything at all, we invite him to help us. Do you girls understand?"

"Yes, Momma," they answered in unison.

* * *

Out in the barn, Willie's father was telling his son how he wanted the stalls cleaned.

"Watch what I do, son," he began. "I will prepare this stall for cleaning. Then you do the same in the one next to it. All right?"

"Yes, Papa."

Mr. Petzold led the cow out of the stall and walked it to the enclosed pasture.

"Now you do that with the cow in your stall, Willie."

Willie did as he was told. When he returned to his father's side, the instruction resumed.

"Now, I take a shovel and pick up all the manure and straw on the floor. I put each shovelful into this wheelbarrow. When it is full, I push it to the manure pile outside the barn and dump it in.

"Watch, Willie," he directed.

While this was going on, Ethan stood a few feet away. Every time Willie looked his way, Ethan would nod his head, but he never spoke or tried to help his friend carry out Mr. Petzold's directions.

Soon, as the three men walked toward the manure pile, Mr. Petzold pushing a wheelbarrow full of manure and straw. After he dumped it, he returned to his stall inside the barn and filled the wheelbarrow again.

After repeating this process several times, he turned to Willie and said, "All right, son. Now it's your turn. Take the shovel and fill the wheelbarrow with the stuff on the floor in your stall. Just like I did in my stall."

Willie looked over at Ethan.

Ethan spoke for the first time since they had been in the barn.

"Go ahead, Willie. You can do it, just like your Papa showed you."

"All right, Ethan," Willie said.

It wasn't long before his stall was emptied. Then, he spread fresh hay on the floor.

"Now, Willie," he said. "You do that in your stall."

And Willie did.

Now that both stalls were cleaned, the cows were led back.

But Willie's father wasn't finished. "Every morning, son, after breakfast, it will be your job to clean out these two stalls. Think you can do that?"

Willie looked at Ethan. Once he got a reassuring nod from his friend, he said, "Yes, Papa. I can do that."

Mr. Petzold turned to Ethan. "You're welcome to have dinner with us, Ethan."

"Thank you, sir," he answered. "But I had better get home. My Momma is expecting me. I'll be back for the milking this afternoon, though."

"Fine," Mr. Petzold said. "Give your mother our regards, Ethan. And thank her for sharing you with us."

"Are you leaving, Ethan?" Willie asked.

"Just for a little while, big guy," Ethan told his friend. "But I'll be back this afternoon to help you and your Papa with the milking."

"All right, Ethan," Willie answered.

* * *

After he washed up outside, Ethan walked into the entryway at the back of his house. There, he took off his shoes, muddy from the Petzolds' barn.

Don't want to get my mother's floors all muddy. I remember her reading the riot act about that before I went into the Army.

With his house slippers on, he opened the inside door.

"Hi, everyone," he greeted.

"Have you been over at the Petzolds' all this time, son?" his mother asked right away.

"Yes, Momma," Ethan answered. "I told everyone there about Willie's experience and made a few suggestions as to how they should treat him. Then I went with Willie and Mr. Petzold out to their barn."

Ethan told his mother of how Willie's father had given his son directions and assigned him the daily chore of cleaning out the barn's stalls.

"Willie needs to be included in that type of thing. He needs to be Given responsibilities, you know."

Mr. Schock walked in from the barn. Joseph was right behind him.

"You're home, I see," he said to Ethan.

"Right," Ethan said. "I need some more of Momma's cooking."

"Well, you three men sit yourselves down," Michelle Schock told them. "I've fed little Mary, and she's napping."

For farm families, the noon meal was called 'dinner'. It was the main meal of the day; the meat and potatoes meal. The evening meal was called, 'supper' and was much lighter; usually leftovers.

"Tell us about prison camp, son" his mother asked.

Between mouths full of food, Ethan described prison life.

"You had to live right out in the open?" his father asked, hardly believing what he had just been told.

"Yes, Papa," Ethan told him again. "A lot of the time, anyway. The worst was at Belle Island, a prison just outside of Richmond in Virginia. There, we were barefoot and wore Confederate cast-off clothing, too. The food was the worst part of prison, though.

"Many days, we got nothing. When we did, it was usually some watered-down soup with some kernels of corn floating around in it. If we were real lucky, we might have a piece of meat or two in the soup.

I won't tell my Momma about putting rat meat in our soup once in a while.

"And the water we drank was too foul to stomach. At Belle Island, it was polluted with the prisoners' waste."

"Are you saying it was polluted with human waste?" his mother said, shocked.

"Yes, Momma; human waste."

"How did you manage to not get sick, son?"

"The men in our mess boiled our drinking water or went without."

"So, what did you drink?"

"We didn't have milk like you have on the table, Momma," Ethan told her. "We didn't have coffee either. Many men came down with stomach troubles because they drank polluted water, and many died as a result. It was a rule in our mess that we didn't drink any water unless it was boiled first."

"And you survived because…?" his father asked Ethan.

"In addition to boiling our water, the men in my mess exercised and prayed together every day, and of course, we were lucky."

"You lost a lot of weight, too, son," his mother observed. "Your clothing is way too big for you."

"But I'm back safe and sound, Momma," he reminded her. "Besides, your good farm food will fatten me up in no time."

"Have some more mashed potatoes, son," his mother urged. "And save some room for pie."

JOHNSON'S ISLAND

"I remember telling you to report back to me in a week, Major," the Union doctor reminded Richard Pope.

"It's been almost a month, and you're still running a fever. You want pneumonia?"

Pope was still coughing, too. Between coughs, he replied, "I thought I was getting better, Doc."

"Well, you were wrong," the doctor told him. "You might be dead wrong, too, if you're not careful."

Pope left the medical tent with more cough syrup and instructions to keep warm and drink a lot of water.

Back at his barracks, Pope took some cough syrup and covered up with a blanket on his bed.

His bedmate, Ed Burke, spoke up. "Jus' remember, Pope, I toll ya to get your sick ass back to the doc. But no, you knew better.

"Is it like that with all you southern aristocrats from Charleston?"

"Afraid so. That's what my older brother, the doctor, would say, anyway," Pope responded.

"What'd the blue-belly doc say fer you to do this time?"

"Take more syrup, keep warm and drink a lot of water."

"Lots 'a luck with that keepin' warm business," Burke snapped. "Thas what he told you last month. See how well that worked."

* * *

But within a week, Pope received word that he was being sent South.

"What the hell?" Burke exclaimed.

"You're going home? How'd you manage that, Pope?"

"I think the Union doc wanted me out of his hair," Pope surmised. "So, he told the commandant we'd all be better off if they shipped me home."

"Their doc just didn't want to get blamed when you died, that's the long and short of it."

"Could be," Pope replied between coughing spells. "Whatever, I can just picture myself in my father's warm kitchen and a table there full of great food."

"I'll be pissed if you recover and spend the rest a' this war enjoying that warm kitchen and all your mammy's cooking."

"Thanks, Burke," Pope snapped. "And good luck to you, too, my friend."

* * *

Johnsons Island's prison had been filling up. The construction crews had kept ahead of the arriving prisoners, erecting a new barrack about every ten days. As a result, just about all of the 3,000 Confederate officers housed at Camps Douglas and Chase Prison were transferred to the officer's prison on Johnson Island before the Cartel parole agreement was ended.

And the strong November winds of Lake Erie were sweeping the small island.

The prisoners were able to keep the barrack stoves hot with the timber they salvaged on the island. But once outside, they suffered from the cold. And when the first sinkholes dug for human waste were filled up, new ones had to be dug further and further away from the buildings, bitter cold or not.

PRISONER EXCHANGES

The first exchanges of prisoners under the terms of the Cartel had been accomplished, but future exchanges were in doubt. Northern leaders had called a halt to mass paroles/exchanges for three reasons.

First: military leaders, like Grant, insisted that to parole/exchange Confederate prisoners only made it necessary to face them in battle again.

Equally important, Federal military leaders, like Grant, believed that keeping captured Confederates in northern prisons and away from the battlefield would damage the Confederate government's war making ability.

Lastly, Union political leaders refused to accept the Confederate treatment of its colored soldiers who were in Southern prisons. The Union objection followed Richmond's announced intention of treating captured Negro soldiers as runaway slaves, not legitimate prisoners of war.

So, in the short run anyway, it appeared that prisoners would remain in place for at least the winter of 1862–1863, except some of the most ill.

RICHMOND

Among the sick Confederate prisoners-of-war sent south was Major Richard Pope, most recently held prisoner on Johnson's Island in Ohio. He boarded a train in Sandusky, Ohio, and traveled south to Harper's Ferry, Virginia, and then to the Confederate hospital in Richmond.

"Richard," greeted Doctor Charles Pope. "Welcome to my little piece of the world."

"Happy to be here, brother," Richard responded. "Actually, I'm happy to be anywhere but on the island prison in Ohio." He could hardly get out the words, he coughed so much.

"Let's get you cleaned up and in some hospital clothes so's I can examine you."

After his brother's prodding and poking, Richard was warmly tucked into his bed. A male nurse was spooning some hot broth to Major Pope as well.

"What's the verdict, Doctor?" he asked and began a deep-seated cough.

"You're full of phlegm right now," Dr. Pope told his brother. "That's what all this coughing is all about. Your system is trying to get it out by coughing."

"The Yankee doc gave me some cough medicine. What can you do about it?"

"First, I'm going to thoroughly sweat you. That should loosen up some 'a that stuff that's clogging up your system. Hot broth should help, too."

"That sounds like our old mammy's cure," Richard teased his brother, the doctor.

"Right now, that old remedy is the best we can do; we don't have a better treatment."

"Let's get on with it, brother," Richard urged. "I'm really tired a' all this coughing."

* * *

There was a sweat house near the hospital. It was heated up and Richard taken there.

Several men were in the sweat house with Richard.

"Are you men in this hot house to sweat out an infection?" Richard asked.

"Ya got that right, buddy," one of them answered.

"I come down with this fever and aches a few weeks ago. My sergeant sent me to sick call, and they sent me here. The doc there said he don't want me to infect all the others in my unit. So, here I am, all cleaned up and nowheres ta go."

"I was a prisoner up on an island in Lake Erie. Cold and windy like I never saw. The Yankee doc sent me here just to get rid a' me, I'm guessing," Richard told his companion.

Another patient added, "Funny, the doctors told me to drink a lot a' water. And here they want me to sweat it all out. Wish they'd make up their minds."

It wasn't long before the men were back in their hospital beds, sweating under a pile of blankets. Hot stones were placed under their mattress cover to continue the treatment.

"Hey! How ya doing, brother?" Charles Pope asked.

"You're gonna have a lighter brother after all this sweating, I can tell ya," Richard responded. "I think I've sweated out a gallon already."

"That's the idea, smart ass!" his brother, the doctor, reminded him. "I sent a telegram to Father. I wouldn't be surprised if we don't see him walking in here to see you before you've melted away."

"That'd be pretty neat to see him," Richard admitted. "I miss the ol' man."

"So do I, actually."

"You know, brother," Richard complained. "This bed is lumpy as a bed a' rocks."

"It should be. You've got a layer of hot rocks under your bed cover," Dr. Charles Pope told his sick brother. "It's supposed to continue the sweating treatment."

"That part of the treatment is working," Richard informed his brother. "It's the bruising of the rocks in my bed I'm complaining about. I can't get comfortable."

"Whine, whine, whine. I give you the best treatment available, and all you can do is complain."

"I warn you, Doctor Pope," his brother responded between coughing spasms. "If I die after all of this miserable treatment, I'll never forgive you."

"When we were kids, Richard, you always found a way to outwrestle me. You always seemed to end up on top. Now, big shot, I'm in charge."

"I knew it," Richard said. "You resented me all this time. Now you've got what you wanted, control. I knew it."

"A blessing this war has brought me." With that, Charles walked away from his brother's bed, laughing heartily.

But it wasn't a laughing matter to Doctor Charles Pope. He consulted with one of his colleagues about his brother's condition.

"My brother, the major, is not responding to the traditional treatment," he reported. "What would you do?"

"You could try bleeding."

"That's barbaric and would just weaken him more."

"Then make him drink more water and broth and just hope."

"I fear his lungs are filling with liquid as it is."

"Pneumonia?"

"That's my fear," Pope conceded. "That's what the Yankee doctors told him."

"If that's the case, I'd say spend your time with someone you can save and pray for your brother."

Elmira Prison

"What do you mean you can't do anything about the human waste situation?" Eastman almost shouted at his Surgeon-in-Chief Major Sanger.

"We can dig latrines every few feet, Colonel," Sanger insisted. "But, the damn stuff seems to seep into Foster's Pond. That lagoon of polluted water has nowhere to go. So, it just sits there drawing all the human waste."

Eastman interrupted, "Since we don't get our drinking water from there, can't we just ignore the thing?"

"Not if you want to get rid of the stink it creates." Sanger responded. "I can't prove it, but seems to me it causes disease, too."

"Hell, Major," Eastman snapped. "My wife already told me that. She's threatening to take the kids ago to back to Ohio if it's not cleaned up."

Sanger continued. "Bottom line is, I can't find a way to drain the thing. Maybe one of Hoffman's engineers could take a look at it and figure out a way to solve that problem."

"All right," Eastman decided. "I'll wire Hoffman and ask him to send me someone to assess the problem."

"Eastman turned to his aide. "What about the barrack roofs and the mess hall facility?" Got any solution for those two problems?

"You heard the builders we had out here, Colonel. Money can solve both problems. The real question is, can you get Washington to cough up the few more thousand dollars?

"They builders said that the leaking roofs can be fixed, the mess facility expanded and stoves put into each barrack. Not a problem. Except they said, it would cost $5,000 for the mess facility, five hundred dollars per barrack building to fix the roofs, and another two or three hundred dollars for stoves to be installed in each of the barracks."

Munger concluded his reports. "Can you get that kind a' money out of Washington?"

"All I can do is try, Captain. I'll send the wire this very day."

* * *

Hoffman's aide Captain Johnson asked. "Have you seen these requests from Colonel Eastman at Elmira Prison?"

'Captain," Hoffman snapped. "I told that whining son-of-a bitch how much he had to spend. How he spends it is of no concern to me."

"That's sort of the point, Colonel," Johnson went on. "He claims that his needs exceed just renovating those barracks. It appears that he feels they need major work on the roofs. In addition, there are no stoves to heat the darn things this winter."

"Tell him that we're not going to run a vacation resort there. Remind him that when his barracks were very recently filled with Union recruits, I heard nothing from him about leaky roofs or the lack of stoves. If his facility was good enough for our boys in the past, it's good enough for rebel prisoners now.

"So, he must make do with the money I've authorized him to spend. It's his look-out if he exceeded his budget."

"Yes, sir. But, there is one other item you might want to take a look at, sir."

"What's that?"

"They've got a pond of some size within the prison that appears to be pretty foul. They're asking for one of our engineers to come over there to take a look at it' an' see if can't be drained; or something."

"Send one to 'em, Captain." Hoffman ordered. "Maybe that will stop all this whining."

Captain Johnston went on. "What about the tents we sent to Elmira to house the additional 5,000 prisoners. Stoves for those tents would sure come in handy this coming winter? It gets pretty cold in that part of New York December through March."

"This is only June, for Lord's sake, Captain," Hoffman snapped. "You can look into the cost, but don't buy any right now. Are you turning into a bleeding heart on me, Captain?"

"It's not that, sir," Johnson protested. "But, I don't want you yelling at me for not mentioning these things when we can still do something about them."

"Point taken, Captain. Off with ya' now."

"Yes, sir. "

ANDERSONVILLE PRISON

The movement of Union prisoners away from Andersonville Prison continued as Sherman's army marched to the sea from Atlanta. Trains arrived at the prison on a daily basis to take prisoners away from the advancing Federal forces.

In the process, thousands of prisoners were moved east toward prisons in South Carolina; others were sent to Savannah. Some were sent south toward Florida. Corey and Ethan McElvain were among those loaded on a train headed south.

Jammed into a boxcar, Cory commented, "I thought everyone was headed east."

"Maybe it's a good thing," Ethan responded. "It's cold by the Atlantic Ocean, don't ya know? Gotta be warmer heading south."

"I 'spose," Corey said "But when we gonna stop? I gotta pee, real bad."

His brother Ethan chuckled. "Somethin' must be wrong with your smeller, brother. Can't you smell all that urine an' such in this car?"

"Oh, I smell it, brother," Corey responded. "I just didn't want to add my smell to the stink."

"Ya!" His brother laughed. "I never thought I'd tell you to pee your pants. But what choice have ya got?"

"None, I suppose."

"Just don't do it on me."

* * *

It did get warmer as the train chugged south. Instead of farmland, though, more and more of the land on both sides of the track was marsh or dense fields of scrub.

"I had thought we could run off at one of the stops the train made," Corey told his brother.

"Hardly," Ethan responded. "It's all marsh an' such. Where in hell would we go anyway?"

"Right," Corey agreed. "The only dry ground I see is what these tracks sit on."

"Best we just wait an' see where they're taking us."

"I suppose."

Their train traveled south for some time. When it stopped, the men were ordered to leave the boxcars that brought them to Thomasville, Georgia.

A Confederate sergeant ordered them to line up.

"As soon as yas line up proper, the sooner yas will get some chow," he shouted.

Food was certainly the key word; the men lined up quickly.

"That's better, lads," the sergeant shouted. "On the other side a' the tracks be the food. I want one file at a time ta move forward on my order. First file, forward, march!"

Ethan looked into the bowl he had been handed.
"My Lord!" he told his brother. "This is little more than warmed up water."

"Don't be so hasty," Cory said. "I see some corn kernels at the bottom of my bowl."

"You always seem to get the best of things, Cory," Ethan responded.

"Probably 'cause I'm the baby of the family."

"Probably."

Over the next few days, the Union prisoners were allowed to rest. But it wasn't all that comfortable. The December weather had turned cold, and there were no shelters available. So, everyone slept in the open field; without blankets.

It had been the Confederate plan to have the prisoners build their own prison stockade on this site. But it wasn't long before they realized their prisoners were too weak to cut enough timber for the construction of the prison's walls.

So, on December 19th, that plan was abandoned. The following day, the prisoners were walked ten miles north. The next day, they marched nineteen miles to just south of Albany, Georgia.

Their march was over very difficult terrain.

"Good thing we have shoes," Cory said as he waded through almost waist deep water in a swampy area. "No telling what we're stepping on here."

Most of the men had threadbare clothing. Only a few lucky ones had shoes. Food was scarce, and the men suffered from the cold as well.

At Albany, they were loaded into boxcars and headed north. When the train stopped on Christmas Eve, the men discovered that they had been returned to Andersonville Prison.

"What a hell of a Christmas present this is," Cory told his brother.

"I never thought I'd be happy to see this place again," Ethan said.

"You gotta be kidding!"

"Think about it, brother." Ethan chuckled. "At least here we're probably gonna get fed."

"Ya got me there."

The movement of Andersonville prisoners to the east stopped. Sherman had taken Savannah and was moving his army north. So, no more Union prisoners were moved that winter.

But Cory and Ethan were kept busy at Andersonville.

"When the Rebs last moved men outta this prison, they left all the sickest back here ta fend fer themselves."

"Best they did, Ethan," Cory judged. "Most a' them would a' died packed into those boxcars like we were. Now, we're about the healthiest prisoners around. Wish we had some medicine and a doctor or two to help the sick prisoners."

"'Least they have you to tend 'em, Corey," Ethan told his brother. "You're our doc around here."

"Wish I really was, brother. I'm glad to try helping the sick boys. But all I know are old home remedies for common problems like puncture wounds, burns, headaches and stomach upsets. Truth be told, I don't even have the herbs I need to treat those ailments."

"You're still better than nothing, Corey," Ethan insisted. "At least the men have someone who knows a thing or two about how ta help."

"Wish I could do more than just boil water and keep cuts an' such clean."

"What we really need is food," Ethan concluded. "We're starving here; pure and simple."

"Surely would help," Corey agreed. "Hot water with some kernels of corn can only go so far."

"Well, rumor has it that we're gonna be exchanged soon," Ethan said.

"How long we been hanging around Reb prisons, brother?"

"I forget," Ethan snapped. "What's your point?"

"As long as we have been prisoners, we've heard rumors of one thing or another, and ain't none a' them been true. Right?"

"Ya got me there, Corey. Sorta fun talkin' about 'em, though."

"Knock your serf out, brother," Corey urged. "My hopes for freedom from this hell have been trashed too many times fer me to bother my head with 'em."

RICHMOND

In December of 1864, there was a closed-door meeting at the Confederate White House.

"General Winder," Jefferson Davis told his guest. "Thank you for coming. Please have a chair, sir. In your request for this meeting, you said something about prisoner release. Do you have a recommendation about the tens of thousands of Union prisoners we now hold?"

"Yes, Mr. President, I do," Winder began." We currently have several prisons in territory behind enemy lines. Andersonville, Blackshear and Macon are current examples. We have virtually no food for the prisoners we hold there. Most are now so emaciated and weak that if they are not seriously ill already, they will be. I despair of ever seeing that situation changing.

"The Federals have chosen to bypass these three Georgia prisons and abandon the Union soldiers we hold there. Prisoners we hold in South Carolina will be next if Sherman moves north as expected."

"I thought you moved most of the prisoners from the prisons you mentioned?" Secretary of State Judah P. Benjamin wondered.

"Yes, we have, Mr. Secretary. Only the sick remain there.

"Back in 1864, we had an exchange with the Federals of sick prisoners. When northerners saw the condition of the released sick prisoner, the public backlash in there was so severe that I believe our soldiers held prisoner by the Union were mistreated in retaliation."

"But, General," Secretary Benjamin asked, "what was the condition of the Confederates soldiers released by the Union?"

"Mr. Secretary," Wilder responded. "You must remember that back then, we released prisoners who were considered seriously sick. So, the Union boys we released were sick, but they were also very emaciated.

"Our boys who were released from Union prisons were sick, too, of course. That's why they were released to our care. But they had been pretty well fed, certainly by comparison. Most of them did not look emaciated."

President Davis interrupted. "My Lord, man! We're not running a popularity contest for Northern public opinion here, General. We're at war!" he snapped.

"Of course, Mr. President. But northern public opinion aside, the fact is we simply can't adequately feed all the prisoners we now hold, and the ratio of deaths to prisoners held is rising alarmingly."

"And what is your suggestion, General Wilder?"

"Mr. Secretary, I suggest we relieve ourselves of the prisoners of war we hold in Georgia and South Carolina."

"Unilaterally, General?"

"Certainly not, Mr. President. I recommend that we should reopen negotiations with the appropriate Federal officials for a mutual exchange."

President Davis ended the meeting. "Thank you for your report and your recommendation, General Wilder. I assure you both will be given serious consideration."

The General rose, saluted President Davis, and left the room.

President Davis and his Secretary of State remained seated.

"What do you think of this matter, Mr. Secretary?"

"Mr. President," Benjamin responded immediately. "I think you should order me to explore precisely the course of action General Wilder proposed."

"I'll think about that over this weekend," Davis promised. "At our Monday Cabinet meeting, I will announce my decision."

"Very well, Mr. President," his Secretary of State said. "Monday, it will be."

Elmira Prison

"Captain Johnson," Colonel Hoffman said. "You have a report for me dealing with Elmira Prison?"

"Yes, sir. It's from the people of the Sanitation Committee who visited there recently."

"Those damn bleeding hearts would rather have us spend more money on our prisoners than on our troops in the trenches at Petersburg."

"Tell me what they had to say."

"The Committee members conducted their inspection during one of the worst snow storms the area had this year; it was a blinding blizzard with below zero temperatures."

"Wouldn't you know it." Hoffman chuckled. "Couldn't have been mild temperatures. It had to be record setting lows."

"It got worse, sir." Johnson reported.

"it seems one of our officers assigned to the prison, a Major Beall forced the men of one barracks to fall in around midnight during that blizzard for roll call."

"Are you serious, Captain?"

"Yes, sir. While the Sanitation Committee members watched, he kept over one hundred prisoners standing in that below freezing snow-storm for over an hour. According to their report, a dozen or more men were barefooted. None of the prisoners had winter clothing."

"Damn!" Hoffman shouted. "We bust our behinds to get stoves in each of the barracks and few for the tents, and some idiot pulls a stunt like this.

"I'm going to see him transferred out of Elmira to a front-line unit."

"That might be difficult, sir," Johnson informed his superior. "Beal is called 'Peg-Leg' 'cause he lost part of one leg early in the war."

"We don't have to keep him around, though," Hoffman told his aide. "Re-assign him to this office. I'll find him a post in a warehouse counting shoes or something until this war is over."

"Yes, sir."

"Anything else in that report I should know about?"

"Not surprisingly, the Sanitation Committee complained about the human waste problem at Elmira. We have similar problems in all our prison facilities. But, Fosters Pond at Elmira is especially bad."

"That engineer we sent there never really fixed that did he?"

"He tried draining it, but the locals complained that he only polluted the nearby river so they could no longer use it. So, we stopped doing that. The Committee estimated that over 3,000 gallons of urine are dumped daily into that stagnate pond.

"Their report also states that the prisoners are not given adequate wood to burn in the stoves we installed, nor do they have warm enough clothing to keep warm."

"I'd remind the Committee that our boys in the field are cold, too. As for stove wood, we have pretty well exhausted the nearby supply. The locals are complaining about that, too."

"One last thing, sir." Johnson offered. "It appears that a Committee member overheard the Chief Surgeon at Elmira, Major Sanger boast to a colleague that, "I have killed more Rebs here than any soldier at the front."

"Are you serious, Johnson?"

'It's in the report, sir.'

"Damn!"

*　*　*

Confederate prisoners dubbed, Elmira Prison, 'Helmira'.

It appears to have been well earned. Of the 12, 123 Confederate prisoners held there between July 6th, 1864 and July 5th, 1865, 2,9632 died. This number of deaths would be the highest of any Northern prison. This death rate would only be exceeded by that of the Southern prison of Andersonville.

So, it would seem accurate to call Elmira Prison, the Andersonville of the North.

THE JOURNEY HOME

"By the Lord in heaven, brother," Cory admitted. "You were right. We're being sent home."

"Gotta have faith sometimes, young fella," Ethan reminded his brother.

"Not gonna waste my energy arguing with ya, Ethan. I'm saving it for what lies ahead."

"Good plan. Let's get some sleep. That empty boxcar will be here early tomorrow."

"Right. We don't want to miss it."

"Funny, brother," Ethan quipped. "Real funny. Get some sleep."

* * *

So, on April 1, 1865, the Mc Elvain brothers were sent north to be exchanged. Prisoners whose homes were in the Midwest were sent to a temporary prison called Camp Fisk, four miles east of Vicksburg, Mississippi, to await exchange.

On that journey, the Anderson and Macon prisoners were first sent to Montgomery by train. Then they went by boat on to Selma, Alabama.

They left Montgomery on the steamboat Henry James. Ethan McElvain and his brother Corey were standing along the portside railing. There, they were enjoying the cool spring breeze and the sights along the shore.

"We never been on a steamboat a'fore. Have we?" Ethan commented to his brother, Corey.

"Don't recall. No, I don't think so, Ethan."

"Hear the noise of the paddlewheel churning up the water? Sort a' calming. Don't ya think?"

"What I think, actually, is that most anything would be better than where we come from."

Chuckling, Corey nodded his head. "Ya got that right, brother. Just getting outta all the stink and mud of Andersonville gives me hope that we might just survive this thing."

"Right," Ethan said. "Gotta admit, though, I've had my doubts a time or two."

"Me, too. Ya know something else? A thought just occurred to me; I hope everyone's all right at home."

"Gosh, I haven't even given them a thought in a long while," Ethan admitted.

"I'm not surprised," Corey said. "It was hard fer me not to be depressed thinking about home or the folks there. So, I gotta tell ya, Ethan, I put all a' that out a' my mind, ya know; Momma's kitchen an' the smell of her bread baking in tha morning. I jus' couldn't bear ta think a' those things."

"You ain't alone with that, brother," Ethan assured his Corey. "But all 'a that's done with, brother. Our war is over. We survived the worst they could throw at us."

"Yup, we did. I never thought I'd see the day. But here we are, both of us headed home.

"I got an idea, Ethan," Corey said. "Let's go up to that clean top deck and just sit in the sun till chow time."

"You're the doctor, Corey," Ethan said with a big smile. "Lead the way."

* * *

On the upper deck, the McElvains found a spot in the sun and sat with their backs against the railing.

"My Lord," Ethan observed. "There are a lot of guys on this boat. Ya think they all be from Andersonville?"

"Could be," Corey answered.

"Hey, buddy," he asked the fellow sitting next to him. "What prison you from?"

"Andersonville. How about you?"

"The same. Where you headed?"

"My name is John Clark Ely, an' I'm from Ohio, an' my buddies here are John Maddox and Romulus Tolbert. They're from Madison, Indiana."

"My name is Corey McElvains, and this here is my brother, Ethan. We're headed back to DuQuoin, Illinois."

"You don't look too sick to me, Ethan; you neither, Corey," John Clark Ely observed. "How come the Rebs didn't send you east with the rest a' the prisoners?"

"You're right, John Clark," Ethan commented. "They didn't send us east. And we're not sick neither, thank the Lord. The Rebs sent us south around Thanksgiving time. When they figured we weren't no good to 'em anymore, they sent us back north."

"Craziest damn thing," Corey added. "They had us walking all over north Florida. I never saw so much swamp; walked through most of it, I swear. We arrived back to Andersonville last Christmas Eve. What a hell of 'a present that was. Rebs acted as though it was all planned to happen that a'way."

"Sounds like the Army ta' me," John Maddox commented. "Some things don't change, no matter which army is running the show."

All the men laughed at that remark.

"Ya got that right, soldier," Romulus Tolbert added.

"We got some other Indiana boys over there." Romulus pointed across toward the starboard railing. "They's from the prison in Macon, Georgia. Ta hear them talk, it seems ta me that place was a paradise compared to Andersonville."

"If you weren't sent east, were you sick?" Corey asked.

"Ya, I was. They left me behind 'cause I had diarrhea, real bad, still do some," John Clark revealed. "Clean water an' rest have sure helped me a lot. But if'n you see me hurrying off to the privy, you'll know why."

"Lot a' fellas died from that," Corey added.

"Ya', I was lucky, fer sure."

"What about those other guys?" Ethan asked, pointing to the guys from Indiana.

"I don't know why these other guys weren't sent east," Clark revealed.

It wasn't long before they were fed a soup full of corn, black beans and okra. It was sort a' mashed into a paste. They even were given some corn bread.

"This is the best meal I've had in I don't know when," Tolbert judged.

"Not bad a'tall," Ethan agreed. "Filled my shrunken belly anyways."

The men slept where they sat under the stars as the boat churned its way through the night.

* * *

The next afternoon, they disembarked in Salem, Alabama. From there, they walked a good deal northeast; took a train some of the way and walked some more.

"Good thing we had that one good meal on the boat," Corey said.

"Right," Ethan agreed. "All we got today was some stale bread."

"Better than nothin'," Talbert added.

"I suppose."

"Move along, you men," their Confederate guard urged. "We got a few more miles ta go yet today."

"Is you a guard or just a guy in a Reb uniform guiding us along?" Maddox asked.

"I don' know which I is, soldier," the man responded. "All I know is, sooner you get to Camp Fisk, the sooner they let me get across the Mississippi to my home in Arkansas."

"That gun a' yours even loaded?" Corey asked.

"It may be," he answered. "But I run out 'a percussion caps a while back. So, it won't fire anyways."

"Well, I'll be." Ethan chuckled. "What come a' your army, Reb?"

"Far as I can tell, Yank," he responded, "General Hood threw it away attackin' Sherman in front a' Atlanta last fall. I ain't seen hide nor hair a' it since."

* * *

"That's the North Star, Corey," his brother said, pointing up to the sky.

"That word, north, has a pretty sound to it, don't it Ethan?" Corey responded.

"Surely does. It surely does."

"That fella who 'sposed ta be guarding us?"

"Ya, what about him?"

"He appears as skinny as us. Barefoot, too."

"Your point?"

"We're the prisoners, an' he's the guard. Seems ta' me he should be better fed an such than us. Don't ya' think?" Ethan concluded.

"Think they's as bad off as we are?"

"That's my thinkin'."

"Good thing for everybody this war's about over," Corey told his brother.

"My point exactly."

* * *

The next day, the column reached Camp Fisk. The camp was located within sight of the Mississippi and the port of Vicksburg.

The men stood on a hill with a clear view of that city's courthouse and the American flag flying from its peak.

John Clark Ely said, "Oh, this is the brightest day of my life, long to be remembered."

"That flag does look good flappin' in the wind over there," Ethan added.

"Yep," J. Walter Elliott agreed. "It certainly does. We is out from the gates of hell – out of the jaws of death. We going home."

Not quite. First, they had to await exchange. And Camp Fisk was where they would wait. It was four miles east of Vicksburg. A temporary holding place, the camp straddled a railroad track in a deep depression on both sides of the track. Brush and such had been piled around the perimeter to create a place to hold the prisoners. These Union prisoners had been freed of Confederate prisons but were to be held by Union authorities until exchanged. Guards from a Colored unit patrolled the camp.

Upon arrival, the men were given clean uniforms, hardtack and boiled cabbage. The food caused many of the weakened prisoners to have diarrhea.

When the McElvain brothers arrived, the ground was muddy from spring rains. So, there was no dry ground on which to sit down or sleep. The men had to stand. More rain made the situation worse. The heavy downpour actually created a water level there that reached the knees of some prisoners.

So, J. Walter Elliott was wrong; their time in hell was not over. To make matters worse, the water became polluted with human waste very quickly.

As a result, the almost 4,700 men held at Camp Fisk either did without clean drinking water or consumed that which was seriously contaminated.

VICKSBURG

"So, what do we have here?" General Morgan Smith asked.

"We've got somewhere 'round 4,700 released prisoners being held at Camp Fisk, sir," Captain Speed responded.

"And?" the general continued prodding.

"And the orders we received early this week directs us to ship them north to Cairo, Illinois, as fast as it can be arranged."

"What are your plans in that regard, Captain?"

"There are several paddle-wheelers available to us, sir. And they all want as many passengers as we can supply them."

"How are you going to pay for all of this?"

"It is my understanding that we have $5 per enlisted man and $10 per officer allocated for this task."

"Have you made any inquiries with the ship owners about what they will actually charge?" the general asked.

"Depending on the deal we cut, we can expect the per head cost to be much less than we have been allocated."

"Why do I have to drag this out of you, Captain?" the general snapped. "I'm the one who will have to sign off on all of this, remember? So, you had better be clear with me about all the arrangements, the expected costs, as well as the payouts."

"I understand, sir," Speed assured the general. "Should I ask Colonel Hatch to advise on this matter, sir?"

"Why would you do that, Captain?"

"Because he is the Quartermaster and must approve any payments, and because he has had experience with these matters."

"Oh, yes. Most of it bad, too." General Smith replied. "I remember something about a court-martial back in 1861 for his selling government goods and pocketing the funds. My information is that a review board wanted to cashier him as incompetent earlier this year, too."

"Right, General," Speed added. "But he's from Illinois, so his White House connections saved him both times.

"And the War Department sent him here."

"Unfortunately for us, Captain," General Smith concluded. "Tell Hatch I want him to negotiate with the shippers and oversee the assignment of the liberated prisoners to the various steamboats. Then, if anything goes wrong we can point the finger at him."

"I will see to it, General."

"You had better, Captain," the general reminded him. "If these boat captains and their agents want military passengers, they will have to deal with Hatch. He will decide which boats get the passengers and which do not. You will handle any payments involved."

"I understand, sir."

"Then see to it, Captain," the general concluded. "And keep me informed."

"Yes, sir."

CHARLESTON

Two household slaves carried Richard's stretcher into the Pope house.

Colonel Pope directed the move.

"Take the stretcher right into my study," he ordered. "Place it on the floor and lift Master Richard onto the bed I had placed there."

"Yes, sur," one of the stretcher bearers answered.

Colonel Pope held on to his son's hand as they moved down the hallway.

"Don't worry, son," he said. "We'll get your health back in no time. Our doctor will be here this afternoon. You just rest."

"Mammy's got a treat for my Richard, Colonel." The family cook announced.

"I've been dreaming of your cooking since the last time I had your treats."

A good-sized Negro lady burst into the hallway from the kitchen.

"Where is dat boy a' mine?" Mammy asked Colonel Pope.

"He's in my study, Mammy; waiting for you."

She entered the room and saw Richard Pope lying on the newly made bed.

"Hi, Mammy," he greeted her. He started coughing again.

"Surely took ya long 'nuff ta get back here ta me," she chided. "What you do to yer-self, boy?"

"I got held up, Mammy," Richard responded. "All that Northern air didn't agree with me. But I'm here now. You gonna take care of me, Mammy?"

"You jus' wait an' see, boy" she promised. "We'll get some a' my good cooking inta you, an' ya'll will be jus' fine in no time."

"Sounds good to me, Mammy."

"We start wit dis hot chicken broth," she said. "I don't want ta see a drop left in dis bowl. Ya hear me, now?"

"Yes, ma'am." Hot as the soup was, he greedily swallowed every ladle-full she pushed against his lips.

"Now, you sleep till the good doctor comes. Ya hear me now?"

"Yes, ma'am."

* * *

After the doctor finished his examination, he spoke with Colonel Pope.

"Your boy has pneumonia, Colonel," he revealed.

"That's what his brother and the other doctors in Richmond told me, too," Pope responded. "What can we do about it?"

"Not much, I'm afraid," the doctor said. "I'll go through my medical journals when I get back to the office. But treatment hasn't changed much in the last decade. Sweating, liquids and rest are still the only steps I know of."

"They took all those steps in Richmond," Pope told his doctor. "Is there nothing else?"

"As I said, I'll check around in my journals and with my colleagues, too. In the meantime, keep him in bed, feed him all the hot liquids he can stand and keep him warm."

"In the meantime, we're just supposed to stand around and watch him die?" Pope almost shouted.

"I'll get back to you first thing in the morning, Colonel," the doctor promised.

"First thing in the morning, then."

* * *

Upstairs, in his wife's darkened room, Colonel Pope told her of Richard's arrival in their home.

"You mean my son Richard is here and you haven't told me?" Mrs. Pope shouted at her husband.

"Calm yourself, dear," Colonel Pope urged his wife. "I didn't want to upset you until our doctor had a chance to examine him."

"Take me to him, right now," she continued to shout. "I'll not wait another moment. You put him in your study? I never heard of such a thing when we have comfortable bedrooms, empty. Now, in my weakened condition, I have to go all the way downstairs to be with him and help him recover.

"I bore that boy, and you have kept me from him. I told you that this war would be the end of this family. I'll never forgive you or that awful bunch in Richmond for getting us into this terrible war."

"Yes, dear," Colonel Pope admitted wearily. "You have told me that many times."

"Take me to my son, immediately."

NORTH FROM VICKSGURG

The steamboat chugged along on its way south from Cairo, Illinois. The Sultana had been built in 1863 and had plied the Mississippi ever since. Captain George Mason was the captain and partial owner of this paddleboat.

During the river war in the West, Union forces sought to gain control of the Mississippi River and its tributaries. As its efforts were successful, the government used steamboats like the Sultana extensively. They were used to ferry troops and to carry supplies up and down the Union controlled river.

Once Vicksburg had been captured by Union forces in July 1863, the Mississippi river was open to Union traffic all the way to New Orleans. As a result, the river had seen a brisk and profitable trade for these independently owned steamboats.

Most of them used boilers to create steam. These were filled with water drawn directly from the Mississippi River. Because of the heavy sediment of that water, there was always a danger of clogged boiler tubes. If that happened, an explosion might result. So, regular inspections were required.

The Sultana had had such a boiler inspection on April 12, 1865, and passed. As a result, Mason was allowed to continue using his boat to carry cargo and passengers on the Mississippi River.

During the spring of 1865, the Sultana was on its way to New Orleans. Captain Mason stopped in Vicksburg to arrange cargo for his return trip north. He had been made aware that the Federal government needed to transport prisoners north on ships like his, by way of the Mississippi River.

Several thousand of them were being held at Camp Fisk, a few miles east of Vicksburg. The government wanted to move them as soon as possible from Vicksburg to Cairo, Illinois. From that port, they would be sent to various cities in the Midwest.

So, during his stop at Vicksburg, Mason sought a contract with the Union authorities to carry released prisoners north. He was licensed to carry 376 passengers in addition to many tons of cargo.

* * *

"Colonel Hatch," Mason greeted. "Thank you for meeting with me on such short notice."

"Not a' tall, Captain Mason. How can I help you?"

"We can probably help one another, Colonel," Mason responded with a smile.

"How so, sir?"

"I had a conversation with Captain Speed shortly after I arrived in Vicksburg this morning. He told me that he might not have any passengers for my return trip to Cairo later this month. I was under the impression that you have more men to transport than you have boats available."

"Captain Speed is mistaken. I'm sure we can work something out, Captain Mason."

"I'm happy to hear that, sir. While you are clarifying the situation, I'd like to ask a question or two."

"Go right ahead, Captain Mason," Hatch urged.

"It is my understanding, sir, that you have been ordered to move the prisoners being held at Camp Fisk as soon as possible. Is that true, sir?"

"You are well informed, sir."

"And," Mason continued. "You want to do that by steamboat?"

"That seems to be the most practical method, yes," Hatch added.

"And," Mason went on, "it is my understanding that you are authorized to pay $5 per head for enlisted men and $10 a head for officers for that transportation to Cairo, Illinois. Is that correct?"

"Yes, that is correct, Captain."

"Since that's the case, I have a proposal for you."

"I just arrived in port from Cairo. So, I am pretty familiar to the river from here to there. I would suggest that you pay me the maximum allowed for enlisted men and officers for the first 1,000 men you load on my ship. Any additional passengers you assign to the Sultana would be at $3 per head."

"That is an interesting proposal, Captain Mason," Hatch remarked. "But doesn't your boat have a limit on the number of passengers you are allowed to carry?"

"I am proposing a cash and carry deal for you, Colonel," Mason responded. "How I manage my numbers is my concern; not yours."

"I see," Hatch responded. "But before this conversation goes any further, Captain, you had best understand something, too. You are one of many seeking to transport former Union soldiers north. If you want any at all, you will be required to meet the requirements of this office. Am I clear on that, sir?"

"Of course, Colonel."

"My records show that your boat is licensed to carry 376 passengers and cargo of various kinds. Is that true, sir?"

"Yes, that's true."

"Therefore, you will be allocated 376 enlisted men and officers to transport north on your boat, the Sultana. You will receive the full amount authorized for the first one hundred of them. For any additional, you will receive $3 per head. All payments will be made here in Vicksburg at the time of loading. Is this clear to you, Captain?"

"Will you handle Captain Speed for me?" Mason asked. "He seemed reluctant to even offer that number for my trip north to Cairo."

"General Smith has told me of your visit with him last evening. He directed me to cooperate with you. You can ignore Captain Speed. Do we have an understanding then, Captain Mason?"

"Yes, Colonel," he responded. "I accept your terms. My boat will be back in port on April 23rd. I just hope you will give me more than 376 passengers, though."

LOADING FOR DISASTER

On the return trip from New Orleans, one of the Sultana's boilers sprang leak seventy-five miles south of Vicksburg. The boat's engineer, Nathan Wintringer, told Captain Mason that it would be necessary for the boilers to cool before repairs could be made.

"Can we wait until we get to Vicksburg, Mr. Wintringer?" Mason asked.

"I think we can make it to that port, Captain. Keep in mind, sir, that an overhaul of that boiler will require about 24 hours to do a proper job."

"Can a temporary repair get us to St. Louis?" Mason asked his chief engineer.

"I doubt it, sir," Wintringer reported. "I might be able to patch up the boiler when we get to Vicksburg. With luck, that will probably get us to St. Louis."

"Good, then do it," Mason ordered. "I want to take advantage of a government contract to carry freed prisoners north to Cairo. I'll probably lose that chance if we stay in Vicksburg more than a day. So, only make whatever repair is absolutely necessary."

"I'll do what I can, sir."

The Sultana had barely reached Vicksburg when one of the boat's firemen ran to the town's foundry. There, he hired a boiler mechanic and the supplies needed to repair the leaking boiler.

Meanwhile, back on board the Sultana, Mason learned that the Henry James had just left Vicksburg with thirteen hundred paroled Union prisoners. This paddleboat was followed by the Olive Branch with seventeen hundred military passengers.

Captain Mason immediately sent his business agent to find Colonel Hatch.

"You remind that son-of-a-bitch colonel that we have a deal," Mason shouted. "Tell him that I will go to General Smith if I don't get at least as many as he placed on those other two boats that just left here."

"Yes, sir."

While repairs were in progress, the Sultana was loading cargo. In addition to passengers and crew, the boat carried several tons of sugar, hogs, and of course tons of fuel for the boilers. The agent returned with good news.

"Captain," he reported, "The colonel says he will get you all the passengers you feel it safe to carry. Captain Speed was present, but he doubted if more than 600 could be provided before you set sail."

"What the hell is the hold up?"

"Something about personnel paperwork. You know, all that government bullshit."

Mason virtually exploded, "You get back up there and tell them I'll tell the Chicago press that they are responsible for delaying transport for these released prisoners 'cause of some damn paperwork."

Within the hour, Captain Speed was on the docks personally seeing to the loading of passengers on the Sultana. The Pauline Carrol was also in port, but all the passengers seemed to be directed to the Sultana. In fact, another empty boat, the Lady Gay, docked and sought passengers, too. But Hatch and Speed continued to load passengers on the Sultana.

Twenty-three sick soldiers confined to cots arrived along with two hundred seventy-seven men unable to walk. Initially they were assigned to the Sultana, but the surgeon responsible had them removed from that boat. He insisted that the crowded conditions on the Sultana made it unsafe for his sick men.

Mason became aware that his boat was getting top-heavy with passengers.

"Captain Speed," he warned. "I think I have all the passengers my boat can handle."

"Look, you slime-bucket," Speed spat. "You went over my head to the General and threatened to go to the press with your damn whining. In return, the General roasted my butt. So, don't talk to me about overloading. I got one more trainload coming. And you're getting every last one a' them boys on your boat."

Sure enough, when the last train arrived that evening, men could be seen hanging over the railings on every deck of the Sultana. Some of the newly arrived prisoners complained and suggested that they be loaded on one of the other two boats in port.

"I believe that some of the passengers on that boat had the smallpox," Speed told the men. "If ya want to get home, you best board the Sultana."

Before that last trainload arrived, the Sultana was said to have almost sixteen hundred military passengers on board. Captain Augustus Williams was in charge of keeping records for payment purposes. He came up with a final tally of nearly 2,000 military passengers. Other passengers and crew swelled that number to 2,400.

At about one in the morning of April 24th, the Sultana left port and headed north on the Mississippi River with a stop in Memphis on its way to Cairo, Illinois.

At the Vicksburg port, the overloaded Sultana is ready to depart on its journy north on the Misssissippi river to St. Louis.

LOWELL

After the noon meal, Ethan knocked on the door of the Petzold home. It was answered by one of his friend Willie's sisters.

"Hi, Mary," Ethan greeted. "Could I speak to Willie?"

"Sure," she responded. "Come on in, Ethan. No need for you to stand outside. Willie's just having a cup of coffee."

Once inside, Ethan greeted everyone.

"Good morning, Ethan," greeted Mrs. Petzold. "Have a seat. Want to join us in a piece of apple pie?"

"I don't want to be any trouble, Mrs. Petzold."

"No trouble a' tall," she responded. "Mary, get Ethan a piece of pie and some coffee."

"You take cream and sugar, Ethan?"

"Yes, I do, thank you. 'Morning, Mr. Petzold. How are you doing, Willie?"

"I'm fine, Ethan," Willie answered. "I just finished my barn chores for the day and am having some pie. My mom just baked it, Ethan. It's still warm."

"That's great, Willie," Ethan told his friend. "My momma has a pie baking right now, too. I stopped over to ask if you wanted to go fishing when you finished your chores. Would you like to go?"

"Yes, I would," he responded. "Is that all right, Papa?"

"You've finished your chores for the day, son. So, it would be fine."

"Let me finish my pie first, though, Willie." Ethan asked.

* * *

The two young men were at the same small lake they had frequented as boys.

"I wonder what Mike Drieborg is doing right now. What do you think, Willie?"

"Where is he, Ethan?"

"He's in Grand Rapids learning to ride a horse. Remember, he wrote his sisters that he will be home on leave for Thanksgiving. We'll see him then. Won't it be great to see our old friend?"

"Yes, it will," Willie answered. "I wonder what he looks like now."

"The last time we saw him was only a year or so ago. So, I don't think he will have changed much."

"Have we changed much, Ethan?"

"You and I have lost a lot of weight, my friend. Our mothers' cooking is sure to put it all back. But right now we're still sort of skinny."

"I forget that part."

"Right," Ethan told his friend. "Oh, I almost forgot. I got a letter from Kelly."

"Is that the Kelly we were in prison with, Ethan?"

"Yes. He and our other prison friend, Tom, are going to visit us here. They're traveling by train all the way from Detroit just to see us. Won't that be great, Willie?"

"I think so."

"I'll talk to your folks about having one of them stay with you, and the other one at my house. Think that will be all right?"

"Why don't you stay with me at my house, Ethan?"

"Because my folks want me to stay with them. We've talked about this before, Willie."

"Have we?" Willie asked. "I forget."

"That's all right. Hey! I think you've gotten a bite."

Sure enough, when Willie pulled on his line, he had a fish on the hook.

"Hey, Willie!" Ethan exclaimed. "I think it's a keeper."

Ethan took the fish off the hook and put it on the line in the water with the other fish they caught. When we're done here, we can take these to your barn and clean them for your momma to cook. Won't that be good eating?"

"Have I eaten fish before, Ethan?"

"Yep. You have. Before we joined up, the three of us, you and I and Mike, used to fish here all the time. Remember?

"Sometimes we'd decide that whoever caught the biggest fish or maybe the most fish would get to take all the fish we caught home. We had some good fish fries back then."

"Have we caught enough fish for a meal today, Ethan?"

"We have, my friend. And you caught the biggest one, so you get to keep the whole mess. We'd best get them back to your place and clean them."

The two friends took in their lines and cleaned up the area before they began the walk to the Petzold farm.

"Hey, you two!" Mr. Petzold greeted. "Looks like you caught a pretty good mess of fish."

"We did, Mr. Petzold," Ethan told him. "And because Willie caught the biggest one, you get to keep all a' them for a good fish dinner."

"That sounds good ta me; as long as I don't have ta clean 'em," he joked.

"Don't worry, sir," Ethan assured him. "Willie and I will do the cleaning. Won't we, Willie?"

"Will you show me how to do it, Ethan?"

"Sure. Mr. Petzold, where do you want us to clean these fish?"

"I've got a bench on the other side of the barn, Ethan. Use that, please. Throw the fish leavings in the hog pen, would you?"

"That will work for us, sir."

The two friends walked to that side of the barn. Ethan gave directions to his friend.

"Come on, Willie. Let's get this job done. You cut off the heads of the fish, and I'll gut 'em." Ethan showed his friend what he meant.

"Then, I'll show you how to take out the bones and scale 'em. Will that be all right with you?"

"Sure, Ethan."

"Well, let's get to it, Willie."

SPRING ON THE MISSISSIPPI

Every spring, the melting snows from Canada and Minnesota flowed into the Mississippi. And this spring flow caused the river to escape its banks and fill the river with debris and sandy soil from the shores. The heavy spring rains only made the situation worse.

Standing on the bow's second deck, the McElvain brothers watched the river flow past the moored Sultana.

"Could you imagine trying to swim in that stuff?" Cory wondered aloud.

"I agree," Ethan said. "It looks pretty bad. This early in the spring, I don't recall we ever took a dip in that lake we used to fish in, either."

"Look at all those logs, trees an' shrubs flowing by," Cory added. "The banks must be really flooded to pull all that stuff into the river."

"Probably happens every spring."

"Want to stay up here tonight?" Ethan asked.

"Might as well," Cory responded. "Too crowded on the lower decks anyway. Remember what that fellow Boor told anyone who would listen?"

"No, I don't. Remind me, will ya?"

"He said he looked inta' all that pounding we heard from near the center of the boat. He said he saw some men trying to put a metal patch on one a' their big boilers. He said it didn't look good ta' him fer us to be sleeping atop that boiler room."

"Oh, ya," Ethan said. "Now I remember. Fine, so we stay here at the front of the boat?"

"I think they call it the bow," Ethan teased.

"What a smart ass you are, brother."

"Just trying to bring a little cheer and humor into your life. I'm happy you are so agreeable today."

"Hey!" Ethan snapped. "Actually, I don't give a rat's ass where we stand or sleep or how crowded this boat appears ta' be, or anything else. All I care about is this boat getting you and me to Cairo, Illinois, as fast as possible."

"Right," Cory agreed. "Only a few hours from there to home. I can almost taste Momma's cooking."

"Stop it! You're driving me crazy here."

The waters of the Mississippi the Mc Elvain brothers were looking at ran fast with whirlpools and cross-currents pulling debris of all sorts under the water as the swift river ran toward the Gulf of Mexico. And it was cold, too, less than 60 degrees this time of year.

It not only looked dangerous, it was. In the water, a person's body temperature would be quickly and dangerously lowered within a few minutes. Thus, if a person wasn't pulled under the water and drowned, he would be in danger of dying of hypothermia if he stayed in the water more than an hour.

* * *

Late the next evening, the Sultana docked in Memphis, Tennessee. There, one hundred-twenty tons of sugar carried from the lower Mississippi were unloaded. In addition, twenty-seven crates of wine and a herd of hogs were taken out of the ship's hold.

The loss of this cargo lost the boat most of its ballast. So, with the upper decks so overloaded, the boat was in danger of rolling over.

"Hey, Ethan," his bother said.

"Ya, what?"

"Let's take a walk into town. I hear there's a place called the Soldier's Home operated by the Sanitary Commission. Soldiers can clean up and get a hot meal there."

"They told us not to leave the ship, Corey."

"What do they know? Come on, let's get some good food."

"The last time I took your advice and did what you told me, I enlisted. Look how that turned out," Ethan reminded his brother.

"Let's at least stretch our legs," Corey insisted. "We got a good half an hour before this rust-bucket leaves."

"I know I shouldn't," Ethan told his brother. "But as usual, I'm going along with you. I promised our momma that I would look after you. So, I can't let you get yourself in trouble alone."

"What are brothers for?"

"I guess."

The brothers trudged up the hill into town.

They found the Soldier's Home by asking people they encountered on the main street of town. By the time they got their meal, they heard the ship's whistle announcing its departure.

"Oh, crap!" Ethan said. "It must be 10:30 already. And the damned boat is leaving without us."

The brothers grabbed what they could carry of their meal and ran for the dock.

By the time they arrived, the Sultana was already out into the Mississippi River.

THE SULTANA DISASTER

"Now you've done it, Corey," Ethan complained. "We've missed our ride home. Damn it!"

"Why is it my fault?" Corey shouted back. "Remember, I didn't drag you off that boat."

"Our momma will skin us alive when she hears."

Cory wasn't buying any of that. "When she sees us, she'll be so happy, it won't matter that we missed our ride."

"Seems like I get into trouble every time I follow your advice. Damn! When will I ever learn?"

"Tell you what," Cory announced. "I'm not going to stand on this dock and complain about something I can't change. In fact, I'm going back to the Soldier's Home and a nice, soft bed. In the morning, I'm going to get me a bath and a hot breakfast, too.

"Then I'll tackle the getting home issue," he told his brother. "Are you going to join me or just stand around here and whine?"

"A soft bed sounds good, I must admit," Ethan agreed. "Once more, I'm with you."

* * *

The Sultana docked across the river from Memphis to take on coal for the journey to St. Louis,. By 1 A.M., they pushed off and into the Mississippi River, heading north.

Men on the Memphis dock watched as the brightly lit and overloaded boat disappeared around a bend north of the port.

Shortly before 2 A.M., the Sultana was seven miles north of Memphis. At about that time, passengers were awakened by a violent explosion. Those on the upper deck were showered with scalding water and debris. Those on lower decks experienced intense heat from the rapidly spreading fires. Some passengers were blown clear of the boat and into the frigid river. Everyone on board was awakened by the boiler explosion.

But not Cory and Ethan McElvain. They were comfortably sound asleep in their beds at the Soldiers Home back in Memphis. They were unaware of the Sultana's explosion.   But not for long.

RESCUE OPERATION

It was still dark outside when the first bodies from the Sultana came floating by the Memphis docks. Because of the water temperature and the river undertows, few swimmers lasted more than an hour in the water, alive.

As soon as bodies were discovered floating down the river and people were seen clinging to debris in the river, the harbor bells rang, calling men to the riverbank.

An alert was sent by telegraph up and down the river as well. What remained of small boats around Memphis were launched, too.

Shortly, the boat General Boyton arrived at the Memphis docks with some survivors. It had been heading south on the river when it suddenly came upon survivors struggling in the swollen river. They picked up as many as they could and continued south to Memphis.

Lifeboats from the ironclad U.S.S. Essex, the U.S.S. Grossbeak, and the U.S.S Tyler, plus a virtual flotilla of small boats soon left the dock to aid the survivors.

Also, three steamboats in the port were ordered to head upstream, the Jenny Lind, the Pocahantas, and the Rosadella.

Awakened, Ethan and Cory hurried to the waterfront.

"What the hell happened, I wonder?" Ethan said as he ran alongside his brother.

"Whatever happened, brother," his brother told him, "you ought to be thankin' me for causing you to miss that boat. You heard that guy tellin' us the Sultana blew up."

"I 'spose I'll never hear the end of this from you."

"Got that right, Ethan," Corey said. "Now, we gotta see if we can help the survivors."

By 4 A.M., the riverfront area was clogged with swimmers and the bodies of dead passengers from the Sultana.

*　　*　　*

Rescuers from the west bank of the Mississippi became involved, too.

Frank Barton was pushing his canoe into the water.

"Papa," Elliot Barton asked his father. "Do you need some help?"

"You bet I do, son," his father answered. Frank Barton had been a lieutenant in the Confederate Navy. In fact, he was still wearing the grey jacket to his uniform.

"But they're Yankees, Papa. Why should we be risking our lives to help them?"

"Because, son," his father answered, "we're river people. And that's what we do for folks in trouble on the Mississippi. Even if they are Yankees."

"If you say so, Papa."

CHARLESTON

Colonel Pope was most agitated.

"I don't give a damn, Doctor, what your journals tell you. I refuse to just stand here and watch my son die."

"Everything we can do for pneumonia has been done, Colonel," the doctor insisted. "My God, man. Do you think I want to tell you that there is no hope for you son?"

"I don't care what how badly you feel. There must be something you can do," he insisted.

"Allow me to remind you, sir," the doctor said, somewhat offended, "your own son, the doctor, and all those other medical experts in Richmond couldn't do anything either."

Mrs. Pope was back in her room upstairs. She was too overcome with grief to remain at her son's bedside.

Mary Jacqueline sat with her father-in-law. She held Richard's sweaty hand.

"Tell my brother," he whispered to her. "Tell him that I know he tried everything he could. I expect that I was too far gone when I got to his hospital in Richmond."

"Don't talk that way, Richard," she responded. "You'll get through this.

"Just tell him, please."

She sobbed at the thought. "I will, I promise."

ON THE MEMPHIS DOCKS

Boats of all kinds and sizes were unloading the dead and nearly dead.

Cory McElvain was helping local medical people sort out those who could be saved from the dead and too far gone.

"How can I help, brother?" Ethan asked.

"There are two things you can do," Cory responded. "Follow me as I examine the newly arrived. Those who are dead, drag over there. Those who can be saved, take over there."

"Got it."

The brothers worked together for several hours on the Memphis docks.

Finally, Ethan had had enough.

"Hey, Cory," he announced. "I've had it. I'm exhausted. And I need to get something to eat as well as some rest."

"I thought you had some biscuits before we left the Soldier's Home," Corey answered.

"I threw that up long ago," Ethan told him. "I've been operating on empty for hours."

"The locals set up a food tent at the base of the hill," Cory reminded his brother. "Let's get some coffee and whatever else they have."

"Good idea," Ethan said. "Then I need to wash all this grime off and collapse someplace."

"Me, too. The smell of death is in my nostrils, that's for sure."

Then, the brothers again went to the Soldier's Home. It was there they were told that the boat, the Belle of St. Memphis, would leave in two days for Cairo, Illinois.

"Are you up for another boat ride, Ethan?"

"I don't know, Cory," Ethan mused. "It depends."

"Depends on what?"

"On if that boat will be overcrowded like the last one."

"You got a point there, for sure," Cory admitted. "Would you rather walk or wait a few weeks for the train?"

"I'm not strong enough to make it walking, and I don't want to wait that long for a train. So, if you're up to it, let's take a chance on the boat. How about you?"

"This time, I'll follow you," Cory responded with a chuckle. "See, it's not always me who leads you astray."

"We'll see how things work out this time."

Once on board the Belle of Memphis, the McElvain brothers noticed two things.

First, the boat was far from overloaded. And second, they saw two soldiers from Camp Fisk.

Ethan nudged his brother. "Hey, look, Cory. If my eyes aren't playing ticks, that's John Maddox and Bill Talbert over there."

"Think you're right, Ethan. Let's check it out."

"Hey, you two," Ethan greeted. "Why you clutching those life jackets?"

"As I live and breathe," John Maddox said, extending his hand for a shake. "You survived the Sultana, I see."

"Sort a', yes," Cory answered.

Then Cory told them the whole story. When he finished, he asked, "What about you two?"

Bill Talbert told the McElvains of their experience on the Sultana.

"We were up on the bow, where you were. Don't ya remember?"

"Ya, so what happened?"

"You went inta town, and we stayed, that's what happened," Maddox added.

"Right," Ethan agreed. "But then what?"

"Not long after the boat people finished coaling up the Sultana, they pushed the boat inta the river. Pretty quick, we lost sight a' Memphis. John an' I had fallen asleep then, the boat just blew up; gotta been the boilers, near as I can figger."

"Don't you think it coulda been a Reb torpedo?" Ethan asked.

"I suppose it's possible," Maddox said. "I don't really know. All I do know is that I got woked up when the center a' that boat exploded and showered us with drops a' scalding water and all kinds of debris."

Talbert picked up their story from there. "We just hung on ta the railing so's not ta get thrown inta the river. All kinds a' guys were already in the river or trying ta jump inta it.

"But it didn't look very inviting ta me, and the bow seemed to keep floating, so we just hung on there."

"Like he says," Maddox agreed. "The river didn't look too inviting ta me either. So, I hung on right alongside a' Talbert."

Talbert continued. "Must a' been an hour later a man and his son came by in a canoe. They asked if we wanted to be taken ta shore. A 'course we took em up on it. Once on the western shore, they fed us, gave us a place ta sleep and they went back to the river. Rescued others, I expect."

"Right," Maddox said. "Then this morning, the same two ferried us across and we got on this boat heading North.

"I was just telling Maddox a' fore you walked over to us. The guy who rescued us was a Reb officer, just returned home. His son told us that his father said they had to help us Yanks; that it was the duty of river people to help those in trouble on the Mississippi.

"Don't that beat all?"

"I suppose," Cory admitted.

"The good Lord was looking after you two," Ethan said.

"You guys, too, it seems ta me," Maddox concluded.

* * *

After a stop in St. Louis, their boat left for Cairo, Illinois. There, the boys boarded a train to take the McElvain brothers and hundreds of others orth.

"What did the conductor say this place is?" Ethan asked his brother.

"Look above ya, for heaven's sake," Cory kidded his brother. The station sign says we're in Matoon City."

"I don't recall ever being here, Cory. Have we?" Ethan asked.

"At least you got that right," Cory responded. "Let's ask the railroad guy over there where's the telegraph office."

The brothers hung around for several hours, waiting for a return message from home.

"Momma says to wait here," Ethan said. "They're coming to get us."

"Probably don't trust us to get the rest a' the way home on our own."

"Can't say I blame 'em," Ethan told his brother.

AFTERMATH OF THE DISASTER

The death toll as a result of the explosion of the Sultana, was staggering. It was the most loss of life in the history of maritime disasters ever experienced in American history.

Almost 2,400 people were aboard the Sultana when it left the Memphis docks. Within twenty-four hours, some 1,700 were dead or dying. Over a thousand of these were missing and never accounted for.

The event was well publicized in the Memphis area, but not in the East. The Lincoln assassination was still dominating the news there. And as the New York Times noted, there were no soldiers lost who lived in the East.

With the end of the war and the return home of several hundred thousand soldiers, there was little public outcry to even investigate the Sultana tragedy.

* * *

But, with almost 1,700 Midwesterners dead, there were some demands for an investigation of the disaster.

Two issues were quickly identified. As first-hand accounts emerged, it was obvious that the boat was overloaded. Also, those same accounts insisted that one or more of the boat's boilers had exploded.

So, the first obvious question was, why was the boat so overcrowded with passengers? Early inquiries had confirmed that the boat was licensed to carry only 376 passengers. Photographs clearly showed the boat dangerously crowded with many more passengers than the number authorized. Why?

Congressional testimony left no doubt that the boilers were the primary problem. Evidence gathered at subsequent inquiries determined that the overloading and subsequent great loss of life was caused by the greed of the private contractors and the criminal cooperation of military officials.

Despite such conclusions, no one was punished.

The boat's captain, Mason, died in the explosion. Mr. Wintringer, the chief engineer, lost his license, only to have it restored

 A military court found Captain Speed guilty of negligence and ordered him dismissed from the service. But he, too, was able to have the verdict reversed. He returned to Vicksburg, where he served as a criminal court judge.

The commissary general of Union prisoners concluded that both Speed and Hatch were the most culpable military officials. Hatch and Speed's political connections shielded them from prosecution.

It would appear that none of the investigations into the Sultana disaster were seriously pursued.

AFTERWORD

With the unexpected beginning of the War Between the States, both sides were unprepared to deal with prisoners-of-war.

Over the history of warfare, the issue of prisoners taken in battle had been settled by the opposing commanders on the field.

But what of a rebellion or civil war? What if one side did not recognize the other as a legitimate government? King George III found himself in this position during the American Revolution. Lincoln found himself in a similar position when eleven-member states left the United States to form a new government.

Like the King of Great Britain before him, Lincoln refused to treat with this new government over the issue of war prisoners. He feared that negotiating with representatives of the Confederate government might lend credence to their claim of being an independent nation. He considered the conflict a rebellion, not a war between nations.

But after the Union loss at the 1st Battle of Bull run in July of 1861, public pressure and Congressional demands moved him to take measures authorizing a formal exchange of captives.

As a result, the first government-sanctioned discussions to authorize exchanges took place in February of 1862. By July 22, 1862, a system called the Dix-Hill Cartel was announced.

Under the terms of this agreement, all prisoners were to be released, and either exchanged or paroled, within 10 days of capture. A system called an equivalency table was devised whereby a certain number of enlisted men could be exchanged for an officer.

Any prisoner not exchanged within 10 days could be paroled upon signing a pledge not to take up arms against his captor until he had been formally exchanged for an enemy prisoner.

The system soon became bogged down in paperwork and complaints. Some parolees sent home to await exchange were simply lost in all the paperwork. Federal officials claimed that many paroled Confederate soldiers were returned to their units prematurely. Confederate officials claimed that the Union sent paroled soldiers to the West or assigned them to non-combat duties, thus releasing other soldiers for service in combat units.

Such actions were contrary to the Hill-Dix agreement, in fact, if not in spirit.

Union leaders like General Grant also complained about the condition of exchanged Union soldiers. He contended that Union soldiers released after confinement in Confederate prisons were in no condition to return to duty.

He also observed that Confederate prisoners, after confinement in Northern prisons, were duty-ready after release.

In the summer of 1863, the Union ended participation in the Dix-Hill Cartel. What finally triggered this action was the Confederate reaction to the North's use of Negro soldiers.

The Confederate government announced it would treat captives who were Negro as recaptured slaves and therefore not eligible for parole or exchange. They also warned that they would, upon capture, execute the white officers who commanded Negro units.

Later in the war, the Confederate government unsuccessfully sought to revive the Cartel. General Grant opposed such a move, saying, "We have got to fight until the military power of the South is exhausted. So, we must kill every prisoner released or exchanged. It simply becomes a war of extermination."

So, despite the political pressure of the 1864 presidential election approaching, President Lincoln supported his military leaders and refused to treaty with the Confederate government on the issue of prisoner exchange.

All prisoners had been released by September of 1865.

* * *

Confederate soldiers held in Northern prisons totaled 214,865. Southern prisons held a total of 193,743 Northern soldiers.

While there are no completely reliable figures on death due to sickness, estimates are available. So, it is estimated that 15% of those held in Southern prisons died while in custody. While 12% of the Southern soldiers held died while in Union prisons.

It is interesting to note that the death rate for soldiers held in the prison camps of both sides was higher than that for soldiers serving in combat units.

CHARACTERS

SCHOCK FAMILY

Carl Schock	Father
Michelle Schock	Mother
Ethan	Son
Joseph	Adopted Son
Mary	Adopted Daughter

PETZOLD FAMILY

Gustov Petzold	Father
Mary Petzold	Mother
Willie Petzold	Son

DRIEBORG's CAVALRY UNIT

Capt. Michael Drieborg	Troop Commander
Sgt. Riley	First Sgt of I Troop

LIBBY PRISON

Colonel Rose   Union Prisoner

Major Hamilton   Union Prisoner

POPE FAMILY

Col. Pope   Father

Mrs. Pope   Mother

Dr. Charles Pope   Son

Richard Pope   Son

Mary Jacqueline   Wife of Charles

Helen   Household slave

David Pope   Son

Andersonville Prison

Union Prisoners:

John Ransom	Battist
Cory McElvain	Pete McCullough
Ephran McDlvain	Capt Wirz: Andersonville Commander
Paul Lewis	
George Hendryx	
Phjil Lewis	
Jimmy Devers	
Sam Hutton	
Joe Sergeant	

Belle Isle & Salisbury Prison

Ethan Schock   Union Prisoner

Tom Novak   Union Prisoner

Willie Petzold Union Prisoner

Bill Kelly   Union Prisoner

Camp Douglas & Johnson Isle Prisons

Major Richard Pope   Confederate Prisoner

Col Randall McGavock   Confederate Prisoner

D>C>McLouth   Mayor of Sandusky, Ohio

James M. Ashley   Congressman from Ohio

Sultana Disaster

Gen. Morgan Smith   General-In-Charge

Captain Speed   In Charge of Prisoner Transportation at Vicksburg

Colonel Hatch   In Charge of Prisoner Transportation at Vicksburg

John Clark Ely   Union Prisoner Returning Home

John Maddox   Union Prisoner Returning Home

Romulus Tolbert   Union Prisoner Returning Home

Cory McElvain   Union Prisoner Returning Home

Ephran McElvain   Union Prisoner Returning Home

BIBLIOGRAPHY

John Ransom's Andersonville Diary: by John Ransom. Berfley Books. 1988. 281pp.

Andersonville: by MacKinlay Kantor. Signet Publishers 1955, 733pp

Camp Douglas: by David Keller. Arcadia Publisher. 2015. 256pp

Civil War Prisons: William Helleline. Kent State U. Press. 1972. 123pp

Hell on Belle Isle: Diary of a Civil War POW. Don Allison Ed. 1997. 191pp

Andersonville of the North: The Myths and Realities of Northern Treatment of Civil War Confederate Prisoners. James Gillispie. University of North Texas Press. 2008. 278pp

Portals to Hell: Military Prisons of the Civil War. Lonnie Speer. Stackpole Books. 1997. 410pp

The Salisbury Prison: A case study of Confederate Military Prisons. 186+1 – 1865.l Louis Brown. 1992. 357pp

Made in the USA
Columbia, SC
11 March 2019